# From
# Needles
## to
# Natural

# From Needles to Natural

*Learning Holistic Pet Healing*

JUDY MORGAN D.V.M.

ARCHWAY
PUBLISHING

Archway Publishing books may be ordered through booksellers or by contacting:

Archway Publishing
1663 Liberty Drive
Bloomington, IN 47403
www.archwaypublishing.com
1-(888)-242-5904

Because of the dynamic nature of the Internet, any web addresses or links contained in this book may have changed since publication and may no longer be valid. The views expressed in this work are solely those of the author and do not necessarily reflect the views of the publisher, and the publisher hereby disclaims any responsibility for them.

Any people depicted in stock imagery provided by Thinkstock are models, and such images are being used for illustrative purposes only. Certain stock imagery © Thinkstock.

ISBN: 978-1-4808-0905-5 (sc)
ISBN: 978-1-4808-0906-2 (hc)
ISBN: 978-1-4808-0907-9 (e)

Library of Congress Control Number: 2014912408

Printed in the United States of America.

Archway Publishing rev. date: 07/15/2014

# Contents

# Introduction

A while back, I joined an online group of cavalier King Charles spaniel lovers. They were a group of people totally committed to the welfare of their dogs. Once they discovered I was a holistic veterinarian, they started asking questions like: Which heartworm preventative is best? What's the best food? Which vaccinations should I get for my dog? Which flea and tick product do you recommend? Once I started answering questions, they multiplied. New people would join the group and ask questions that had already been discussed, and I would repeat the answers or someone would find the old posts. Finally, they started saying this all needed to be written down somewhere for access. So here you have it.

I have been a practicing veterinarian for more than thirty years, and I like to believe I've learned a few things along the way. I have formed many opinions, and that is what this book contains: a collection of my opinions. Many of those opinions are backed by solid research, some are gut feelings, and some just come with experience. This book is by no means meant to replace visits to your regular veterinarian. It is written to give you some knowledge and tools for discussions with your veterinarian.

I am grateful to my parents and family for standing behind me along the way, especially my children who grew up in cages in veterinary clinics pretending they were dogs while I worked long hours. I appreciate every animal that has taught me something along the way and the clients who have been gracious enough to allow me to treat their precious pets.

I am particularly indebted to all the rescued dogs and cats that have crossed my path. They are a source of inspiration, showing trust and love where many times it was undeserved. I'm so lucky to have my partner in rescue, Hue, who has a bigger heart than any person I know. If I left it up to him, we'd have every sad puppy face in the kingdom camped out at our house. As my mom says, "You can't save them all." But we are going to try our hardest!

# The Beginning

W hen I arrive, there is already a long line of dogs straining at the ends of their leashes. Some are barking and carrying on while others cower behind their owners. Cats in boxes and cages are hissing and growling, unhappy with the crowd of dogs. I am loaded down with boxes of syringes and vials of vaccine. Today, I am the veterinarian in charge of the rabies vaccination clinic in a small town in rural southern New Jersey. I chuckle as I struggle to open the firehouse door, remembering the first vaccination clinic I ever attended; I was a small child standing in line with my mother, sister, and our cocker spaniel/Irish setter mix, Toby. Looking back on my first few experiences with veterinarians, I still marvel that this is my chosen profession.

When I was growing up, we always had at least one pet of some sort in the house. My mother adopted Toby before I was born. He was a bit feisty and hated all the neighborhood kids that taunted him and threw rocks at him. He was a good guy for the most part and was kind to my sister and me. I think my mom really wanted the dog to bond with my big sister, but he became so attached to my mom that he really didn't care about the kids.

My mom grew up on a farm, so she has always loved animals and has tried to instill that love into us. Besides the dog, there always seemed to be a goldfish in a bowl, won at carnivals or bought from the dime store. I think my mom replaced those goldfish every month after we killed them by overfeeding them. Then there were the ever-present dime-store turtles. Those little guys are illegal to sell now because they carry salmonella and make little kids sick. Not really much of a pet, but it was fun to design their little habitats.

My mom was a first grade schoolteacher and always had pets in her classrooms. She started with gerbils in a fish tank. She'd bring them home on weekends and school holidays and over the summer. We got to care for them and learned the hard way not to pick them up by their tails, which will instantly break off (a defense mechanism to protect them from predators). After the gerbils came hamsters, then guinea pigs, then dwarf rabbits. My father was not really a big fan of all the pocket pets, but he tolerated them as long as they stayed in their cages (they didn't) and didn't pee on the furniture (they did).

We lived on a lake when we were growing up, and one day a woman rang our doorbell with a small mallard duckling in her arms. She said she had found him waddling down the street a few blocks away and wanted to know if we could keep him and raise him. I'm not sure if she had tried other houses and we were the only people who answered the door or if she knew we were animal people. Dad wasn't home, so mom agreed to take him.

My sister, Sally, and I named him Peep Peep and commenced building a pen out of chicken wire that was partly onshore and partly in the lake so he could learn to swim. We would take the rowboat out every day and collect lily pads and lily pad flowers to bring back for Peep Peep to eat. Some days we would take Peep Peep out with us in the boat and let him practice swimming in the lake around the boat. I'm not sure why it never dawned on us, but there were snapping turtles in that lake that loved to eat small ducklings. I don't know how we got lucky enough not to have him eaten in front of us.

Sally and I loved to go fishing in our backyard in the lake (classified years later as the second most toxic waste site in the country). We made dough balls out of flour and water, put them on hooks, and dropped them in the water. The good news is that we were awful fishermen and rarely caught anything. The bad news is that when we did catch something, we'd have to run and get Mom or Dad to get it off the hook and set it free.

One day while fishing, Toby was wandering around the backyard and keeping an eye on us. He started digging for something along the bulkhead. Suddenly, he started yelping, screaming in pain, and hopping around on three legs. We ran for the house, and Mom came running, worried about her poor baby who was obviously in pain. She packed the three of us into the car, and we hurried off to the veterinarian. We were lucky because the veterinarian was in the office and agreed to see our "emergency." But it went downhill from there.

Toby was not a big fan of strangers, and as far as I know, had never been in a veterinarian's office before. The doctor tried to grab the sore paw and was rewarded with a quick bite from Toby. The doctor yelled at my mother and said she should have warned him the dog was a biter. (Were we supposed to know he would bite him? It seemed reasonable that he would react when he was in pain. It seemed to me, even as a small child, that the doctor should have been more careful.) After a quick muzzle, it was discovered that Toby had torn off his dewclaw and needed a simple bandage and some antibiotics. Unfortunately, my mom was so traumatized from being yelled at she was crying hysterically when she left the office, along with two crying young girls and a whimpering dog. Strike one for the veterinarians.

Not long after that incident, my sister and I were staying at my grandparents' house for the day. They had a beautiful English setter hunting dog. She was older and had never been spayed (it wasn't done nearly as commonly back then). She had developed mammary cancer, and the masses had gotten so large they were open and bleeding. My grandfather placed the dog in the trunk of the car (oh my, that seemed mean), and off we went to another veterinarian. I really had no idea what was about to happen, but suffice it to say, we went home without the dog. This time, my grandmother was crying—along with two crying young girls. Strike two for the veterinarians.

When I turned twelve, we moved away from the home we had known for years, heading south to Virginia. My sister was thirteen and was already a typical teenager, belligerent about moving away from friends and relatives and the school she knew. For years, she had collected horse statues and horsey toys. I guess she really wanted a horse because with all her whining, my dad agreed to buy her a horse in Virginia if she would just stop complaining and go willingly. That girl must have whined better than anyone I've ever known because that was a huge step. My dad wasn't even a big fan of small pets; I couldn't imagine what he would do around horses.

With the agreement in place, we packed our belongings and our dogs and headed south to a strange world where people had funny accents. We were moving into a new development with big lots and woods and streams. Unfortunately, with woods and streams and new developments, come snakes and other forest creatures. My dad was bound and determined to clear the land around the house, and every weekend, there would be a snake finding, mostly copperheads. Did I mention my dad was totally and completely afraid of snakes? It was terrifying to see him out there with his metal rake and shovels, trying to get them before they got him. Luckily, he never ended up on the short end of the stick. When we moved away later, we found out that a copperhead had been living under my mom's washer and dryer in the laundry room. The moving men picked up the washer, and then they dropped it faster than you can imagine. They ran from the laundry room, screaming and pointing. Lucky for the snake, and everyone else concerned, the snake slithered out of there and out the garage door faster than anyone could grab a metal rake or shovel. One snake spared.

Virginia was a strange new world for us. Besides the snakes in the yard and woods around us, there were a lot of small lizards. The lizards liked to climb the chimneys and come into the house through the fireplaces. Every day, there seemed to be a lizard somewhere in the house. My dad traveled a lot for work, which left mom and two girls to fend off lizards. We were afraid of them, but luckily, there was a family down the street with a couple young boys. Every time we had a lizard in the house, Sally and I would run down the trail through the woods to get one of them to save us from the lizard. I don't know if we caught a new lizard every day or the same one just kept coming back in the house. By the end of the year, I was a little braver about herding lizards into boxes or onto papers so I could carry them outside and set them free.

In addition to lizards and snakes, there were also strange little creatures called flying squirrels. They would soar through the trees around the yard and woods and were really fun to watch. At least they were fun when they were *outside*. One evening, a flying squirrel somehow managed to get into the house. Dad happened to be home that day, but as mentioned previously, he was not exactly an animal person. That squirrel was so frightened that it flew all over our new house, leaping around furniture and off walls and lamps, being followed by two screaming girls and two flustered parents. Finally, my father grabbed a crocheted afghan off the sofa and threw it at the squirrel. The poor thing got its feet so tangled up it couldn't fly anymore, but it sure made a lot of frightened squirrel noises. At least we could carry the gyrating afghan outside, and after a while, the little guy got himself untangled and headed for the woods.

So, back to that horse deal my dad made with my sister. Being true to his word, within a few weeks of moving south, my dad bought my sister a horse. My mom found some old horse dealer who sold us a pony for $165, including a saddle and bridle, and he would even deliver the pony! I don't know how my mom did it, but she really has a good nose for a bargain (she's the one you want with you when you go to a department store sale). Did I mention we knew *nothing* about horses?

My mother had found a gorgeous thousand-acre farm along the James River where we could keep the pony. She went to the caretaker's house and asked if they would consider boarding horses there. The owner of the plantation thought it would be regal to have horses (okay, one pony) grazing in his fields, so he agreed. We would pay ten dollars per month, including all the hay in the old barn. We were in heaven.

Mom took us out to the barn every day for a month; the three of us took turns riding the pony, and sometimes all three of us would ride at the same time. That poor pony struggled to lug us around, but she was just as docile as could be. We wouldn't know until much later that she was probably thirty years old! We named her Spooky because she was white like a ghost.

It soon became clear that one little Spooky pony was not going to suffice. So back we went to the old horse dealer. For another $165, we purchased a second pony with saddle, bridle, and delivery included. This one was brown; we named her Goblin, staying with the Halloween theme. We didn't know until much later that she was only three and not very well trained. Since Sally was the better horsewoman, she adopted Goblin, and Spooky became my pony. Now we had two ponies we could ride, and life was a little easier for the ponies.

My dad got conned into building stalls in the old dairy barn for our ponies (he is not one who enjoys construction or any project of that type). But with the help of my grandfather, the project was handled. Soon, others got wind of the barn, and new horses and boarders started to arrive. Weekends were filled with building more stalls, and we were thrilled to have other kids to ride with us and teach us more about horses. Luckily, one of the new people was a riding instructor who got us all going in the right direction, taught us a lot, and kept us from getting killed or killing our horses.

By the end of the year, the place had turned into a riding academy with a beautiful arena (built by the parents; poor dad got rooked into that too), forty stalls in three barns, and kids everywhere. It was run as a co-op, and everyone took turns feeding and cleaning the stalls. The instructor took us to watch horse shows, and my eyes lit up with envy. Someday I wanted to be able to do that too. We took group trail rides for miles along the river and through the plantation fields. We learned to swim our ponies in the river and streams and had great picnic lunches in beautiful fields. This place was truly magnificent.

But, all good things must come to an end. At the end of the year, Dad announced we were moving back north. This time, he had two whining daughters, insisting the ponies must move with us. Needless to say, it cost more to move the ponies than it did to buy them and care for them for the whole year.

But Mom worked her magic again and found another old rundown farm where we could keep the ponies for twenty dollars a month (oh no—the board had doubled!). It was only a mile from home, so we could ride our bikes or row the boat across the lake from our house to the farm. Mom decided we should join 4-H so we could actually learn something about horses. I loved 4-H, but in those first few months, I felt like the dumbest kid alive because I knew so little about how to really take care of my pony. The learning curve was pretty steep, but we learned more than I ever thought possible over the years.

The big highlight for a kid in 4-H was taking a horse to the county fair at the end of the summer. Our county fair was at the local rodeo grounds, and we would get to keep our ponies there for three nights (and we would sleep in the stalls with them!). Unfortunately, about ten weeks before the fair dates, Spooky was found dead in the field. No one really knew the cause, but we had discovered by that point that she was probably in her early thirties. I was devastated and desperately wanted another pony I could show at the fair. I started riding another pony at the farm, but he too was found dead in the field a few weeks later. Things were not going well. I guess my parents felt sorry for me because they agreed to take me to the local horse auction to pick out a new horse. I bought a gorgeous big palomino for $225. He was nice to look at, but he was way too much horse for me. He used to race back to the barn with no warning, and I would hang on for dear life. Somehow, I survived. When it came time to go to the fair, we loaded up the palomino and my sister's pony and headed off to camp out for a few days.

Those were the best days ever. We knew nothing about showing our ponies and absolutely were not competitive in any of the show classes. We loved watching the real riders jump over obstacles and show their gorgeous horses that were shiny, clipped, and braided. The only things we had a chance to compete in were some gaming classes and the costume class. That first year at the fair, we each won our costume divisions and got our photo in the Philadelphia newspaper, "Alloway Sisters Win Riding Honors at Fair." We were celebrities! We were ready to start learning as much as we could about horses and riding, hoping to be able to show in the real competition the next year.

However, that was not the case. A few weeks after the fair, both our horses became ill. Every time a fly or mosquito bit them, blood would run down their legs. They had fevers and wouldn't eat. They were losing weight. The veterinarian came a few times and prescribed some antibiotics, but he couldn't seem to figure out the cause of the problem. Other horses on the farm were also sick.

After a couple visits from the veterinarian, he suggested running a Coggins test. We had never heard of it (this was years before mandatory testing began). This blood test determines if a horse is infected with Equine Infectious Anemia. EIA is a virus that is carried by flying, biting insects and is transmitted between horses. There is no treatment, and horses that are positive for the disease must be euthanized. A few days after the blood was drawn, the bad news arrived; all the horses on the farm were infected. They all had to be sent to slaughter.

Dr. Leroy Coggins, the veterinarian for whom the test was named, came to the farm along with the state veterinarians, and they put all the horses in quarantine. It was the largest single outbreak recorded in the state. Our hearts were broken. Strike three for the veterinarians.

Now, after all these bad experiences with veterinarians, you might wonder how I ever ended up becoming a veterinarian. Let's just say that I was about to have a better experience.

# A Pony for Christmas

We lost our horses the day before I started high school. My parents said no more horses. They were too expensive and heartbreaking. Sally and I moped around, not being able to go to the barn every day. We had had to destroy all our grooming and feeding equipment, just in case any diseases could be carried on them. We had nothing to show from our two-year foray into the horse world, except our blue ribbons from the fair and some photos that made us cry.

When Christmas came around, we begged and begged for horses. We promised we would never need another vacation or another gift if we could just have horses again. That year, under the Christmas tree, we found buckets and brushes and barn gear, but no horses. How could our parents be so mean? Who gives horse gear to kids without horses? We sadly headed off to Christmas breakfast with the grandparents. I thought I'd never have another happy day.

After breakfast, my mom handed each of us an envelope. Inside the envelope was a poem. I can't remember my whole poem, but the first two lines were:

*I am your brand new pony.*
*My name is Bo-Ca-Kee.*

Now, you're probably smiling, because you got it. I must have been the dumbest kid on earth because I read the entire poem (a whole page) three times before it dawned on me I had a new pony! At that point, craziness broke out, and we made everyone jump in the car and head to a new barn. (Mom had worked her wonders and found a new barn, but Dad had to build stalls again!) We played with and groomed our new ponies until everyone was so cold they insisted we head home. We were back in the horse business!

There was only one problem with my new pony. He was eighteen years old—and pretty darned lame. He limped all the time. My mom had bought him from a friend of mine who had shown him for years and done very well. He could be shown and wouldn't limp, as long as he was given a drug called Bute, which is basically horse aspirin. People thought we were crazy for buying a lame pony, but my mom somehow knew that this pony could teach me how to ride and become a horsewoman (and he fit in our $250 budget). So we bought a boatload of Bute tablets and gave them to Bokee four days every week. Three days were so I could practice riding and jumping and one day to show. Then he got three days off.

The hardest part of dealing with a lame pony was getting the Bute into Bokee. It's very bitter and tastes like aspirin. Mom hid those huge pills in apples, applesauce, and bran mash with molasses—you name it. Bokee got pretty smart, so after a while, Mom just started shoving them down his throat like you would pill a dog. (Did I mention my mom is four-foot-ten and weighs about a hundred pounds?) Most people would never consider shoving their hand down a horse's throat, but again, we didn't know any better. Somehow, this process worked out pretty well, and my little Bokee pony took me to many championships and even the state finals. By that time, we had moved to a new barn with a lot of 4-H kids and show horses (where our board doubled again to forty dollars per month, but my dad did not have to build stalls), which was owned by our riding instructor, Mr. Bell.

Mr. Bell had been afflicted with childhood polio and had shriveled legs. He drove around the farm in an old station wagon with a public address system and loudspeakers. He must have had eyes everywhere because if we were doing something wrong, we'd hear his voice over the PA speakers yelling how to get it right. He knew more about horses than anyone I had ever met. He bred world champion racing ponies and had the world's fastest stallion in the barn. Mr. Bell gave free lessons to all the 4-H kids every Sunday and let us rent a horse trailer to go to shows for two dollars for each use. He took our group of kids to shows almost every weekend and coached us to become champions. Unfortunately, after a couple years of this, Bokee was so lame he just couldn't be ridden or jump anymore.

Mr. Bell's daughter, Mary, was an equine veterinarian in Canada. As luck would have it, she came to spend the summer at the farm. Mary let me help her when she worked with horses, and I thought she was great. She told me she could do a surgery on Bokee's front legs to help him walk better. She would remove part of the nerves to his front feet so they would be somewhat numb. It really wouldn't make it so I could ride and show him again, but it would make him happier so he could be turned out in the big fields for his retirement. My parents agreed to pay for the surgery, and Mary let me assist. Surgery was performed in the field next to the barn. Mary taught me how to change Bokee's bandages every day. She told me how much to walk him each day and when he could be turned out in the small paddock, and eventually the big field. I used to go out in the paddock and pick grass to take to Bokee in his stall when he was on stall rest. He was my best friend. I used to sit on his back and read books for hours. Eventually, he did well enough to go out to the big field with all the racing ponies and lived out his years grazing out there.

Bonus for the veterinarians! I was so enamored with what had been done for my pony that I decided this was what I was destined to become ... a veterinarian who took care of horses. My future was planned. Now I just had to get there.

# The Long Road

Once I decided I wanted to be a veterinarian, I was possessed. I read all of James Herriot's books (the veterinarian from England), studied biology and anatomy, and read every horse book I could find. I was pretty sure I wanted to be a horse veterinarian, but I really liked dogs too. I always wanted a cat, but my dad really didn't like cats (my grandfather once gave me a book *101 Uses for a Dead Cat*). I figured my chances of having a cat were pretty grim, but I did get to spend some time with small animals at least.

There was a pet rabbit in our neighborhood that someone had turned loose (not a great idea since they're pretty incapable of defending themselves). One day, my father noticed the big white rabbit had a nasty wound on its leg. He told me I should catch it and try to help it. Catching that big bunny was quite a chore, but somehow we managed. I put the bunny on the trunk of the car in the garage and examined the wound. There was a large "bug" looking out at me from the wound! I pulled the "bug" out (I really don't remember how), and the bunny seemed happy to hop away without a care in the world. After some reading, I discovered the "bug" was a Cuterebra, a large maggoty type worm that causes a wound in flesh and grows in there until it falls out and later becomes a large fly. Most people would have thought it was gross, but I thought it was really cool.

I took every science and math class I could in high school, managed to graduate with a 4.0 GPA, and was class valedictorian. I just needed to figure out which college would give me the best chance of getting admitted to a veterinary school. Back in the late 1970s, it was pretty hard to get into veterinary school. It required four years of undergraduate college, which was followed by four years of veterinary college. There were many more applicants than spaces for students, about a thirteen to one ratio. Women were only filling about a quarter of the spaces; veterinary medicine was still pretty much a man's field.

After much research and debate, I decided on Cook College, which is the agricultural college at Rutgers University in New Brunswick, New Jersey. I'd like to say it was a great undergraduate experience, but it was very competitive and stressful. I did have a great time riding on the student mounted police patrol and got to have my horse at college for two years. However, I was so anxious to become a veterinarian that I took extra credits and went to school in the summers so that I could graduate in three years instead of four. I learned about all kinds of animals, including classes in swine management, poultry, equine science, dairy cattle, and small ruminants. The animal science degree at Cook College was only nine credits shy of a degree in chemistry. I'll admit inorganic chemistry, organic chemistry, and biochemistry were not my favorite classes. I struggled the most with physics, but I managed to get through everything with A's and B's. I just had to hope it would be good enough to get me into graduate school.

My last year at Cook College was filled with writing essays, taking entrance exams, and filling out applications for veterinary school. I flew around the country to interviews, hoping to find a college that would accept me. The interviews were filled with questions that were sometimes easy and sometimes left me speechless. Some schools had us take tests; others had us write essays on subjects like "What does organized veterinary medicine mean to you? How important do you feel it is to take part in the governing bodies for veterinary medicine?" Huh? Oh boy.

I was stumped at Cornell when they asked me to identify my best and worst attributes. I came down with a major head cold at my Purdue interview and sneezed, sniffled, and wheezed with puffy eyes during my question-and-answer session. At Illinois, the good old boys on the interview panel decided that since I was a little girl who liked horses, they would only ask me questions about pigs. Little did they know that I had just taken a swine science course, and I nailed every one of those questions. By the end of spring, I had been to seven colleges for interviews and had my fingers crossed that one school would accept me.

My parents were trying to figure out how to pay for another four years of college. They offered to take a second mortgage on the house, but I decided I would have to cover the expense myself. That meant more applications and paperwork trying to get scholarships and loans.

By the time graduation rolled around, I had been accepted at Michigan State University College of Veterinary Medicine and I was ready to go. I spent the summer teaching at a great riding camp in the Poconos, knowing I would soon be on a great adventure toward becoming a veterinarian. I was scared to death that the classes would be so hard I couldn't cope or the hours would be so long I'd never sleep again. During the interview process at the different schools, I had talked to bleary-eyed students about long nights of staring through microscopes in the microbiology and histology labs. They talked about the long nights in the emergency rooms and large animal clinics doing treatments. I was petrified. I was also determined.

At the end of the summer, I was called to the pay phone at the camp. (Many years before cell phones.) It was the admissions office at Cornell University, saying someone had backed out, which left an opening in the entering veterinary school class. I was amazed. It was so awesome to actually have a choice about which college I wanted to attend. I wasn't sure what to do; however, I really hate cold weather. Michigan was going to be cold. Cornell, in Upstate New

York, sounded even colder. I politely declined, saying I would stick with Michigan. But, it gets even stranger.

The next day, I received the same phone call from the University of Illinois. They too had an opening. Now, geography is not my best subject, and I am pretty sure no one has ever decided which veterinary college to attend based on the weather, but I was pretty sure mid-state Illinois was going to be warmer than upstate Michigan.

The registrar said, "That's great! We'll see you in two weeks!"

What? Wow. I had to pack up the horse, leave camp, buy books, get a trailer, pack furniture, and find a place to live. Holy cow! This was really happening!

I headed home, and my parents helped get everything together. As luck would have it, one of my friends from Cook College had not gotten into veterinary school when she graduated the year before, and she had gone to Illinois for a year to establish residency. She had also been accepted to start at the veterinary college the same year that I was. She was from New Jersey and was coming home to collect everything she needed for another four years in Illinois. We would have a car/trailer caravan out to Illinois. I had never driven that far, and I was really excited.

So, two weeks later, we were on our way. Somewhere in the middle of Ohio, the weather became awful. In the distance, I saw my first tornado. As we drove, it seemed the tornadoes were following us and popping up all around us. Was this an omen of the next four years? Heaven help me!

# Four Long Years

At the time, the four years of veterinary school seemed like the longest years of my life. Looking back, it really wasn't that long. I was homesick most of the time and couldn't wait to get back to the East Coast. The strangest part of Illinois for me was that all the roads were laid out in a grid system; everything was straight lines and squares. In New Jersey, our roads went all over the place with curves and bends and angles. I also couldn't get used to the size of the state. Back home, I could leave New Jersey and drive through three states in an hour. In Illinois, I could drive all day and still be in Illinois. I did master the long drive from Illinois to New Jersey, and I traversed that long highway many times each year, coming home any chance I got.

I was determined to do well in veterinary school, but I didn't really think about the fact that everyone there was a good student who had worked just as hard as I had to get there. We had all competed heavily to get in, and everyone was used to working hard. The first two years of school were all classroom learning; very little time was spent working on animals.

I was pretty overwhelmed by the work, but I devised a system to get through. Classes were taught from eight until five on Monday through Friday. The class of ninety students was split into two groups for labs and one group for lectures. That meant there were forty-five lab stations with microscopes. Competition for microscope use was pretty tough in the evenings when everyone wanted to study. So, at five o'clock, I would head home to grab dinner. I went to bed and slept until one or two in the morning. I would head back to school and study until six o'clock.

I would grab a quick nap on a sofa in the ladies lounge until 7:30. Arriving students would wake me up, and I would grab coffee and a donut before heading to lectures. It was a crazy existence, but since there weren't too many people trying to study at four o'clock in the morning, I had the place to myself.

On weekends, I had a job as a lab assistant for a physiology professor to help cover expenses. I cleaned glassware in the lab, and I also had sheep barn duty. I got to feed and water the sheep and spend time in a barn, which made me happy.

The third year of school, I was able to garner a coveted position as a student intern living in the small animal veterinary clinic. There were six students, and we rotated being on call from midnight until eight in the small animal emergency room. It was great experience, and I got free housing, which was a huge weight off my overburdened debt load.

For my senior year, I was able to transfer over to the large animal clinic, where only two students rotated night emergency call. I loved it. I was able to assist in hundreds of equine emergencies and equine colic surgeries in the middle of the night. The cow emergencies were a little more out of my realm, but luckily, farmers didn't bring cows in the middle of the night very often. I was pretty short on sleep, but I was excited to be doing what I had worked toward so long and hard. I had applied for a scholarship from the Illinois Equine Council and was rewarded with enough money to get me through my last year, along with my free housing. I was still going to graduate with a huge amount of student loan debt, but I was going to make it through.

The perks of veterinary school included a long weekend trip to

Kalamazoo, Michigan, courtesy of a large pharmaceutical company. They gave us a tour of the drug manufacturing facilities (very impressive and makes me feel better about quality control maintained in this country) and wined and dined us for the weekend. They gave us free samples of just about everything. They did this in the hopes that we would recommend their products when we were in practice in the real world.

The large pet food companies also courted us. They supplied free food to the school for animals in the hospital and free food for students with pets. Again, they wanted us to recognize their names and recommend their products. Lectures about different animal diseases always included a recommendation for which prescription diet would treat the disease. The pet food companies put a lot of money into research and development of pet foods and prescription diets, so this all made sense.

In early December of my senior year, I found out I could sit for my national board exams prior to graduation. Most states would not allow us to take the exams until after graduation, but Kentucky was one of the few states that allowed December testing. A dozen of us headed south to try our hand at the dreaded exam. I was pretty much in panic mode. In order to prepare, I read and underlined the entire *Merck Manual of Veterinary Medicine* prior to the test. The manual is a few thousand pages, covering every disease known to animals throughout the world. I think I destroyed some brain cells in the process. The exam took two days, and we were all sure we had failed.

While we were there, they offered to let us take the Kentucky state board exam as well. Most of us figured it would be good practice, and we didn't have anything to lose. By the end of the two days, I was pretty skeptical about my chances at passing, but I was glad I had taken the opportunity to practice taking the exam. I headed home for Christmas, thinking I would be a very lucky person if I passed. Imagine how happy I was six weeks later when I received the news that I had passed my national board exams, and I was also certified to practice veterinary medicine in the great state of Kentucky! I didn't think I wanted to live in the Midwest, but, at least they had lots of horses there!

During our senior year of veterinary school, we were required to spend two six-week terms doing an "externship," where we would work as an intern in a real-world veterinary practice. I wanted to come home for Christmas, so I took one of my terms from mid-December to the end of January. It was a cold, snowy winter in New Jersey. I was able to get an externship with a local equine veterinarian who did mostly racetrack work with standardbred horses (they race pulling carts). Since I had never worked with standardbreds, it was a great opportunity to see something new. I also had an externship at night at a local small animal emergency clinic. It's like working in the human ER—sometimes slow, sometimes one big adrenaline rush.

I loved both externships. There was only one problem … I hate cold weather! I froze to death in those racehorse barns all day and couldn't figure out how this doctor had his hands in buckets of cold water all day, rarely even bothered to put his coat on, and didn't seem fazed by the weather. There was another student riding along with us, and she seemed just as cold as I was. I wasn't so sure I could handle working New Jersey winters outside with horses. A cloud on my horizon.

As if my senior year of veterinary school was not stressful enough, a few months later, while working in the small animal emergency ward at school, I received a strange phone call from my aunt one evening. My grandfather was on a lot of medications for his heart. He had had a major heart attack when I was in high school and was lucky to have survived. He stopped smoking, lost a lot of weight, and ate a better diet after his brush with death. He did well all through my college years, but my aunt was calling because he was having trouble. It seemed he had had diarrhea for months, and the doctors had not been able to find a way to get it under control. They tried many medications, including Valium, thinking it was due to anxiety. Nothing helped. His symptoms seemed to be worsening, including blurred vision, double vision, yellow vision, and dizziness. He thought his glasses were the wrong prescription, but they had checked out okay.

My grandfather ran his own business and was a worrier. He was always afraid he would run out of something, having lived through the Depression and not knowing from where his next meal was coming. Thinking in that vein, he had been dumping his medications into little bowls and giving the empty bottles to my aunt to take to the drugstore to get refilled. The pharmacist obviously was not paying attention to the number of refills because my grandfather had over a year's worth of medication stockpiled. What my aunt had discovered that night was that he had the pills mixed up and put them back in the wrong bottles from the bowls. He was taking the once-a-day pills three times a day and the twice-a-day pills once a day and whatever else he had gotten confused. She asked me if his symptoms could be related to taking too much or too little of one of the drugs.

I carefully looked up each of the drugs in my clinic formulary. I soon discovered that every one of his symptoms matched digitalis toxicity. Digoxin is an extremely strong medication that is lethal if taken in large amounts. I cried and told my aunt to take him to the hospital that night, not tomorrow or the next day. He was lucky to be alive since this had been going on for months already. How had his doctors not seen the correlation?

My grandfather was admitted in the cardiac intensive care unit that night. His kidneys were failing, and his heart arrhythmia was life threatening. He was on intravenous fluids to cleanse his system, and the prognosis was guarded. I was so distraught that I hopped on a plane and headed home for the weekend. I had to see him and make sure he would be okay. I surprised him when I walked into his hospital room, and he was instantly cheerful. His doctor came in, and my grandfather proudly introduced me and announced that if it weren't for my diagnostic skills, he would have died. He was so proud that I was going to be a doctor.

The doctor smiled and asked me which medical school I was attending. My mother piped up and announced I was going to be a veterinarian and was attending the University of Illinois. The reaction was amazing. The doctor pursed his lips, squinted his eyes, his face turned red, and he looked like he was going to have a stroke right then and there. He announced that a veterinarian was not a "real" doctor, and this was just ludicrous. He stormed out of the room. Wow. So, there you have it. Eight years of college education, but I was not going to be a real doctor. Humph. I am happy to say my grandfather survived and left the hospital a few weeks later, even if he did have to be diagnosed by a soon-to-be veterinarian.

# Decision Time

M ay of 1984 finally arrived, and it was time for graduation from
veterinary college. Our class of ninety students had lost a few
along the way, but for the most part, we arrived unscathed. Relatives
came from near and far to help the students celebrate becoming
doctors of veterinary medicine. There were parties and champagne
and smiles all around. There was never any question about where I
would practice after graduation. I was headed home to southern New
Jersey, near my family and friends. I had been offered two jobs and
needed to decide which one I would take. Both paid the same amount
of money, so that was not part of the decision process.

One offer was with a small animal practice close to home. It was
not a fancy clinic, and the medicine being practiced was mediocre.
The practice had one owner, and he had worked alone for years. It
was cats and dogs only, no fancy surgeries, nothing very challenging.
I had worked there one summer, and I knew everyone and knew I
could work alongside them with no problems. There was heat in the
winter and air conditioning in the summer. It was a thirty-five-hour
workweek. Emergencies at nights and on the weekends were sent to
the emergency clinic in the area. The worst injury I could sustain was

a bite wound from a dog or cat (although, those can be tragic and painful). I had interviewed at quite a few other small animal clinics and found the "good old boys" attitude still prevailed, and it would be difficult to work in those clinics. The owner was much kinder and would allow me some free rein to update conditions in the clinic.

The other offer was with a local equine practitioner. It was an ambulatory practice, no hospital to go to everyday, just farm calls. The owner of the practice would supply me with a truck, and off I would go to small and large farms to treat whatever came up. This doctor had a large clientele, and some of the horses were fairly expensive show horses and racehorses. He did a lot of reproduction work, palpating mares for pregnancy (no ultrasound in those days), and deciding which horses were ready to breed. It was the opportunity of a lifetime.

Of course, I was trying to make this decision in the spring, when the weather was nice. There were three huge factors that made my decision for me: I hate cold weather, so winter was going to be torture; I could get seriously hurt doing rectal palpations on kicking mares; I would be on call for emergencies all day and night, every day and night. A life outside of veterinary medicine would be pretty tough to find.

So after weighing all the factors, small animal medicine won out. I was hoping to be able to go back to riding and showing horses, as soon as time and money were available. I still had a pile of student debt to pay off and couldn't live at home with Mom and Dad forever. When I received my first paycheck, I thought I had won the lottery and could never spend that amount of money. Boy, was I wrong. Real life was just a moment away.

# The Early Years

My first day as a real doctor was met with great anticipation. I had a fancy new white lab coat with my name embroidered on it, preceded by the letters "Dr." I had my fancy new pen that belonged in a desk set with my name engraved on it (but I had no desk at the clinic to put it on). I had my new stethoscope, new clothes, and I was ready to roll. Or so I thought.

When the first client arrived and placed their pet on the examination table, I froze. I was now the decision maker. I was in the hot seat. What if I got it wrong? What if I didn't know the diagnosis? Worst of all, what if I made a mistake? Luckily, my new employer was also in the building, along with a couple of seasoned veterinary assistants. Any time I had a question or wasn't quite sure what I was seeing, one of those wonderful folks would seem to appear out of nowhere to lend a hand and help guide my decision making. The clinic wasn't anything fancy, and we didn't practice high-powered medicine. Most of the cases were fairly routine—annual exams, vaccinations, laboratory testing, fleas, and parasites. When I was truly stumped with a patient, one of the assistants would suddenly "need me in the back room" to gently guide me with a direction to pursue. My employer was a nice enough guy, but he really didn't like to work up difficult cases.

My employer also did not enjoy surgery, and he was a pretty mediocre surgeon. He and the staff were thrilled there would be someone else around to take over some of the surgery load. I'm pretty sure my employer didn't remember back to veterinary college, or maybe it was different when he was in school, but the actual number of surgeries performed by a student in those days was very few. I had never been totally in charge of the surgery from start to finish.

In school, there were teachers, interns, residents, and other students to help. We had three people running anesthesia, one surgeon, and a couple assistants. In real practice I had ... me. Oh boy. The first few surgeries were gut-wrenching, nail-biting, nerve-wracking hours. I was slow, the work was tedious, and I breathed a sigh of great relief with every success. Luckily, by the time I had done a dozen spays, I started to get faster and more relaxed with the process. Routine surgeries started to become just that. I never stopped worrying about my patient while I was in surgery. I always made sure an assistant monitored them, and I stayed with them until they were awake. But I stopped being a wreck walking into the surgery room.

After two weeks on the job, my employer announced he was leaving the next week for a trip to a national veterinary conference with an extended vacation added on. He would be away for three weeks. *What? Wait! You're my mentor! You're the one with experience! I don't know what I'm doing! What if an animal dies?* I was panic-stricken. I would be left alone to perform the surgeries, diagnose the cases, and handle all the clients. And it was summer, our busy season! He must have sensed my impending panic because he made a concession: he would call every evening to go over cases and answer any questions I had. That sort of seemed reasonable to me at the time, so I relaxed a bit and assured him I would muddle through. I learned the hard way that someone who was on the other end of the phone hundreds of miles away (probably with a drink in his hand while waiting to go out to dinner with friends), who couldn't see the patients in front of me, really couldn't answer any tough questions. Somehow I made it through, and I'm sure it made me more confident in the long run. However, I'm pretty sure that's when I started going gray.

When I think back to how we practiced medicine then compared to what we do now, I am grateful our patients survived. Since we didn't have any intravenous catheters in the clinic, we never gave intravenous fluids. Since we didn't have in-house laboratory equipment, we had to send out any tests we wanted to run. Sometimes it would be days before we had answers. Our old x-ray equipment was basically in our back storage room loaded down with boxes. When we wanted to take x-rays, we had to move the boxes, take the pictures, and hand-develop the films in the "darkroom," which was our mop closet. If we didn't get the animal's positioning right on the first try, there was no way we were going to go back, take another film, and start the hour-long process over again. We had no monitoring equipment in the surgery room, no EKGs, no blood pressure monitors, and no pulse oximeters. Once the animal was put under anesthesia, it was pretty much on its own.

Our survival rate was incredibly good. Looking back, I can only remember losing one animal under anesthesia. That was one of the few days that I questioned whether I was capable of staying in this field.

# Pet Food Salesman

I stayed at my first job for a year and a half. I had become a decent surgeon and felt better about my diagnostic skills. We used a lot of antibiotics in those days, as there was no talk of resistant bacteria, MRSA, or flesh-eating bacteria. We also used a lot of steroids for allergies, itchy skin, lameness, and just about any inflammatory condition. We didn't have much else to offer. We didn't diagnose cancer very often, and when we did, it was basically a death sentence. Sure, the big university hospitals may have had more to offer, but not many folks were interested in pursuing those options. Pets were fed whatever was available in the grocery store pet aisle, and we gave it our approval. If the pet was diagnosed with kidney disease, we had a prescription diet to recommend. Otherwise, we pretty much didn't care what they ate.

I left my first job and moved an hour north to marry a veterinary school classmate. I searched out and managed to find a job with another small animal clinic, only a few miles from my new home. This clinic was much more advanced than the one I had left. We had in-house laboratory equipment, proper anesthetic monitoring equipment, and an automatic x-ray processor that only took five minutes to develop an x-ray. We had trained technicians and receptionists who wore uniforms. The hospital building was newer, well laid out, and had a true kennel room, storage room, dental room, surgery room, and an office with my own desk where I proudly displayed my professional pen set with my name engraved on it. My new employer was fairly nice, but he ran a tight ship and had a lot of rules. He did allow me to take over the routine surgeries since I had really come to enjoy surgery by that point. I was able to improve my diagnostic skills under his tutelage and learned to delve further into cases. This clinic was in a much more affluent area, and people were willing to spend more money on their pets.

Next door to the clinic, connected by a hallway, the veterinarian's wife ran a pet boutique. She sold cute doggie clothes, collars and leashes, treats, pet décor, and lots and lots and lots of pet food—but not your usual pet foods found in the supermarkets. She sold Hill's pet products. Hill's is the maker of Science Diet products, and at that time, they made formulas for puppies and kittens, adults, and seniors. Hill's also spends a lot of time and money on research and development of veterinary prescription diets. We like to call them "alphabet soup" because they are named with letters standing for the condition being treated. At that time, I remember P/D (pediatric diet), G/D (geriatric diet), K/D (kidney diet), C/D (calculolytic diet for cats with urinary tract disease), R/D (reducing diet for obese animals), D/D (dermatitis diet for skin allergies), and H/D (heart diet).

Since that time, Hill's has used up most of the letters in the alphabet. Anyway, my employer realized that not only was the science and research behind the diets sound, but the diets were also an incredible profit center for the practice and the pet store. Every animal that came into the clinic was prescribed one of those diets. The compliance rate was high. Our clients would do anything we recommended.

The sales rep for the Hill's company used to stop by the clinic fairly often, at least once a month. She brought us lunches and clinic supplies like posters, anatomy models, and whatever perks came down the pipeline. My employer received trips to conferences and lower prices for mass quantities of food purchased. I became good friends with the sales rep, as well, and she would take me out to dinner and buy me drinks when I went to conferences. I was the poster child for prescription pet food sales.

I stayed at that clinic for almost five years. I was happy to work close to home, and I learned a lot from a good veterinarian. But it was time to start a family, and I left the job when I was eight months pregnant. My employer may have been a good veterinarian, but he wasn't a nice enough person to hold my job for me. I was officially unemployed with a growing family. We would be able to get by for a few months, but I knew I would soon have to return to work. I was lucky enough to stay home with my son for two months. Then we hired a Swedish nanny, and I was off on a new adventure.

# On the Road Again

U nable to find another position as an associate veterinarian close to home, I signed on with a temp agency. As a "relief" veterinarian, I would be sent to clinics throughout New Jersey and Pennsylvania when an extra doctor was needed to cover vacation or sick leave. I was sort of like the substitute teacher. I found this to be rather challenging and really enjoyed it. I liked having the freedom to choose where I wanted to work and what I wanted to do. I met a lot of great doctors, staff, and clients along the way. I was offered permanent positions at many of the clinics where I worked, but I was enjoying the freedom of not having to answer to a boss every day.

In addition to working as a relief veterinarian, I took on a regular job at the local emergency clinic where I had done my senior externship and had sent emergency patients while working at my first job. The emergency medicine was challenging and pushed me to think fast and learn new things. When I was the only doctor available at two o'clock in the morning and a dog had a bleeding tumor in the abdomen, it was up to me to solve the problem. This was where I did my first splenectomy (removed the spleen), first nephrectomy (removed a kidney), first bloat surgery (twisted stomach), and many other procedures that pushed me to new limits. I also learned to really trust and use my staff. I loved my technicians, and they worked very hard at what they did. I learned to assign tasks and expect results. I stayed at that emergency clinic for ten years, working Fridays overnight and Sundays during the day. I combined working there with whatever other relief positions I had at the time. I would probably have stayed there indefinitely, but the clinic was eventually sold to a corporation when the owner was nearing retirement. Most of the doctors working there left at that time, as we discovered corporate medicine was not something we enjoyed.

By the time I left the emergency clinic job, I had stopped traveling around so much as a relief veterinarian, had my second child, and had settled into a small animal clinic in southern New Jersey, not far from my parents. The practice was small, but the medicine and surgery practiced there were excellent. My new employer was fairly easy to work with, and I loved the staff. I commuted an hour each way, but I often took my kids and dropped them at my parents' house so they could have grandparent-grandchild bonding time.

As luck would have it, two years later, a new proposal fell onto my desk.

# A Place to Call Home

One day at work, I saw an advertisement from a local Realtor on my desk. There were photos of an old, rundown veterinary hospital for sale. The hospital was only five and a half miles south of the practice where I was working. This was too good to be true. I didn't have any money and didn't know if a bank would back me, but I had to at least take a look. I made an appointment to look at the property and was astonished to find it was even more rundown than it looked in the photos. This was going to be a long road of construction, loans, and time with no income. There was no way I could undertake this project on my own. I was also struggling with the moral dilemma of opening a practice only five miles away from the practice owned by a man who had been good to me over the previous five years. So I went to him with a proposal.

The practice he owned had outgrown the building. We were crammed wall to wall with employees, clients, and patients, and we had to carry animals and products up and down the stairs to the kennels and storage in the basement. Many of our clients lived in the area south of the new property I had seen. I proposed that we buy the old clinic down the road, rehab the building, and split the practice into the main hospital and a satellite hospital. We could do outpatient appointments at the newly purchased hospital, and send all hospitalized, surgery, and radiology patients to the hospital he already owned. At first, he wanted nothing to do with the project. He said he had enough on his plate and didn't want to expand. I persisted and told him I really wanted to take this on and would find a way to do it without him if he wasn't on board (even though ethically, it was a struggle for me to be competing with the person who had been kind to me for so long).

Luckily, with a little pressure, he decided it would be a good project. We became partners. I ended up being the minority partner, but at least I was finally a practice owner! With his good track history running a practice, the loan from the bank was easy. I borrowed money from my grandfather for my part of the down payment. My new partner loved construction work, so he redesigned the building, hired a helper and an electrician, and rehabbed the entire building for a fraction of what it would have cost to hire out all the work. We were up and running in no time. I worked at the new clinic, he worked at the original hospital, and the other two doctors on staff rotated between the two hospitals. Since he was the managing partner, I just had to show up and practice veterinary medicine.

Once I became a partner, I needed to work more hours because we now had two clinics to cover six days a week. The long commute was draining, and I talked my family into moving south. We would be closer to my parents, who were extremely helpful with childcare. When they weren't available to babysit, I could take the kids to work with me. They loved hanging out at the clinic and would pretend they were dogs by putting blankets and water bowls in cages and curling up to sleep. I would be able to spend more time helping the clinic grow without the long commute. We built a house on a three-acre property. The best part of all was that I could finally get back into riding horses. Finances were a little better, and my student loans were finally paid off. As a partner in the practice, my income was a bit better, so we thought we could handle the expense.

# Finally Back into Horses

I started by finding someone to give my children lessons at a local farm that had good ponies for them to handle safely. My daughter was only twenty months old, but when she saw her four-year-old brother riding, she demanded to do the same. It was so much fun to be back in a barn and to watch my kids learn.

After a year of having them ride twice a week, I was determined to find them a pony of their own. I had been out of the horse business for ten long years, so I had no idea what I was going to have to spend to find a good pony. I started the search, thinking I could find one for fewer than five hundred dollars. Ha! After a month, I had raised my price to one thousand dollars. Ha! I started talking to old riding friends who were still in the show world, and I was politely informed that a good show pony to get them started would cost somewhere around ten thousand dollars! I was crushed. My husband said there was no way we would be spending that kind of money on a pony. Of course, by this time, I had promised them a pony, so I was going to have to find one somewhere.

After a lot of searching, I managed to buy a fat gray pony that had come through an auction in central New Jersey for just a little over a thousand dollars. He had been a driving pony and had the nicest personality. He was going to need a lot of training, but I thought he was safe enough to get started. Even though he had been used as a driving pony, he could at least walk and trot under saddle with the kids on him. He was sick and had green discharge pouring from his nose after coming through the auction, but a local veterinary friend was nice enough to loan us the use of a paddock at her veterinary clinic where he could be quarantined for a month. The kids named him Smokey, with the show name Puff of Smoke (after we ruled out NASCAR Bob, which was my son's choice). Once Smokey was healthy enough, we moved him to the lesson barn, and my kids had their new best friend. They taught Smokey how to canter and jump and took him to shows almost every weekend. Eventually, he won more championships than any other horse that had ever gone through our barn.

A year after buying the pony, I knew I wanted a horse of my own to ride and show again. After the pony search the previous year, I knew it wouldn't be easy. I didn't have ten thousand dollars to buy a show horse. I was going to have to sacrifice some of my horse requirements to get one that fit my budget. I would have to get a young horse that needed a lot of training or an older horse that may have some health issues.

After months of looking, I found the perfect horse. I went to a barn in Delaware to look at a young off-the-track thoroughbred. As I watched the rider put him through his paces, I knew he was too much horse for me. I couldn't afford to get hurt and be unable to work and care for my children and their pony. Luckily, there was another horse working in the arena. I asked about him and learned he was a twelve-year-old quarter horse with a ton of show experience. His name was Auto Pilot. That seemed like a good sign. I asked to ride him, and it was true love within five minutes. His asking price was out of my range, but the owner told me he needed to be sold because his arthritis was getting bad—and they didn't know how much time he would have left in the show ring. Because I was a veterinarian and she knew I would take good care of him, we were able to negotiate a lower price. I had my new best friend.

We ended up building a barn on our three acres and had our horses at home. It was the first time in my life I was able to take care of my horses without boarding them, and I was in heaven. There was no electricity or running water in the barn, but every morning at five, I carried my lantern to the barn and cleaned stalls in the dark. I ran a hose from the house to fill water buckets and troughs. I sweated in the summer and froze in the winter while breaking water on ice buckets, but I still loved it. I set up jumps in our field, and the trainer came to our house twice a week to give lessons to us. We bought a truck and a horse trailer and pulled the horse and pony all over New Jersey, Pennsylvania, and Delaware to horse shows, piling up ribbons and championship points everywhere we went. My life was full, and I was happy.

# Life before Alternatives

When my kids were growing up, we always had a dog. When they were born, we had a red Doberman named Astro. He was a big goofball, and my kids learned to walk by hanging onto his legs and climbing on his back. When he was about two years old, he ran out the door one morning—straight into the side of our car parked in the driveway. It seemed he had lost his vision overnight and was completely blind. Other than not being able to see anything, he seemed perfectly normal. I was stumped as to the cause, so I took him to a specialty veterinary practice where the neurologist diagnosed him with Granulomatous Meningoencephalopathy. I had never heard of it. The cause was unknown, but the neurologist said it was an inflammatory disorder that some clinicians theorized could be related to vaccinations given for distemper. The only treatment was a heavy dose of steroids along with a heavy dose of another chemotherapeutic immune-suppressing drug.

Luckily, Astro's vision came back fairly quickly with the drugs, but the side effects were awful. The steroids made him drink and pee constantly. He would just stand there and stare at me as the urine ran out of him. He couldn't get outside fast enough, and we spent a lot of time cleaning up accidents. He took the medications for a year before we were finally able to wean him off the drugs—but not before he developed a secondary fungal infection due to his suppressed immune system. I didn't vaccinate him anymore, as no one was sure of the association, but I didn't want to take a chance. Maybe that was a sign I was destined to be against over-vaccination of our pets.

Poor Astro also had horrible gas all the time. He could clear a room and was a total embarrassment when friends came to the house. I fed dry kibble because that was the "preferred" form of pet food. This was during my days as a dog food salesman, so I tried every prescription diet available, as well as every dry food I could find made by the major pet food companies. I finally found a pelleted, no-soy formula made by a smaller pet food company, which seemed to help a bit, but he never really thrived on anything I fed.

As a result of all the drugs he was given, the inflammatory process in his body, and the food that didn't agree with him, poor Astro always suffered with low-grade liver disease. His liver enzymes were never normal, and every year or so, he would spike a high fever and extremely elevated liver enzymes, requiring antibiotics and more anti-inflammatory medications. He would spend a week curled in a shivering ball, nauseous and anorexic with each episode. He suffered a second bout of blindness a few years after the initial episode and had to be given another round of steroids and immune suppressants.

As he aged, Astro became slower and slept more. I thought he was just getting old. He would lie around a lot and didn't want to chase the kids around our three-acre property. It was around that time that the new wonder drug, Rimadyl, came on the market. It was marketed as the newest, greatest gift for old dogs with arthritis and pain. I didn't know for sure that Astro was sedentary because he had arthritis pain, but he was eight years old, and it made sense that he would. I decided to try him on the new drug. The results were amazing. Suddenly, he had more energy than I had seen in years. He would race around the house and yard, chasing deer through the fields and playing with the kids. I thought it really was a miracle.

What I had assumed was old age was actually pain keeping him from being active.

What I did not know when Rimadyl first came on the market was that some dogs could have adverse reactions to the drug. A dog belonging to one of my veterinary technicians died from liver failure two weeks after starting the medication. It is now recommended that dogs with liver problems should not be given the drug. Had I known that at the outset, I doubt I would have used the drug for Astro, given his long history of liver disease. Somehow, I got lucky, and Astro was able to take the medication for two years. He did finally die at the age of ten from liver failure. I'm not sure if it was related to the drug or if it was just the final throes of his long-standing liver problem.

Unfortunately, all of Astro's problems occurred before I started using alternative treatments for my patients. Looking back, if I owned him later in life, I never would have given him vaccinations once he became an adult. Perhaps that would have prevented the Granulomatous Meningoencephalitis that plagued him. Instead, I would have performed blood titers to determine immunity to distemper and parvovirus. I would have given vaccinations only if the titer was low. I would not have fed Astro dry kibble. I would have fed him a raw meat diet, with some home-cooked food added for variation, including foods to help soothe and strengthen the liver. I would have given him herbal therapies to help combat his chronic liver disease (although perhaps he would not have developed the liver disease without being over-vaccinated and overmedicated). I would have treated his arthritis with herbal and nutritional supplements, laser therapy, chiropractic care, and acupuncture. I like to think he would have lived longer than ten years if he had had the luxury of having a mom using alternative therapies.

# A Strange New World

In my world of veterinary medicine, I am always searching for new things to learn, new procedures, and better ways to get things accomplished. After our new clinic had been open for about five years, we were doing well and it was always busy. One day, an advertisement came in the mail for a course called Veterinary Orthopedic Manipulation. It talked about therapies that could help animals recover faster from surgery, help with lameness issues, and even help some internal medicine problems. My partner did a lot of orthopedic surgeries, so this looked like a good course to take so that I could help those animals after surgery. My partner agreed, and we sent in my course registration.

A month later, I arrived at the course. There were about forty people in the room, and a veterinarian was all set to start the lecture. About forty-five minutes into the lecture, it became apparent this doctor was talking about doing chiropractic manipulations on animals. This was not what I thought I had signed up to learn. At the first break in the lecture, I started talking to people in the room and discovered about half of them were actually human chiropractors, not veterinarians. I was stumped. We had paid a lot for this course, so I figured I should stick it out and see if there was anything useful I could learn. I had only been to a chiropractor a couple times in my life, when I was pregnant for my son. I have to admit that the doctor solved some big issues for me at the time, but I wasn't sure how much stock I put in this healing therapy. The lecturer was talking about using this therapy on horses, and I couldn't see how that was going to be possible, given their size and my size (five feet four). I settled back to listen and learn, feeling pretty skeptical.

After two days of training, I bought one of the chiropractic tools from the lecturer. I took it home and headed off to visit my parents to tell them about this strange new thing I was learning. My parents had a fifty-pound standard schnauzer that was about seven years old. I asked them if she was having any issues with running or jumping. My mom reported that Sparky couldn't jump into the car anymore, so she had to lift her. (Yup, hundred-pound woman, fifty-pound dog.)

I took my newfangled gadget, called an activator, and did a treatment on Sparky's spine. We headed out to the car in the garage to see if Sparky could get in the car. We opened the car door and stood back to see what would happen ... and a miracle occurred! Not only did Sparky jump into the back seat, she jumped over the front seat into the front of the car, then back over into the back seat, repeating this motion three or four times. We all stood there with our jaws open, thinking it was the coolest thing we had ever seen. I couldn't wait to try the thing on more cases.

On my first day back at the office after finishing my course, I was excited—and a bit nervous—about trying my new technique on some patients. I wasn't sure how receptive clients would be to this new therapy, but I figured I wouldn't charge for the treatment the first few weeks while I learned more about the technique. As luck would have it, one of my first patients that morning was a German shepherd that couldn't walk. We had never seen the patient before, and the owner sounded upset when he called. His dog was huge, older, and couldn't get up from lying down. He had someone help him get the dog in the car and headed to the clinic.

When the man arrived, he walked in bent over, using a cane. He had to have been ninety years old. My technicians carried the dog in on a blanket and placed him on the exam room floor. The old man and I had a conversation that went something like this:

Him: "Doc, I think he's got arthritis, and that's why he can't get up."

Me: "Sir, could your dog walk yesterday?"

Him: "Sure, he was running and playing yesterday."

Me: "Sir, I don't mean to be rude, but do you have arthritis?"

Him: "I sure do, that's why I use this cane."

Me: "Sir, could you walk yesterday?"

Him: "Of course, don't be silly."

Me: "Sir, can you walk today?"

Him: "Of course, you saw me come in."

Me: "Okay. It seems to me that arthritis would not come on suddenly and make your dog unable to walk. I think we may have something bigger going on here."

Him: "Okay, doc. Just get him walking. He's too big to carry."

Oh, boy. I really wasn't sure what was going on, but the dog was painful in his mid-spine when I touched him. We didn't have an x-ray machine at the clinic, and the man was unwilling to take the dog to our main hospital. I gave the dog an injection of steroids, which would hopefully kick in and allow the dog to start walking in a day or so. I also got out my wonderful new gadget and did a treatment along the dog's back. I didn't expect anything great to happen, but I also figured I didn't have anything to lose. I asked the technician to stay with the dog while the man paid his bill and then to carry the dog back out to the car. I went on to my next patient in the next exam room.

When I came out of the exam room a few minutes later, I was incredulous as I watched my technician chasing the huge German shepherd down the hall! I asked her what she had done to get him up, and she said, "Nothing! He just got up after you left the room and started running!" I was flabbergasted. Maybe there really was something to this new technique!

During that time, I was teaching pharmacology and pathology to the veterinary technician students at a local community college. I was so excited about this new therapy I had found that I spent a whole hour in pathology class talking about and demonstrating this new technique. The students were very excited, and many of them brought their dogs to the next class session to have them adjusted. They reported their dogs felt great and wanted to keep bringing their pets to my office for future treatments. This was great; my new therapy was building momentum!

But not everyone was happy about my new teachings. The next week, I was called into the head administrator's office at the college. He wanted to know if there was any truth to the rumor he had heard that I was teaching the students about "chiro-quack-tic." I assured him it was not quackery and explained how the therapy was helping many of my patients. I was told not to mention it again in any of my classes. I guess not everyone has an open mind.

From that point forward, I tried my activator on just about anything with four legs and even some with two. (My dad became one of the biggest fans of the treatment!) Usually the results weren't quite as miraculous as my new German shepherd friend, but I was getting results in just about every case. I had finally found a way around using steroids for all those arthritis and inflammation cases. Steroids have many side effects, and I had never been happy about using them.

I started using the activator on my horse and the kids' pony, and the results were amazing. Our pony had never been able to lift his head higher than his shoulders until I adjusted him with the activator. After one treatment, he was totally different. My horse had been getting steroid injections in his joints to keep him sound. Once I started adjusting him, he never needed another injection.

I wanted to learn more. I wanted to know what else was out there in the land of alternative medicine that might help my patients feel better and live longer.

# Too Many Options

Once I started researching alternative therapies, I discovered an amazing number of options. Not all the options had been used on animals, and many were still in their infancy and not practiced by many veterinarians. I started reading about acupuncture, acupressure, flower essences, Chinese herbals, American herbals, Ayurvedic herbals, raindrop therapy, essential oils, aromatherapy, homeopathy, glandulars, vitamins, folk remedies, animal communication, T-Touch, Reiki, and Craniosacral therapy; the list was endless! How was I ever going to be able to learn all this? I was disheartened.

My sister had been taking and teaching courses in Reiki, T-Touch, and Craniosacral therapy for years. I always thought Sally was a bit "odd" for believing in and using those therapies. I had attended some classes she had given about T-Touch, and I thought it was something useful that people could practice on their own pets. I just didn't see how it could help in a veterinary practice. I attended a Craniosacral class that Sally was giving for first-level practitioners. I couldn't really get the hang of it. I had her treat my elbow, which was sore from using the activator, and the pain was gone permanently after one treatment. I just didn't think those treatments were therapies I would enjoy performing.

Trying to be practical, I figured I would have to start by getting better at performing chiropractic adjustments. I had started treating more horses (finally back to my original goal of helping horses!), and I wanted to learn more about adjusting horses. Since my husband was also a veterinarian and a horseman, we figured this was something we could do together. We scheduled a trip to Missouri for a course about equine chiropractic. There, we worked with about thirty other veterinarians who were doing this type of work. We got to work on a lot of horses while we were there and felt pretty confident with what we were doing.

When we came home, we started lining up clients with horses and headed out on farm calls. Mostly we had to do calls in the evening and on weekends since I had to work in the small animal clinic during the week, and my husband had a full time job with the state Department of Agriculture. It took a long time driving to farms, and we were getting exhausted. We needed a bigger farm so horses could come to us.

After convincing my husband we *needed* it, we bought a forty-acre farm a few months later. Soon, we were on a roll. In order to pay for the farm, we took in horses for boarding and lessons. Within a year, I had fifty lesson students, and we had twenty-five horses at the farm. The farm was interfering with my practice. My husband's job was an hour away. We needed help. We hired a friend to help with lessons and farm maintenance. I reworked my clinic schedule so I could be there two long days each week, leaving the other five days available for chiropractic work, farm work, horse shows, and lessons. Every year, when a new class of students wanted to learn equine chiropractic, we offered our farm and horses for practice. It allowed us to keep learning, and it felt good to help train others so more animals could get treatment.

Unfortunately, the strain of running a busy farm, working at the clinic, and my husband's long commute took a toll on our family. My son had stopped riding horses, and he and his dad spent weekends at soccer tournaments, while my daughter and I spent weekends with horses. Our family broke apart, and we were divorced. The farm was sold, and I moved six of our horses to another farm where my daughter could continue riding and I could continue teaching. It was a very sad time in our lives, but the good news is that my ex-husband and I managed to become good friends again a few years later. He actually works in my clinics occasionally when I am away, and we attend horse shows together to watch our daughter compete.

# Treating Horses Holistically

While I never got back to my original plan of becoming an equine veterinarian, I have had the pleasure of being able to work with horses again. Besides riding and showing for myself, I had the joy of teaching others, holding horse shows at our farms, and training horses and riders. But my biggest joy has been helping horses recover from injuries and misuse. The use of chiropractic care, acupuncture, herbals, homeopathic remedies, and saddle fitting has allowed me to help hundreds of horses over the years.

Lameness and bad behavior are the most common concerns I hear when I am called to treat a horse. On the whole, I'd say there is no such thing as a mean horse. Horses exhibiting bad behaviors are generally in pain or have been mistreated. Owners who don't know better use stronger bits, whips, chains, and other abusive items to try to control an ill-mannered horse, which usually just makes things worse. Many times, the horse has been through a thorough veterinary examination, and nothing has been found to indicate a medical problem causing the poor behavior. Commonly, chiropractic care or acupuncture can solve these issues.

I find one of the biggest issues for horses with pain is a saddle that doesn't fit. Many riders have no idea how to properly fit a saddle to the horse. Riders buy saddles that feel comfortable for them, never considering whether it is comfortable for the horse. I see riders using multiple saddle pads to try to make the saddle fit better. My favorite comparison (told to me by my sister) is that if your shoes are too tight and you put on more socks to give them more padding, you are just making the shoes tighter and they hurt even more. The same goes for saddles! I see riders, whose bodies are uneven, riding with one stirrup three inches longer than the other. They put more weight on one side of the saddle, and their horses become unevenly muscled, eventually developing back pain and lameness. I've sent many owners off to see their own chiropractors!

Ideally, the saddle would be custom made to fit the horse, and the saddle would stay with the horse its entire life. But this never happens. Generally, the saddle stays with the rider, or it gets sold when the rider outgrows it. Even if the saddle stayed with the horse, it would still need to be looked at annually with a critical eye because a horse's muscling changes with exercise and training.

Horses that have been well trained and well mannered, that suddenly start having behavior issues, are generally horses in pain. They don't just suddenly become evil. A bucking horse is usually a horse with back pain. Horses that won't hold up a hind foot for cleaning are generally horses with hock or stifle pain. Horses that suddenly start to shy or be fearful commonly have pain that is distracting them. A horse that bites or kicks when the girth is tightened may be a horse with stomach ulcers. There are acupuncture points associated with stomach ulcers and pain in each of the joints. Acupuncture is a great diagnostic tool, as well as a treatment modality.

Lifestyle changes have created problems for our big friends. Many horses do not have the opportunity to walk in large fields and graze many hours a day. We have artificially tailored their lives to meet our requirements. Horses are being kept in stalls, sometimes around the clock, only being taken out when ridden. Horses are herd animals and should not live in solitary confinement. Stomach ulcers have become an overwhelming problem because horses worry and become bored, developing bad habits like stall weaving, pacing in circles, pawing, and kicking at walls. Because these horses do not have access to fields for grazing, they are fed hay, which can be variable in quality. Large quantities of sweetened grains are fed to increase energy and weight. Metabolic diseases like insulin-resistance and Cushing's disease stem from these sweetened, high-carbohydrate diets. Colic, colitis, stomach ulcers, and laminitis have also become big problems for horses.

The key to good health for horses would include a return to a more natural state, if that were possible. Unfortunately, a growing population and increasing need to use land for housing have left less land available for grazing. Some show horses and racehorses have become so valuable that their owners wouldn't think of letting them run loose in a field with other horses where they might get hurt. I can only recommend consideration of a more natural lifestyle, if possible.

# On Pins and Needles:
# Learning Acupuncture

After two years of using chiropractic treatments on my patients, I was ready to move on to another therapy. I chose acupuncture as my next foray into the alternative world. There were only a few places available to learn animal acupuncture. One of the newest places to learn was in Florida, at an institute started by a veterinarian from China, Dr. Xie. I was sure that learning Chinese acupuncture from a Chinese veterinarian was the best I could do.

The course took a year to complete and required a weeklong trip to Florida every three months. This was going to be an expensive endeavor and require time away from the office, the farm, and my family. My business partner at the clinic was not very happy about my desire to learn alternative therapies, so I would pay the bills—not the clinic—but I was determined to continue learning and signed up for the course.

I admit I knew nothing about acupuncture when I started the course. I read three books about Chinese theory and acupuncture to get some background. I was still overwhelmed. It was like starting veterinary school all over again because it was a totally different way of thinking from traditional medicine. In Chinese medicine, we use things like the characteristics of the feel of the pulses or the colors and coatings of the tongue to make a diagnosis. Areas of warmth or cold in the body, the animal's personality, the season of the year, and the pet's diet all play into the diagnosis. Terminology like blood, phlegm, damp, qi, yin, and yang had different meanings than in Western medicine. Organ systems included spleen, triple heater, and upper and lower Jiao, which were not organ systems I had dealt with previously.

In addition, I soon learned that traditional Chinese veterinary medicine was not just about performing acupuncture. The other branches of Chinese medicine included food therapy, Tui Na (a form of chiropractic and massage), and Chinese herbals. There was much more to learn than I originally thought. I was also fascinated by how every disease can be correlated to a season, a personality, and diet. Again, I couldn't wait to begin treating patients with my new therapies.

During my journey into alternative therapies, I did take time to learn a little about modalities that would not be my area of expertise—but would at least allow me to understand a bit about their uses. I had used Bach flower essences many times during my years with horses, most commonly Rescue Remedy. Rescue Remedy is a very popular product used during times of stress and trauma. It can be given by mouth or sprayed on the animal or person.

One time my daughter was riding her pony, and he was spooked and spun and ran. She became off balance and fell, but her foot got caught in the stirrup. I was horrified to watch the pony running around the arena while she spun from her ankle hanging upside down. The stirrup finally released as the pony jumped over a fence in the arena. When Gwen hit the ground, I was ecstatic to hear her make a tiny squeaking noise because I knew she was alive. I was sure she had torn all the ligaments in her knee and had a concussion from hitting the ground. I sent someone to grab the Rescue Remedy and gave her a dose before I let her sit up. It was miraculous to see how quickly she regained her wits after being given the remedy. Incredibly, she had no torn ligaments, no broken bones, and no concussion. A homeopathic salve of arnica, applied to her knee three times daily, cleared the bruising within two days. She was back to riding within three days. The doctors at the hospital had prescribed crutches and Tylenol with codeine, but she never used either of them.

At that point, I was pretty convinced the essences had real merit, and I read a bit about other flower essences that are used to treat emotional issues. I found a company (Botanical Animal) owned by a woman who was trained in the use of flower essences, and she made her own remedies and packaged them with clear instructions, which made my life much easier. I still commonly use flower essences for animals suffering emotional distress.

I had also used essential oils and aromatherapy for my family and my patients in the past. Eucalyptus oil on a light source or in a vaporizer helps clear the sinuses. Lavender oil is soothing, calming, and antibacterial. Peppermint and ginger oils can sooth the digestive tract and combat motion sickness. Tea tree oil is antibacterial. Many essential oils repel fleas. There are hundreds of oils used for everything imaginable. Again, I found a good company (Young Living) that makes high-quality oils and oil combinations. I don't use them all the time, but sometimes it's the extra product I need.

I read about homeopathy, which is the famous Dr. Pitcairn's area of expertise. He has written wonderful books about natural pet healing using homeopathic remedies. One of my clients is a homeopath, and she does phenomenal work using that therapy. She even gave me more than a hundred hours of audiotapes made by Dr. Pitcairn, along with workbooks to learn about homeopathy. Unfortunately, it was too overwhelming to grasp so much information while I was learning about Chinese medicine, and I never made it through all the tapes. I did learn enough to be able to converse with clients about homeopathy and be able to recommend some common remedies. There are companies that make combination homeopathic products (Homeopet), and I commonly use those for my patients. A true homeopath will tell you combination products are not ideal, but using them gives me one more tool in my toolbox (and I've had good success with them).

Once I started treating more patients with alternative methods, I started seeing the problems associated with over-vaccination of pets. I started discouraging my clients from vaccinating every year. I recommended against using topical flea and tick preventatives and heartworm preventative medications year round since we lived in an area where fleas and mosquitoes disappeared during our long cold winters. It no longer made sense to me to apply chemicals to our pets every month. I no longer recommended prescription diets that were made with poor-quality ingredients when I knew I could make the pet healthier with an alternative raw or home-cooked diet using whole foods.

Unfortunately, those parasite preventative and prescription diet products provided a huge revenue stream to our veterinary practices. My clients were becoming confused because I would recommend one thing and the other doctors in the practice would recommend something different. My partner was not very happy with what I was preaching to our clients. He accused me of practicing voodoo veterinary medicine. Alas, another closed mind.

# Finally, My Own Clinic

S ince my partner was dead set against my new way of practicing medicine, we decided it would be better to split up. I could no longer push vaccinations and medications, and he could no longer tolerate me talking clients out of profitable treatments. He sold his share of the clinic to me, and we parted ways. Strangely, we had originally bought the practice from a doctor who practiced homeopathy. I remember we used to laugh and be amazed at the "black magic" that used to be practiced in that building. It just goes to show how everything comes full circle eventually. So whether I was practicing chiro-quack-tic, voodoo, or black magic, it didn't really matter, as long as I was caring for my patients in a healthier manner.

Once I owned the clinic, I had a new set of frustrations. I had never been in charge. I had no idea how to do all the "business" of running a business. Suddenly, I was completely in charge of everything. I needed to learn about taxes and payroll and insurance and inventory and building maintenance. This was totally foreign territory! It took me two years to find the right consultants to teach me how to run a business. Thank goodness we survived while I was figuring it all out. I had to find the right staff who believed in what I was doing with alternative medicine. I was practicing holistics before it was "cool" to be holistic. It was a challenge.

Even though my focus became more about holistic medicine, traditional medicine continued to play a huge role in the treatment of my patients. I never wanted them to be in pain, and if a traditional medication needed to be part of their therapy plan while we were working on natural healing, I wouldn't deny them the medication. I have always joked that if I get hit by a bus, please give me some real drugs.

I integrated traditional and alternative therapies, trying to find the right balance for each patient. No two patients were the same; since their illnesses and symptoms were never the same, no cookbook treatments could be used. Sometimes it took perseverance to find the right combination of therapies to solve the problem. When I first started using alternative therapies, it would take me hours to figure out which approach would be best. The poor clients who came to me for holistic consultations in the early years were in the exam room for a very long time while I figured out which acupuncture points and herbals might solve the problem. Looking back, I am so grateful for their patience!

Many times, by the time I got to see a new patient, they had run out of options with their traditional doctors. The medications weren't working—or the pet was so sick from all the medications that the owners were looking for something different. I enjoyed the challenges and the research of finding the best options for each pet. Most clients who seek out alternative therapies understand that it takes time for the body to heal itself, especially after years of poor diet, over-vaccination, and over-medication.

We live in a stressful world where everyone is busy, and no one takes time to slow down and enjoy life. Our stress is passed to our pets, and their health suffers, just as ours does. They need good food, a healthy environment with minimal pollutants, and interaction with others. Many pets spend most of their time home alone, many times crated for hours, and their only interaction with their human is the one minute taken to pour dry kibble into a bowl or open the door to let them outside. These are the living conditions that contribute to stress and ill health. So when I see a new client, time is spent talking about vaccinations, medications, diet, environment, and social interaction.

When it comes to diet, one of the benefits of home cooking is the interaction between the pet and owner. Taking time to plan a diet and put together variations helps clients bond with their pets. Watching the reaction to a home-cooked meal instead of dry kibble in a bowl is priceless. Taking the time to play with pets in the yard or going for a walk around the neighborhood is great exercise for everyone involved. Leaving work a little early because your pet has been home alone all day is good for both of you. Animals, like people, are social creatures.

It's a balancing act to find the right treatments that work for both the pets and their owners. Sometimes owners are limited by time, sometimes by finances, and sometimes by a pet that refuses to take medications or supplements in any form. Physical limitations of the owner can make it difficult to care for disabled or weakened pets. All variables must be taken into consideration to find the perfect options for each family. I love watching the transformation of the pets and their owners when we find the right balance and see improvement in their lives.

I have found good companies to work with over the past twenty years that carry American and Chinese herbals, glandular products, and vitamins. With every patient I see, I end up researching possible treatments for the symptoms, which has ended up being my best learning method since it is much easier to remember treatments when they go along with certain cases.

The great thing about alternative medicine is being able to treat the *whole* animal as an individual, not just treating "kidney disease" or "seizures." There really is no "one-size-fits-all" therapy. Each pet that comes in for a consultation is looked at as an individual. I look at diet, environment, vaccine status, medications, symptoms, and the smell, feel, and look of the animal. I use all six senses when diagnosing and treating pets.

# Integration: East Meets West

I ntegration combines the use of traditional veterinary medicine with complementary therapies. It involves minimizing the overuse and misuse of conventional medications (just say no to drugs). Integrating chiropractic, acupuncture, craniosacral therapy, physical therapy, magnetics, homeopathy, homotoxicology, nutritional therapy, and Chinese or Western herbal therapies may allow the use of far fewer traditional medications.

Unfortunately, many of the pets presented to my office are suffering from chronic infections, chronic inflammation, and degenerative diseases. I commonly use traditional medicine for a "quick" fix (which may still take months) while adding alternative therapies to achieve long-term health. Once the inflammation has decreased and the immune system is strengthened, the body will, ideally, be able to remain healthy. While each pet is different, there are some common points that must be followed to raise your pet this way.

First and foremost, feeding the proper diet is the foundation upon which any integrative pet care program begins. Simply put, your pet *is* what he or she eats. Minimizing harmful byproducts and chemicals is essential. You need to become a label reader. Know which ingredients are good and which are bad. Whether you are feeding commercial, home-cooked, or a raw diet, whole, fresh, organic food ingredients are best. If a food is suitable for human consumption and is something you would consider part of a healthy diet, your pet can probably share with you. You should avoid grapes, raisins, chocolate, macadamia nuts, and onions because these can be toxic. If something qualifies as junk food for people, it will also qualify as junk food for pets (think chips, pretzels, candy). Each pet is different, and there is no "one-size-fits-all" diet that I can recommend across the board.

The second step in working toward a more holistic treatment plan for your pet is to minimize vaccinations. In the past, the veterinary community has advocated annual vaccinations for dogs and cats for common diseases like distemper, parvovirus, leptospirosis, and Lyme disease. More recently, research has shown that immunity from vaccination may last years, and some veterinarians now recommend vaccinating less often (although I recently saw a statistic that stated 80 percent of veterinarians still recommend annual vaccination of pets).

Vaccinations do not give instant protection from disease. The injection contains small amounts of the virus or bacteria that are killed or modified to prevent the injection from causing disease. The animal's body recognizes the components of the disease and builds an immune response against the disease. Unfortunately, when the body is constantly bombarded with disease particles, the immune system can go into hyper-drive, causing an overzealous response. This overzealous response can cause the immune system to react against the cells of the body. Diseases like autoimmune hemolytic anemia, lupus, arthritis, cancer, or any other inflammatory disease can be related to the constant stimulation of the immune system. It only stands to reason that less stimulation will allow the body to have a healthier immune system to respond to future attacks by outside invaders.

Chronic use of medications can degrade the body's ability to recognize disease-causing organisms. The liver and kidneys are the filtration system for the body, constantly weeding out toxic substances.

While medications may help treat one symptom or disease, they may cause other symptoms or set up a cascade of events that may eventually result in the demise of the individual.

Chronic use of heartworm preventatives and topical or oral treatments for fleas and ticks can also affect the long-term health of your pet. I will devote a chapter to this topic, but suffice it to say that I do not recommend overuse of these products. Depending where you live, internal and external parasites may be a big threat. Again, it's all about judicious use of these products or using alternative, safer products.

In addition to feeding good food and minimizing toxins for your pet, you need to know what is normal for your pet. The physical examination by your veterinarian, performed at least once a year and preferably twice a year, particularly once your pet is a "senior," is the most important part of the veterinary visit. Detecting a heart murmur, aging changes in the eyes, high blood pressure, or small tumors allows you to get an early start on diagnosis and treatment of problems. Rather than waiting for an illness to become life threatening, you may be able to make changes in food or lifestyle that will prevent further problems.

Laboratory diagnostics should be included in the annual visit. I recommend a complete blood count (CBC) to look for signs of anemia or increased white blood cells that could indicate infection, inflammation, or possibly cancer. A complete chemistry screen will detect changes in liver or kidney function, electrolytes, blood sugar, heart muscle inflammation, and pancreatic function. A baseline thyroid hormone level can be used to help determine thyroid function, which is commonly low in any dog that is stressed or has another disease process in the body. Take a urine sample to be analyzed for blood or protein in the urine, which could be signs of infection, bladder stones, bladder cancer, or kidney disease. A fresh stool sample should be tested twice a year for intestinal parasites. A heartworm test should be run at least once a year (twice if you live in a tropical climate with abundant mosquitoes) even if your pet is on preventative.

Older pets or pets with heart or kidney disease should have blood pressure monitored every six months. High blood pressure can cause heart and kidney disease, but it can also be the result of these diseases. Eye pressure should be measured with a tonometer at the annual exam. Breeds of dogs with short noses (brachycephalic breeds) are more prone to glaucoma than other breeds. Any redness, bulging (more than normal), or irritation should be checked immediately. Once the pressure rises in the eye, this is a very dangerous situation and can result in loss of vision in only a few hours.

Middle-aged to older pets may benefit from survey radiographs of the spine and hips to detect early signs of arthritis. If caught early, lifestyle and diet changes can be made to stop the progression of arthritis. There are many supplements on the market that can be beneficial for these pets.

Do not ignore dental disease in your pet. Dental tartar and bacterial infection under the gum line can contribute to heart and kidney disease. The bacteria in the mouth travel through the bloodstream and lodge on the heart valves or in the kidneys during blood filtration. Take care of your pet's teeth daily and have a professional dental cleaning at least once a year as soon as you start seeing the first signs of plaque or tartar. Use a daily cleaning agent like MaxiGuard Gel, a natural zinc ascorbate cysteine gel, to decrease plaque and tartar. It's like my dentist always said, "You only have to floss the teeth you want to keep."

Large breeds of dogs tend to have stronger enamel and less dental disease than small breeds. Healthy pets with a good diet also have stronger teeth and will develop less plaque and tartar. Genetics play a role in dental health, and some dogs will lose teeth no matter how well you care for them.

Non-anesthetic dental cleanings are a new fad. Groomers, pet "dental health technicians," and veterinarians are using manual techniques to scrape tartar from the teeth without sedation. This may seem like a great idea, but I have some concerns about the procedure. Even the most well-behaved pets will rarely allow their mouths to be held open long enough to allow thorough cleaning of the insides and backs of the teeth. Cleaning the visible tartar from the outer dental surfaces is nothing more than a cosmetic fix. Bacteria reside in plaque under the gum line, which is difficult or impossible to remove with hand scaling in an awake pet. Scraping the teeth without polishing will result in etching of the enamel, which will cause even more plaque to adhere to the teeth. Currently, I do not recommend this procedure.

In addition to addressing food, medical, and dental needs, a pet should have an active, happy lifestyle to achieve good health. Positive human interactions, exercise, and healthy weight, all contribute to good health and longevity.

In summary, to follow an integrated plan for your pets:

- Feed a species-appropriate diet with no preservatives, dyes, or chemicals.

- Feed high-quality proteins and low-carbohydrate diets.

- Limit the use of medications.

- Limit the use of vaccinations. Perform titers when possible.

- Limit the use of topical and systemic parasiticides.

- Know what is normal for your pet by having your veterinarian perform annual examinations and laboratory testing.

- Know the problems encountered for your specific breed, and take action to monitor and prevent problems.

- Take care of dental disease by brushing, using Maxi/Guard Oral Gel, and having professional dental cleanings.

- Provide regular exercise.

- Keep your pet lean rather than heavy.

- Provide environmental stimulation and human interaction. Pets are social animals.

# Alternative Healing to the Rescue: Wobbler's Disease

W hen Astro died, we decided not to get another dog right away. It was the first time in my life (except while living away at college) that I can remember not having a dog. My children had never known life without a dog either, but we were busy buying a farm and working with horses and didn't think there was time available to train a new puppy.

After a few years with no dog, I decided it was time to get a new farm dog. I went out and bought another Doberman from a private backyard breeder. Yeah, I know it was probably not the best source. The kids were excited and my son, Andrew, named him "Blink" after the popular band Blink 182. Blink was a typical Dobie: goofy, playful, and extra big. He had already had his tail cropped, but we decided to leave his ears long, the way nature made him, which gave him an extra-goofy appearance.

We always thought Blink was extra clumsy because he was an extra-big Doberman. But when Blink was about three years old, we noticed he seemed to wobble when he walked, sort of like a drunken sailor out for a stroll. I was worried he might have a condition called "Wobbler's syndrome," which is very common in Dobermans and Great Danes. It's a malformation of the neck vertebrae that causes compression on the spinal cord at the base of the neck. When I took x-rays of Blink, the condition was confirmed. We would have to be extra careful with Blink. I started him on an herbal formula that would help decrease inflammation in his spine in the neck area, and I was careful not to use a neck collar when he went for walks on the leash.

When my husband and I divorced, I got custody of Blink. He moved with me to my new home and was great company. When Blink was about five years old, I met Hue Grant (I know, cool name, huh?). Hue and I hit it off, and he moved into my house, bringing his extra large, goofy, one-year-old giant masso (a cross between a cane corso and a mastiff), Harley, with him. Harley had absolutely no training because he and Hue were just two bachelors living alone. Hue saw no need to train Harley to do anything other than drool and sit on the furniture. Harley had never seen cats before and thought my two cats were great-looking chew toys.

One day, I heard Hue screaming at Harley. When I came running, Harley was on the floor—and Hue was bent over him trying to pry his mouth open. To my dismay, I saw a gray cat tail hanging out of Harley's mouth. I screamed, and we managed to pry open the jaws of steel just enough to allow our gray cat to leap out, soaking wet, and mad as … well, a wet cat! She took off, and Harley gave us the evil eye for taking away his toy. Amazingly, he didn't hurt the cat; he really just wanted to play. He would see a cat and fly through the house, going under and over furniture, knocking me off my feet, just to get to a cat. One time he went between my legs, and I ended up riding Harley through the house because my feet couldn't reach the floor to get off. Ugh!

Luckily, Blink loved Harley—and Harley loved Blink. They loved to chase each other and wrestle all the time. Unfortunately, Harley outweighed Blink by a good fifty pounds. One day, the two boys were playing, but they started to get a bit rough and aggressive. I grabbed Blink by the collar and, without thinking, pulled him backward. The boys stopped playing, and I didn't think much more about it.

The next day, I noticed Blink was a little slow going up the stairs. He weighed 125 pounds, and I just thought he was moving slowly. The day after that, he couldn't get up the stairs at all. It dawned on me that pulling on his collar two days earlier had probably set in motion a cascade of events that was causing increased pressure on his spinal cord—and he was about to be in big trouble. I took him with me to the office that day, after a struggle to get him into the car.

By the end of the morning, Blink was completely paralyzed on all four legs. I was devastated, thinking I had played a role in causing the problem. I immediately started therapy for Blink. I gave him a chiropractic adjustment and performed acupuncture. He had almost sixty needles inserted and was hooked up to the electro-acupuncture unit to stimulate his nerves. He fell asleep during treatment.

Blink stayed at the clinic for three days, receiving chiropractic and acupuncture treatments daily, along with more herbals added to his regimen. On the fourth day, he could move about well enough that I could bring him home. I continued his daily treatments at home for another week. Within two weeks, Blink was walking and running around the house like nothing had ever happened. Within four weeks, he was back to being my running partner, putting in two to three miles a day with no problem.

Unfortunately, the close brush with paralysis for Blink and death for the cat made us realize Harley needed a different home environment. He had come from a good breeder in Virginia who lived on a farm and was willing to take Harley back. With tears in our eyes, Harley was driven back to his home in Virginia where he has a wonderful life with no cats.

Thankfully, my training in alternative healing methods had pulled Blink back from certain demise. But this brush with disaster made me realize that having a dog that weighed over a hundred pounds was a huge issue for me when the dog was unable to get up on his own. I was too small to lift him; even if he only needed a cart for his hind end, I wasn't capable of getting him into one. I realized Blink would probably be the last large dog I would own.

Options for treating Wobbler's syndrome or Cervical Vertebral Instability include:

- steroids (prednisone or dexamethasone)

- nonsteroidal anti-inflammatory medications (Rimadyl, Deramaxx, and others—do not use with steroids)

- muscle relaxers (Robaxin or methocarbamol 30 milligrams per pound divided into three doses daily)

- herbal supplements (Cervical Formula by Jing Tang Herbal 0.5 gram per ten to twenty pounds of body weight, twice daily)

- herbs for pain and inflammation (Dog Gone Pain—one tablet per thirty pounds, once daily)

- antioxidants (CoQ10 30 to 200 milligrams daily)

- omega-3 fatty acids (20–30 milligrams per pound of body weight daily)

- joint supplements (hyaluronic acid 10 to 20 milligrams daily, MSM, glucosamine, chondroitin each at 15 milligrams per pound of body weight, daily)

- species-appropriate diet (good quality protein, low carbohydrate)

- do not use choker collars

- acupuncture or electroacupuncture

- gold bead implants

- chiropractic therapy or veterinary orthopedic manipulation

- cold-laser therapy

- physical therapy (including use of an underwater treadmill)

- ❧ hind-end lifts or slings (www.ruffwear.com and www.gingerlead.com)
- ❧ boots to protect toes from abrasions if feet are dragging (www.therapaws.com or www.ruffwear.com)
- ❧ surgery to stabilize the vertebrae

Dogs diagnosed with Wobbler's syndrome should be removed from breeding programs.

# Rescue Pups

My daughter had heard me talk about cavalier King Charles spaniels many times over the years. When clients would ask what small breed would make the best pet, I would always recommend cavaliers. They weren't very popular back then, were very hard to find, and were very expensive. Gwen started researching cavaliers and soon became the resident expert.

We had Blink, but Gwen wanted a small dog she could sleep with, train, and call her own. After the divorce, I think Gwen just needed a special friend. Gwen started searching online and trying to find a cavalier to rescue because she couldn't afford to buy one. She was saving her money to buy her own dog. The rescue groups kept turning her down because she was a kid, even though she kept telling them her parents were okay with this and her parents were veterinarians. She never asked me to speak to anyone for her. This was her project.

When Gwen was thirteen, a huge puppy mill in Pennsylvania was closed down. More than three hundred dogs were liberated. Ninety-five of those dogs were cavalier King Charles spaniels. The dogs spent nine months in shelter care, waiting for the legal dust to settle so they could be adopted out to new homes. Gwen was sure this would be her chance to get the small dog she so desperately wanted. One day I heard on the radio that the dogs were ready for adoption. There was only one problem; there were already more than five hundred people in line to adopt the ninety-five cavaliers. There was no way I was going to join that long line. I told her she'd have to wait some more.

As luck would have it, a friend of mine was a veterinarian at one of the local shelters that were handling the spaying and neutering of those dogs. When she heard Gwen's dilemma, she said she could easily get one of those dogs for Gwen to adopt. Gwen was ecstatic! The next day, a three-year-old tri-color female cavalier found her way into Gwen's arms. Gwen paid the adoption fee with her own money, and Dalilah became Gwen's shadow.

At first, Dalilah was so shy that she wouldn't let anyone near her (except Gwen). We used a flower essence called "Angel of Mercy," which is made for dogs that have been rescued, to help Dalilah come out of her shell. She bonded to Gwen completely, following her everywhere, sleeping with her, learning tricks and how to walk on a leash. She went everywhere with Gwen and was possibly the saddest animal ever seen each morning when Gwen would leave for school. Dalilah went to horse shows with Gwen and to dinners with the grandparents. She became everyone's favorite little dog. In fact, I was so in love, I wanted a cavalier of my own. So I started my own search.

My search led me to Lucky Star Cavalier Rescue, a cavalier rescue group that also assisted with adoption of English toy spaniels. English toys are similar to cavaliers, but their noses and tails are a bit shorter. Ideally, they only weigh ten to twelve pounds. My first English toy weighed in at twenty-two pounds (not well bred, but she really needed to be rescued). Lora Lu was five years old and had been used as a breeding dog at a puppy mill in Missouri, having lived her whole life in a small wire cage hanging above the ground. She had luxating patellae (hind knees out of place), no hair, was partially deaf, and didn't see very well. She was also very shy and liked to hide in corners. She wasn't nearly as smart as Dalilah, but I loved her dearly. She became my shadow and would stare at me with a look that said she was just so happy I had saved her from her life of misery.

When I drove to Indiana to pick up Lora Lu from her foster home, they also had a second English toy. Jazmine was eight years old and had been used as a breeding dog at a puppy mill in Oklahoma. Most dogs that live that long in a two-by-two cage have their spirits broken, but not Jazzy. She was the most confident, outgoing small dog I had ever met. She really didn't have any major health issues, which was shocking. Her personality was so overpowering that I took her home too. I was hoping her outgoing personality would make it easier for Lora Lu to adjust, which was exactly what happened.

# Puppy Mills

For anyone not familiar with puppy mills, they are basically puppy-producing factories. Dogs of all breeds are housed in barns or large buildings and kept solely for breeding. Female dogs come into heat twice a year, and a good breeder of high-quality dogs will only breed on every second or third heat cycle. Puppy mill owners breed their dogs every heat cycle for maximum production. Many of the puppy mill owners are Amish, and many puppy mills are located in areas where there is a large Amish population. There are many puppy mills in Pennsylvania, Ohio, Indiana, Missouri, West Virginia, and Oklahoma, but they can be found in any state. State regulations for humane treatment of the dogs vary, and even when good regulations exist, they are rarely enforced.

For a puppy mill owner, the only value in the dogs is their ability to produce puppies that can be sold to pet stores. They have no emotional attachment to the dogs. When dogs are no longer capable of producing puppies, either from age or illness, they are disposable. Some dogs are killed, but some of the "lucky" ones are sold at auction or given to rescue groups. The dogs sold at auction can be any age. Sometimes young dogs are sold, and other puppy mill owners will buy them to become new breeding dogs. The old or sick dogs will hopefully be bought by rescue groups who go to the auctions undercover. If they are not purchased, they will be killed because they are no longer "useful."

The biggest issues facing puppy mill rescue dogs are a long history of poor nutrition, lack of exercise, lack of grooming, lack of veterinary care, and lack of human interaction. I don't think there is such a thing as a "good" puppy mill, but some are worse than others. Cheap dry kibble is the only food the dogs will ever be fed. They are housed in small stalls in a barn or wire cages hanging from the ceiling or stacked three or four levels high. The dogs never leave their crates, which are only a few square feet in size. They eat, sleep, urinate, defecate, and raise their puppies in those cages. The dogs unfortunate enough to be in cages below another row of cages have urine and feces raining down on them through the wire bottoms of the cages. The only human interaction is when someone puts food in the cage or pulls out puppies for sale. If dogs get injured in the cages, they do not receive veterinary care; they are left to heal on their own or die from infection.

Puppies that come from puppy mills are sold on the Internet and to pet stores that resell them. Puppies are vaccinated and dewormed repeatedly, in the hopes they will not fall ill before being purchased. Their immune systems are usually on overload by the time they are bought by a new owner. High prices are paid in pet stores for puppies that usually come with parasites and health defects from poor breeding, poor nutrition, and over-vaccination early in life. Good breeders have no need to have their puppies sold in pet stores since they can easily sell their puppies to knowledgeable buyers.

Many of my clients buy puppies from pet stores, and some of them are healthy. But for those that do come with health issues, knowing their backgrounds helps me get them to a position of better health much more quickly. The puppies that come in sick are given vitamins, herbs, and nutritional support to help them heal. These are puppies that were lucky enough to find their way into loving homes. Even though clients feel they are "rescuing" these puppies by buying them from pet stores, there are actually supporting the pet store and puppy mill industry. I beg you to not fall prey to this scam.

For those dogs not lucky enough to leave the mills as puppies, it can take a long time to build trust and teach them to do the simplest things that we usually take for granted with dogs. Since they have been urinating and defecating in the cage they lived in for years, they have no idea they are supposed to go outside to potty. They have never walked on a leash or been taught the simplest commands. They have never been groomed or bathed or had their nails trimmed. They have never received veterinary care. All of mine have been afraid of men in caps or hats.

I am so happy I have gotten into alternative veterinary medicine so that I can use that new mindset with my rescue dogs. We have fostered and adopted dozens of dogs since our first wonderful girl, Dalilah. The first order of business with a new dog is a complete physical exam and lab work to test for parasites and diseases. I run vaccination titers on them to see if they need to be vaccinated for distemper or parvovirus, which most of them don't, probably due to natural exposure in the kennels. I spay or neuter them if they are healthy enough for surgery. Most of them have teeth that are rotten and need to be pulled. Many need to have their matted, malodorous coats shaved off completely. I start all my new dogs on raw or home-cooked food as soon as they arrive. They have been fed very poor-quality dry kibble their entire lives, and they usually don't recognize the raw meat as food. It usually takes a couple days to get them to eat, but once they discover how good it is, they eat with gusto. If they absolutely refuse to eat, I will transition to the raw or home-cooked food by using a high-quality canned food first.

By not adding vaccination stress to their already stressed immune systems, feeding a healthy diet, and providing love and a clean environment, these dogs start to feel and look better within weeks. Once infected teeth and skin are addressed, their health improves immensely. There's nothing better than seeing a rescue dog the first time they set foot on grass in a big yard. One of our dogs took over a year to discover she could actually run. It took her three years to learn how to bark. When she does bark, it is usually a high-pitched squeal, which must be something she heard in the mill. She is still not well housebroken, even after four years of trying. I dream of the day when puppy mills cease to exist.

If you are interested in helping rescue puppy mill dogs or to learn more about puppy mills, check out www.milldogrescue.org. Any donation of money, time, or help spreading the word about puppy mills is greatly appreciated!

# Critical Care

Two years after Jazzy came to live with us, she became very ill. She started vomiting and wouldn't eat for days. Her lab work and x-rays revealed nothing unusual, and I was stumped. I packed her little bags and set off for the local veterinary college to have her seen by the experts.

After two days in critical care and three ultrasounds, they were finally convinced that she had a foreign body in her small intestine. Jazzy had never eaten anything strange around the house, and I was surprised by the diagnosis. I agreed she should go to surgery for an exploratory search of her abdomen. I was shocked when they called eight hours later to say they had removed one-third of her small intestine due to a sock being wedged tightly in place. She was critical, and they gave her little hope of survival. I was devastated.

Little Jazzy spent eight days in ICU with three plasma transfusions given every day to elevate her protein levels. I visited her daily, and she was the saddest pup I had ever seen. She had a feeding tube placed directly into her small bowel to give her some nutrition. She hadn't eaten in twenty-one days. But, amazingly, after eleven days, the doctors said she was healthy enough to go home. There were two problems: she had developed glaucoma in both eyes from all the stress, and she had a resistant bacterial super-infection around her feeding tube. She was sent home with a bag of medications and antibiotics.

This was all fairly early in my years with alternative therapies, but I was determined to get Jazzy off all the drugs as soon as possible. Her feeding tube was pulled, and she was starting to eat. I made her a home-cooked stew that would be easy to digest and would help rebuild her strength. I used an herbal paste around her feeding tube and never gave her any of the antibiotics. I put her on probiotics (a powder containing healthy bacteria for the bowel) to stimulate her immune system and herbals to decrease the inflammation and pressure in her eyes. She did amazingly well and was back to normal within a few weeks, having gained back all her weight. Luckily, little Jazzy's incredible personality and will to live brought her through a terrifying experience.

About a year later, she started having strange symptoms again. This time, her vision seemed to be deteriorating. She would start out on her leash walks with a funny marching gait in her left front leg. She seemed to work out of it as she got going, so I didn't think too much about it. I chalked up her vision issues to the damage done from her brush with glaucoma. We learned to be Jazzy's guides when we went for walks, teaching her that an upward tug on the leash meant to step up on a curb and a backward tug meant to stop and wait. She always wanted to go for her walks even though she eventually became completely blind. She was such a tough little thing.

Little did I know she was brewing something much more lethal. Jazz was developing a brain tumor that would eventually take her life. I had spoken with a neurologist and had her scheduled for a CT scan to definitively get a diagnosis. Two days before her scheduled scan, she started to have uncontrollable seizures. I tried everything I knew to get them under control, but I had no luck. We decided it was better to let Jazz go than to watch her suffer. Sadly, we were only fortunate enough to have dear Jazzy for a few years. She gave us a lot of joy, and we were very sad when we lost her.

# Not Enough Tears:
# Treating Dry Eye

O ur distress over the loss of Jazzy spurred us to adopt another little toy spaniel. Toys are much harder to find than cavaliers, but we were lucky enough to see a photo online of a pair of young boys rescued from a puppy mill in West Virginia. Paul and George were adorable, except George had something wrong with his eyes. They were all crusty and matted shut in the photo. When we contacted the rescue group, we discovered Paul had already been adopted, but no one would take George because his eyes were such a mess. He had a condition called KCS (keratoconjunctivitis sicca) or dry eye. He couldn't make any tears. George required a medication called Cyclosporine be put into his eyes twice daily for the rest of his life. The medication is fairly expensive, and no one wanted to take on that responsibility. George had been in foster care for nine months.

I was sure there was something I would be able to do to help George to get him off his medications. As luck would have it, he was being fostered in Indiana, close to where I had gone to adopt Lora Lu and Jazzy. Lora Lu, Gwen, Dalilah, Hue, and I headed out to pick up our new boy. We were going to have a reunion with Lora Lu's foster parents and let all the pups have a playdate. We arrived to a house full of cavaliers and toy spaniels. It was heaven. Of course, by the time we left, we also had two other cavaliers that we couldn't resist. Our little family was growing.

Once we had our new family back in New Jersey, we started George, Shayna, and Pookie on the raw food that we were feeding Blink, Dalilah, and Lora Lu. As usual, it took a couple meals for them to figure it out, but they loved it. Feeding six at once took some strategy figuring out who could eat next to whom without stealing and who needed to eat in a different room.

I was very strict about giving George his eye medications twice daily. His eyes still looked awful and had to have the crusts cleaned off at least twice a day. I researched food therapy to find a diet that would help him make more tears. It wasn't very hard to come up with a solution.

KCS is a condition where the eyes do not have enough fluids to make tears, so they produce mucous or "phlegm" to coat and protect the cornea. It actually doesn't protect the eyes very well because many dogs with this condition end up with corneal ulcers and erosions. Many dogs become blind with time. The solution seemed simple enough. We needed to feed George moist foods that would be blood tonics so he would have plenty of fluid available. We needed to feed him phlegm-draining foods so the mucous in his eyes would become thinner and more liquid. Not that I fed dry kibble anyway, but dry kibble would have caused more drying to George's little body and would not have allowed his body to heal.

Many foods drain phlegm, but I had to find things that George would like. I used clams (canned, minced, rinsed, and drained), pears (canned, in their own juice), a splash of almond milk, and fresh peppermint ground in his food. For blood tonics, I added hard-boiled eggs, grated carrots, and sardines in water. I started him on omega-3 fatty acids to decrease inflammation and probiotics to help his immune system. All this was mixed with his raw meats. I used beef as his main meat source, as that is also a great blood tonic, but I rotated in different meats to avoid deficiencies and keep him interested in his meals.

Within a few weeks, I was able to decrease the medication for George's eyes to a once daily treatment. Within a few months, his eyes looked great, and he no longer needed any medications. His coat had grown in thick and shiny, and he was the picture of health.

George's diet is now a staple in my clinic, and we have used it to treat many dogs with dry eye. This was a perfect example of using food therapy to treat a disease that had been described as incurable and requiring lifelong drug therapy. I couldn't wait to start using food therapy more often for my patients!

The most common eye disease I see in practice is dry eye or Keratoconjunctivitis Sicca. This disease is actually easy to treat if the owners will agree to discontinue dry food and increase the moisture in the diet. Cyclosporine, Tacrolimus, and artificial tears may need to be used in the eyes until the body starts producing more tears.

KCS can be genetic, showing up early in life, or it may show up later in life. Either way, high-moisture diets with foods to soothe the liver (which rules the eyes) are the way to treat the problem. The liver likes green foods; spinach, kale, broccoli, string beans, and other green vegetables are good additions to the diet. Blood tonics to increase moisture (after all, blood is moisture in the body) include bloody, red, rich foods like beef, heart, and liver. Whole eggs, sardines, carrots, parsley, kidney beans, and dates are also good blood tonics. Kidney beans and eggs should always be cooked before feeding. Raw kidney beans are hard to digest, and raw egg whites bind B vitamins, making them unavailable for absorption. Phlegm-draining foods like clams, ground almonds, pears, and kelp will help thin the mucousy secretions covering the eyes. Once the new diet has started working, dry eye should no longer be a problem, and medications can be slowly decreased.

# George's Dry Eye Diet

## Morning Meal

- 2 ounces Stella N Chewy's frozen raw beef warmed to room temperature
- (Primal, Darwin's, Oma's Pride, and other commercial products are also available)
- 1 sardine
- ½ hardboiled egg
- 1 chicken liver
- 1 chicken heart

## Evening Meal

- 2 ounces Stella N Chewy's frozen raw beef warmed to room temperature
- 1 slice canned pear in its own juice
- 1 teaspoon fresh ground almonds or almond milk
- 1 tablespoon canned clams, rinsed
- 1 tablespoon cooked spinach
- 1 tablespoon cooked carrots
- 1/2 teaspoon fresh ground peppermint

This will feed a ten-pound dog. Just make more for bigger dogs!

# The Eyes Have It:
# Treating Eye Disease

The eyes are the windows into the body, commonly showing inflammation and disease when there is a systemic problem. In Chinese medicine, the eyes are linked to the liver; when there is a problem with the eyes, the liver should be examined as well. When treating eye disease with acupuncture and herbs, the liver should always be treated.

Glaucoma, or elevated pressure within the eye, is another common problem, particularly in certain breeds. Primary glaucoma can be associated with a genetic predisposition in cocker spaniels, shar-peis, chows, Labradors, basset hounds, and Australian shepherds. Secondary glaucoma can occur secondary to high blood pressure, cataracts, inflammation in the eye, or trauma; any condition that may lead to elevated pressure within the eye.

One of our rescue spaniels, Lora Lu, developed secondary glaucoma while spending the day at a local town festival. We took five dogs with us to walk through town and visit with friends and local businesses. While chatting with a friend in front of the local music store, we did not realize a band had formed and was about to start playing. Lora happened to be sitting right next to a speaker and jumped three feet in the air with the first extremely loud strum of the bass guitar. When I looked down, she was trembling. Her eyes were bright red and bulging out of their sockets. We quickly left the area, but the damage was already done. Her blood pressure had skyrocketed, along with the pressure in her eyes.

Symptoms of glaucoma include cloudy, bulging, red eye or eyes, a dilated pupil, pain, and blindness. If not caught early and treated immediately, blindness is irreversible. Intravenous mannitol can be administered to help lower the pressure. Whenever your pet has any symptoms of eye disease, you should request a pressure measurement be taken to be sure glaucoma is not brewing. If the pressure in the eye is elevated, a blood pressure measurement should also be performed.

Supplements can be given to help prevent glaucoma in breeds prone to this disease, as well as any pet suffering from the disease. These include CoQ10, Lutein, beta-carotene, and vitamins A, C, and E. Ocu-Glo, which contains all of these ingredients, is currently the best eye supplement on the market and is available online direct to consumers.

Avoid choke collars or anything that will put pressure around the neck as these can cause increased pressure in the eyes. Breeds at risk should have blood pressure and eye pressure measured at least twice annually to detect any early increases that can be addressed prior to development of full-blown glaucoma.

Once glaucoma develops, acupuncture can be utilized to help decrease blood pressure and drain liver heat and stagnation. Topical eye drops, like Dorzolamide and Latanoprost, and oral medications, like Methazolamide, may be used to lower the pressure as well. If normal pressure is not attainable, the eye will remain painful and blind. Once the pet is blind, an injection of a caustic antibiotic, gentamycin, can be placed inside the eye to decrease fluid production, which decreases pain. This will also guarantee no return to vision.

One study showed 39.5 percent of dogs undergoing this procedure had tumors in the eyes at the time of enucleation or death. Rather than subject my pet to this procedure, I would have the eye removed if it was completely blind and had no hope of regaining vision.

Fortunately, Lora Lu did recover from the initial incident of glaucoma. She was treated with oral medication (Amlodipine) to lower her blood pressure and drops (Dorzolamide and Latanoprost) in her eyes three times daily to lower her eye pressure. Unfortunately, three years later, her glaucoma became uncontrollable, and she had both eyes removed within a three-month span of time. While it took me some time to adjust to the thought of having a dog with no eyes, Lora Lu adjusted rather quickly. She no longer had the painful eyes causing her to be anxious, and she was much calmer immediately after surgery. She does, however, get a bit annoyed with me when I do the housecleaning and move the furniture around!

Corneal ulceration (a scratched eye) can occur due to fighting (particularly cats), rough play, foreign bodies, or dry eyes. Any time a corneal ulceration occurs, the tear production should be tested to be sure the eye is producing enough tears. Treating the ulcer and not treating the dry eye will result in reoccurrence of the ulcers. In cats, corneal ulceration is commonly seen secondary to viral respiratory infections. For this reason, steroids should never be used to treat eye problems in cats. Even if the virus is not currently active, the dosing of steroids may suppress the immune system, allowing the virus to activate, which will cause more damage. Cats with corneal ulcers that occur due to upper respiratory infections should be given oral lysine at a dose of 500 milligrams daily, for a minimum of thirty days. Scratches on the cornea are always worthy of a visit to the veterinarian; an infection can cause the eye to perforate, causing permanent damage and blindness. Corneal scratches can be extremely painful, and many pets will require medication to help with pain. Do not allow your pet to rub at the eye; use an Elizabethan collar if necessary.

Cataracts are a whitening of the lens of the eye. Left untreated, many will eventually become so dense they will impede vision.

Cataracts can be congenital (present at birth) or can develop later in life as part of the aging process. They are very commonly seen secondary to diabetes. Sometimes these are the first things the owner notices in a diabetic dog. Cataracts can also develop from toxins introduced into the dog's system, like vaccines, drugs, and pollution. The liver filters all toxins, and the eyes will be affected if the liver is burdened. Cataracts can rupture, leaking lens contents into the eye, which is highly inflammatory and painful. Mature cataracts may need to be removed before reaching this point. Currently, there are new eye medications undergoing investigation to prevent maturation of cataracts, particularly in diabetic dogs. Some owners have reported good results using Natural Ophthalmics Homeopathic Cineraria Eye Drops for Cataracts.

Progressive Retinal Atrophy (PRA) is an inherited disease that causes slow degeneration of the retina and leads to blindness. It is most commonly seen in poodles and cocker spaniels, but different forms of the disease have been seen in many breeds. Genetic testing and selective breeding may be the best methods for avoiding this disease.

Suddenly Acquired Retinal Degeneration (SARDS) and Immune Mediated Retinitis (IMR) are two diseases that can cause sudden blindness. These inflammatory conditions are often indicators of a much more serious systemic disease. They have been associated with autoimmune disease, Cushing's disease, cancer, and stresses on the immune system. From a Chinese medicine viewpoint, this makes perfect sense. If we keep stressing the liver with vaccinations, toxins, chemicals, and poor diet, the eyes are going to suffer.

I have only seen this disease in patients that have been over-vaccinated, are suffering from concurrent disease like cancer, or have other immune system dysfunctions. One of my clients has two pugs, Parker and Hudson, who were both afflicted with this condition. One of them had been undergoing treatment for mast cell tumors, and they both had been over-vaccinated and over-medicated, causing severe immune system dysfunction. Both were able to maintain at least a little vision for a few years by changing to a better diet, using topical drops like Dorzolamide and Latanoprost, and oral supplements like Ocu-Glo, SAM-e, and milk thistle.

Traditional treatment consists of high doses of steroids and immunosuppressive drugs along with topical eye medications. Ultimately, the underlying problem needs to be addressed. These pets should no longer receive vaccinations of any kind, and they need to be fed a healthy diet, including probiotics to get the gut immune system functioning at a higher level.

In summary, for any pet with eye disease:

* Feed a healthy diet with plenty of leafy green vegetables like spinach and kale to support the liver.

* Minimize toxins and stress on the liver; minimize vaccinations.

* Supplement with antioxidants like CoQ10 at 30 milligrams for small dogs, 100 milligrams for medium dogs, and 200 milligrams for large dogs.

* Provide Ocu-Glo vitamins.

* Give milk thistle (silymarin) at 5–10 milligrams per pound of body weight daily.

* Give SAM-e (s-adenosylmethionine) at 90 milligrams for small dogs, 225 milligrams for medium dogs, and 400 milligrams for large dogs once daily.

# Foster Failure: Treating Syringomyelia and Chiari Malformation

O ur first "foster failure" (a foster dog that wins your heart and you can't possibly send them to another home, so you keep them) was a ruby red cavalier from Indiana. A puppy mill breeder in Indiana walked into a veterinary office and "dropped off" five old females and one old male that were no longer capable of producing puppies. At least she didn't send them to auction.

A woman who was on vacation in Illinois saw the ruby red boy, thought he was cute, and adopted him. By the time she drove him home to Pennsylvania, she had decided she didn't want to keep him. He snored (heaven forbid!), and he only had five teeth. He didn't fit her idea of the perfect dog. Ugh. She called the adoption group in Illinois, and they were willing to take him back, but she would have to deliver him. She couldn't be bothered. The one good thing she did was contact the local cavalier rescue group. They contacted the Illinois group, and an agreement was made that Charlie would go into the cavalier network. We agreed to pick him up in Pennsylvania immediately.

Charlie stayed with us for a few months, and we fell in love. He didn't snore (at least not as loudly as anyone else in the house) and he actually lost a tooth, so he was down to four. His x-rays showed he was extremely arthritic. His spine was fused in many places, and his hind legs were awful. Half the time, he scooted around instead of walking. He would wait at the top or bottom of the stairs to see if we were coming right back so he didn't waste a trip up or down. He was a grumpy old man with the other dogs at times, but he loved his girls (after all, he was a breeding male for a lot of years).

With Charlie, I had another chance to use my alternative treatments to help him. I gave him omega-3 fatty acids in large doses to reduce inflammation, an herbal pain-relief medicine, and a tablet containing colostrum from hyper-immunized cows for his arthritis. Laser therapy decreased the pain and inflammation in his back and legs. We put rubber "toe grips" on his nails to help him slide less on the hardwood and tile floors.

In addition to arthritis, Charlie also has a disease called SM or syringomyelia. It's very common in cavaliers and English toy spaniels, but other brachycephalic (short-nosed) breeds can be affected. In SM, part of the nervous tissue of the spinal cord in the neck is replaced by a fluid-filled cavity. The disease is commonly combined with Chiari malformation, a condition where the back of the skull compresses the brainstem and top of the spinal cord. Symptoms vary and usually include pain and scratching at the neck or "air-scratching." Veterinarians unfamiliar with this disease will commonly treat these dogs with steroids and antihistamines for nonexistent allergies. Unfortunately, steroids sometimes help relieve symptoms, leading owners to believe their pet does have allergies when in reality, they are dealing with something much more significant.

Charlie does not scratch much; instead, he has very strange seizures where he howls and screams at the top of his lungs with his head thrown back. They can occur at any time, but they tend to happen mostly in the middle of the night. Sometimes he can go days without a seizure; other times, he will have a dozen in a day.

Treatment for SM can include surgery on the spine, but it is expensive, dangerous, and doesn't always decrease symptoms. I have opted not to treat Charlie with surgery, so he takes a combination of medications. I use gabapentin because it actually has pain-relieving properties to help his arthritis pain and functions as an anti-seizure medicine. Pre-gabalin, or Lyrica, is another option if the gabapentin is not effective. He takes furosemide, which is a diuretic to help decrease the fluid accumulation around his brainstem and spinal cord. He is on omeprazole, which also helps decrease the fluid production. The hyper-immunized cow's colostrum (Duralactin) that he takes for his arthritis also helps decrease the inflammation in his spinal cord.

Charlie's protocol is a good combination of therapies to help him live a comfortable life, and he is a very happy boy. He has learned that we will come running to pick him up and soothe him when he has a seizure episode, and now he is the king of "fake" seizures. When he wants to be lifted on the sofa or carried up or down the stairs, he throws his head back and screams. We have become pretty adept at knowing what is fake and what is real, but sometimes we are fooled.

He runs around the yard with the other dogs on occasion and is a joy to watch. I like to think the last years of his life are his best years, and I'm glad we failed to send him out the door.

Current therapies used for SM and CM:

- Gabapentin (11 to 22 milligrams per pound two or three times daily)

- or Pre-gabalin (Lyrica) (2 to 3 milligrams per pound twice daily)

- Furosemide or Spironolactone (1 to 2 milligrams per pound once or twice daily)

- Prednisone or Dexamethasone (0.25 to 1 milligram per pound once or twice daily, weaning off as soon as possible)

- Non-steroidal anti-inflammatories (Rimadyl, Deramaxx, Metacam) – cannot be used with steroids

- Duralactin (1/2 tablet twice daily)
- Dog Gone Pain herbal pain medication (1 tablet per 30 pounds daily)
- Omeprazole (10 milligrams once daily)
- Amitriptyline (0.5 to 2 milligrams per pound once or twice daily)
- oral opioids
- MSM (methyl sulfonyl methane) (15 milligrams per pound daily)
- Pea-Pure, a natural anti-inflammatory and pain killer (15 to 20 milligrams per pound of body weight twice daily) treats nerve pain
- Canna-Pet – organic hemp without THC, neuroprotective, anti-inflammatory, analgesic, anti-epileptic
- cold-laser therapy
- acupuncture to decrease pain and inflammation
- avoid use of collars or pulling on leashes
- surgery
- removing affected dogs from breeding programs

If you suspect your pet has SM or CM, you will need to work closely with your veterinarian to determine which therapies are the best for your pet. Not all dogs need all medications, and not all dogs are candidates for surgery.

# Tremors: Treating Seizures and Epilepsy

D isorders of the nervous system of animals are varied, including congenital, infectious, traumatic, toxic, inflammatory, metabolic, nutritional, degenerative, and cancer. Many neurologic diseases have been effectively treated with traditional medications, and others have had lackluster responses. In acute situations like sudden paralysis or cluster seizures, Western medications can play a pivotal role in treatment. More chronic diseases are sometimes better treated by alternative forms of therapy. Patients with seizures, chronic back pain, intervertebral disc disease, degenerative myelopathy, and limb paresis or paralysis may find more long-term healing and relief when treated with acupuncture, chiropractic care, herbals, and nutritional therapy.

Seizures have many causes. Genetics play a large role; any pet diagnosed with epilepsy should be removed from breeding programs. Severe infestation with parasites or Lyme disease can cause seizures. Nutritional deficiencies, including vitamins A, D, and B6, folic acid, taurine, magnesium, and calcium should be considered, along with low blood sugar. Head trauma, brain tumors, and liver disease must be ruled out. Vaccinations and many chemicals, including those found in flea and tick preventatives, are known to contribute to seizure activity. While not as commonly diagnosed in epilepsy, thyroid disorders and kidney failure can also be causative factors. Any pet having seizures should have complete blood testing performed to rule out infections, thyroid, liver, or kidney disease, and nutritional deficiencies. Diagnosis of brain tumors requires MRI or CT testing.

Pets with seizures and epilepsy are commonly treated with phenobarbital, which is a wonderful drug and has saved many pets from a seizure-filled life. Unfortunately, the liver is the primary organ responsible for filtering and detoxifying phenobarbital in the body. Pets receiving phenobarbital become thirsty, hungry, and sleepy for the first three weeks when taking the medication. The symptoms subside or diminish after three weeks because the liver makes a new enzyme-converting system that handles the drug. Unfortunately, most pets will develop cirrhosis of the liver with chronic phenobarbital usage.

Any pet receiving anti-seizure medications should have liver enzyme values monitored frequently and should be fed a diet of food and herbs to support the liver. Liver is the organ of spring, which is associated with the color green. Deep green, leafy foods like spinach, kale, mustard greens, and liquid chlorophyll will help keep the liver happy. Milk thistle (silymarin) and SAM-e (s-adenylmethionine) help protect and regenerate liver cells.

Luckily, there are other methods available to deal with seizures, for those interested in using alternative medicine. I have successfully treated many pets with seizures using food therapy, herbals, and acupuncture. There is no "one-size-fits-all" herbal remedy for seizures. Clients often purchase online products to treat seizures, which can be harmful. From a Chinese medicine perspective, seizures can be associated with internal wind, liver stagnation with phlegm-fire, blood stagnation, liver yin and/or blood deficiency, or kidney Jing deficiency. An explanation of each of these conditions is beyond the scope of this book, but suffice it to say that it would be impossible to choose the correct herbal formula without the correct diagnosis by a veterinarian trained in traditional Chinese medicine. Please do not be misled by online testimonials claiming one product will cure all pets with seizures. In addition, if you don't straighten out the diet being fed, the herbals will have no effect. I do not vaccinate pets with epilepsy or other seizure disorders.

One of my patients, Breeze, is a Border collie who has a very active life as a search and rescue dog. He can search for people who are lost or killed. He developed a seizure disorder that could have ended his career. Search and rescue dogs go through years of training, and it would have been a shame to lose such a valued member of a team. His owner was very concerned about medicating with phenobarbital, which could affect his tracking abilities, so she sought out alternative therapy for his treatments. His diet has been changed from dry food to a high-quality commercial frozen and freeze-dried raw product. Instead of vaccinating, titers are run to test immunity level to distemper and parvovirus. He receives dry needle acupuncture treatments to drain his liver excess and stop internal wind. He takes a combination of herbal medications, including Di Tan Tang, Long Dan Xie Gan Wan, and Epimedium. This combination has kept him seizure-free for over a year. Before treatment, he was having seizures every two to three weeks. Unfortunately, the work he performs requires vaccination against rabies once every three years, and he will have to be vaccinated. His heartworm preventative was changed from ivermectin to low-dose milbemycin. Ivermectin, moxidectin, and selamectin may lower the seizure threshold and may increase seizure frequency when given; therefore, I do not recommend using products containing these ingredients in pets with known seizure history.

Current recommendations for pets with seizures include:

❧ judicious use of anti-seizure medications, including phenobarbital, potassium bromide, leviteracetam, felbamate, or zonisamide

- monitoring thyroid, liver and kidney function every few months

- a healthy, species-appropriate diet free from dyes, preservatives, or chemicals; feed diets with high-quality proteins and low in carbohydrates

- liver-supporting foods, including dark leafy greens like spinach and kale

- herbs to support the liver, including milk thistle at 5 to 10 milligrams per pound and SAM-e at 90 milligrams for small dogs, 225 milligrams for medium dogs, and 400 milligrams for large dogs once daily

- limited use of vaccinations

- Chinese herbals based on tongue and pulse diagnostics by a veterinarian trained in traditional Chinese veterinary medicine (check www.tcvm.com to locate a veterinarian in your area)

- acupuncture to repair imbalances, drain liver fire or stagnation, and decrease internal wind

- limiting or eliminating use of topical and systemic parasiticides

- using milbemycin for heartworm prevention (Sentinel, not Trifexis, as spinosad in Trifexis can contribute to seizure occurrence); avoid ivermectin and selamectin products

# My Aching Back: Treating Disorders of the Spine

One of our wonderful rescue cavaliers came to us with some issues associated with her spine. Her owner had turned her over to rescue because Shayna would cry every time she was picked up and sometimes when she would run or jump. The owner could not afford to have diagnostic testing to determine the problem and potential surgery for treatment. Shayna's owner had confined Shayna inside for two years, forcing her to use piddle pads, and never taking her out to play.

When Shayna arrived in foster care, the first thing she discovered was the doggy door. She would run outside to play, but she would not come back in through the door. She would sit outside and bark. It wasn't that she couldn't come back in; she wanted everyone else to come out to play. It was spring, and the maple tree seed "helicopters" were falling from the trees and floating on the wind. Shayna would chase them for hours, if allowed. By the time we adopted her, Shayna had already earned the nickname Crazy Shayna.

Of course, since I was a veterinarian, the rescue group thought I would be the perfect person to adopt Shayna. Maybe I would be able to cure her pain with chiropractic care or acupuncture. I wasn't so sure that was an option. You see, Shayna is very crooked. When she looks at me, her head is a bit cocked to one side. One eye is always looking up, and the other one is always looking down. When she lies down, her hind end lies on the side and her front end lies on her sternum. Her spine is as straight as it can get when she is in that position. X-rays of Crazy Shayna's spine showed the worst case of scoliosis I have ever seen. Her spine is an S-curve. One side of her rib cage is shorter than the other. There is no acupuncture or chiropractic manipulation in the world that will fix this problem! In spite of her affliction, Crazy Shayna has a very normal life. She takes supplements and medications to manage her pain and only gets to play with her soft frisbee (her absolute favorite pastime) for a few minutes at a time.

In addition to scoliosis, Wobbler's syndrome, Intervertebral Disc Disease, Degenerative Myelopathy, Degenerative Lumbosacral Stenosis, infections, cancers, and inflammatory diseases of the spine are commonly seen in veterinary practice. Some disorders have specific breed predilections, and others are widespread. Sometimes, high doses of steroids or anti-inflammatory drugs can provide relief for these disorders; other times, pets are rushed to surgery.

Recent studies of Intervertebral Disc Disease have shown alternative therapies combined with medication or surgery have a superior response and recovery when compared to medical or surgical treatment alone. Alternative therapies can include acupuncture, electrical stimulation, cold-laser therapy, and physical therapy, along with herbals and food therapy. A speaker at a veterinary conference for acupuncturists recently referenced quite a few studies showing the same rate of return to function for dogs with ruptured discs with or without surgery. Some dogs will never walk again, even with surgery. Some dogs with complete loss of hind-end function will relearn to walk, even without surgery. I have had pets in both categories.

Dogs with complete loss of deep-pain perception in the limbs (pinch the toes to see if they respond) are generally thought to do better with surgical decompression of the spine. Surgery must be performed within the first forty-eight hours of pain loss to have the best outcome. Unfortunately, up to 50 percent of dogs suffering one ruptured disc may have a second or third episode in the future. Proper diet, weight loss, and controlled exercise are important in preventing recurrence.

Last year, we held our first annual clinic "Bark-B-Q" on a very hot day in July. We invited a couple dozen rescue groups and pet vendors to set up tents and raise money for their rescue groups. The event was incredibly well attended, and our traffic clogged the entire north end of town. Partway through the day, there was a commotion at the driveway entrance where Hue was attempting to direct traffic. A car came flying in the driveway and Hue started waving his arms to get my attention. I ran over to find a good client cradling her dachshund, Schultz, with tears streaming down her face. Schultz had suddenly become paralyzed and was unable to use his hind legs. His owner kept apologizing for interrupting our day and said she just needed to know where to take her precious boy. Of course we went inside and started treatment for Schultz.

Schultz had minimal feeling in his back legs when I pinched his toes. He was panting and obviously had pain in his back. His tongue was purple, indicating blood stagnation and pain. He needed immediate care. I started with injections of steroids to decrease inflammation, muscle relaxers to decrease muscle spasms, and pain medications to give him some relief. Chiropractic adjustment in the area in front of the painful lesion was performed to increase nerve and blood flow and get some motion back into the spine. Schultz had acupuncture needles inserted along his back, and they were attached to electrodes to decrease the pain and spasms. We finished with cold-laser therapy to stimulate healing.

An hour later, Schultz was more relaxed—and his mom was feeling a little better too. We discussed the possibility of surgery, but we decided to opt for medical management. Schultz came for acupuncture and laser therapy twice a week for a few weeks. His mom worked very hard at doing physical therapy with his hind legs at home and made sure he was urinating and moving his bowels regularly. She tried taking him for professional physical therapy, but she stopped when he seemed pained after the first session. I am happy to report that within three months, Schultz was walking very well. By six months, he was running. He had a bit of a funny waddle, but he was a happy boy.

On the other hand, Roscoe, a basset hound, originally came to me with back pain and decreased function of his hind legs, but he was still able to walk. Roscoe was obese, weighing in at over seventy pounds. He had been over-vaccinated for years and was eating a very poor diet. I treated Roscoe with chiropractic care, acupuncture, and herbals that helped his back pain, but the more important problem was obesity. Roscoe's parents took on the weight-loss challenge and succeeded in having him lose more than twenty pounds by using healthy, home-cooked meals. Along the way, Roscoe also tore an anterior cruciate ligament in his hind leg and needed treatment with herbs and laser for that. He did very well for over a year and then became very painful again. Over a course of a few weeks, his condition deteriorated to the point where he was unable to walk. His parents opted for surgery on his back, and within a few weeks, he was up and running.

Obviously, long-backed breeds like dachshunds and basset hounds are predisposed to disc disease. But many other breeds are prone to similar problems, including beagles, cocker spaniels, and shih tzus. All these breeds are prone to obesity, which may contribute to the disease. The best prevention is to control weight, feed a healthy diet, and avoid things that will cause inflammation in the body (sugars and chemicals, including preservatives and dyes). Disc problems can occur in the neck as well as the back; avoid the use of choke collars if your dog pulls on the leash when walking.

Treatment for degenerative disc disease can include:

- cage rest (baby playpens can work well if you do not have a crate)

❖ steroids or nonsteroidal anti-inflammatory medications (these cannot be used together—pick one or the other!)

❖ muscle relaxers like methocarbamol at 30 milligrams per pound divided into three doses daily

❖ American or Chinese herbal medications (choice will depend on tongue and pulse diagnosis performed by a trained veterinary herbalist; check www.tcvm.com to find a veterinarian)

❖ herbal pain medications like Dog Gone Pain given at one tablet per thirty pounds once daily

❖ traditional pain medications like Tramadol or Gabapentin

❖ acupuncture and electroacupuncture

❖ cold-laser therapy

❖ chiropractic care or veterinary orthopedic manipulation

❖ physical therapy (including underwater treadmills)

❖ carts (www.eddieswheels.com)

❖ hind end lifts and harnesses (ruffwear www.ruffwear.com and gingerleads www.gingerlead.com)

❖ puppy stairs to decrease jumping or falling off furniture (my favorites are the original puppy stairs which can be ordered from www.puppystairs.com)

❖ surgical decompression

Degenerative Myelopathy is another spinal disease that can benefit from alternative therapies. This is a slowly progressive disease seen most commonly in German shepherds and Pembroke Welsh corgis, but the mutated gene for the disease has been found in more than forty breeds. Onset is usually seen after the pet is seven years old, beginning with weakness in the hind limbs, progressing to complete paralysis with fecal and urinary incontinence.

Saliva samples can be tested to determine if a dog carries the gene. Check out DDC Animal DNA Testing (www.vetdnacenter. com). Any dogs testing positive should not be used for breeding. Besides the genetic component, many currently believe the cause of the disease may be the immune system attacking the protective myelin sheath that surrounds the nerves and spinal cord, but this has not been proven. There are currently no treatments that will stop the progression of disease.

- The best therapy for these dogs is exercise. This can include leash walking, swimming, physical therapy, and underwater treadmill.

- Hind-end support lifts can make life easier for the owners and pets. There are many great products available. I really like those made by Ruffwear, which are available from many online outlets.

- Carts can be helpful (www.eddieswheels.com).

- Electroacupuncture for nerve stimulation seems to help these dogs retain feeling in their feet.

- Walking on rough surfaces for tactile stimulation may be helpful.

- If the pet is dragging its feet, protective boots should be used to avoid abrasions and wounds. Ruffwear (www.ruffwear. com) and Therapaws (www.therapaw.com) are two good sources for these.

- The use of cold-laser therapy is still being explored for these dogs.

Since this disease may be caused by immune system dysfunction, a healthy anti-inflammatory diet and supplements can play a key role in treatment. A raw or home-cooked diet free from preservatives, dyes, and chemicals can help decrease inflammation. The diet should contain high-quality proteins and be low in carbohydrates.

Supplements can include:

- N-acetylcysteine at 75 milligrams/kg divided into 3 doses per day for 2 weeks, then 3 doses every other day (Dilute the solution 1:4 with chicken or beef broth so stomach upset doesn't occur; Westlab Pharmacy in Gainesville, Florida, can compound this product.)

- Aminocaproic acid (Westlab Pharmacy may be a good source for this as well)

- B-complex vitamins (100 milligrams) daily

- Vitamin C (up to 3000 milligrams) daily

- Vitamin E (up to 2000 IU) daily

- selenium (up to 100 micrograms) daily

- CoQ10 (up to 200 milligrams) daily

- omega-3 fatty acids dosed at 20 to 40 milligrams per pound of body weight (best source for this case may be borage or evening primrose oil).

- ginger (1 teaspoon dried, ground) twice daily

- garlic (1 fresh, crushed, raw clove) twice daily

- bromelain (400–500 milligrams) twice daily

- curcumin (400–500 milligrams) twice daily

- grape seed extract (50 milligrams) daily

- green tea (1 capsule twice daily)

- Avoid the use of chemical parasiticides like topical flea and tick preventatives and oral ivermectin

# Snap, Crackle, Pop: Treating Degenerative Joint Disease

Another name for arthritis is degenerative joint disease. Pets with arthritis may show pain or discomfort in many ways. Commonly, they become less active, sleeping more and interacting less with the people and animals around them. Some pets will become more aggressive and snap when approached. Some pant a lot or pace because they can't find a comfortable position to lie down. They may be slower getting up, have a difficult time using stairs or jumping into the car, seem stiffer when walking or running, or may occasionally limp. Some will be so painful they will stop eating.

Diagnosis of arthritis is based on physical examination and radiographic evidence of degenerative joint disease. Cats suffer from arthritis as often as dogs, but they are less likely to show symptoms. It is common to see severely arthritic joints when taking radiographs of cats. There are many treatments available for arthritis, including surgery if the problem is severe.

The most important treatments for arthritis are weight control, exercise in moderation, and pain management. Ideally, a pet with arthritis would maintain a very lean body mass since extra weight will put more stress on the joints. Even a 5 percent weight loss can have dramatic effects on mobility scores. The easiest way to help your pet lose weight is to lower the amount of carbohydrates in the diet, meaning little or no dry food, adding meat protein and vegetables to decrease calories.

Generally, arthritic pets will already be limited in their activities because of pain, but these pets still need exercise. If the pet remains inactive, the muscle groups will start to shrink because they are not being used. As the muscle groups shrink, the pet becomes weaker and more inactive. This then becomes a cycle of inactivity. Exercise is needed to maintain muscle tone and to promote joint health. Controlled walks, swimming, and physical therapy are good exercises that can promote muscle tone and joint mobility. High-impact activities, such as chasing a ball for prolonged periods, may cause too much pain. The key is controlled exercise. Swimming and the use of underwater treadmills are excellent forms of exercise that don't put pressure on painful joints.

Pain management is a broad category that includes multiple aspects of traditional and alternative medicine. Many owners will give aspirin or over-the-counter anti-inflammatory medications to pets— without realizing that aspirin commonly causes stomach ulceration— and many of the medications are toxic in pets. Some doctors have used steroids, but I prefer to use them for very specific cases involving degenerative nerve issues, and only as a last resort. There are many side effects associated with steroids, including liver damage, diabetes, obesity, and increased thirst and urination.

Newer nonsteroidal anti-inflammatory (NSAID) medications are available through veterinarians, but many pets cannot tolerate these medications. Also, many pet owners are afraid to use them due to possible side effects, which can include bowel ulceration and perforation, liver disease, kidney damage, and death.

From a more holistic way of thinking, there are many alternatives available to treat the pain and inflammation of arthritis. I recommend any pet with symptoms or evidence of degenerative joint disease should be started on a nutritional joint supplement containing glucosamine, chondroitin, and hyaluronic acid. There are, literally, thousands of products available on the market. When choosing a product for your pet, be sure to do the research on the product you want to use. Human supplements can be used in pets, but they may not be as readily absorbed and used by the pet's body.

Since nutraceuticals (nutritional supplements) are not regulated by the FDA, you are at the mercy of the company selling the product. Do not rely on website testimonials! (After all, I'm pretty sure my mother would write a pretty good testimonial for me on my website.) The product may, or may not, contain the ingredients listed on the label. One study done years ago showed very few products contained the same level of therapeutic agents in the supplement as they showed on the labels. Some had none, some had more, and some had less.

There are a few good products on the market, and more are emerging all the time. Currently, I like Cosequin, Glycoflex, and Conquer K9 Plus; these have all been proven to be effective in my practice, and the companies that make them have great reputations. These products may help improve lubrication within the joints by increasing joint fluid production and thickness, decrease inflammation in the joints, as well as help to repair joint cartilage.

Studies have shown that starting these agents early for breeds that may be prone to developing arthritis may have a protective effect for the joints. Dosage for glucosamine should be around fifteen milligrams per pound of body weight per day (1,500 milligrams for a hundred-pound dog, 750 milligrams for a fifty-pound dog).

There is some dispute over whether diabetic dogs should be given glucosamine because it breaks down into a sugar molecule, which could make it more difficult to regulate the diabetes. If in doubt, use a hyaluronic acid product instead of glucosamine. Hyaluronic acid should be dosed at two to twenty milligrams per day, depending on size of the dog. I dose any dog over fifty pounds with twenty milligrams per day. Chondroitin should be given at a dosage of ten to fifteen milligrams per pound of body weight daily (about the same as the glucosamine). MSM (Methylsulfonylmethane) is found in many joint supplements and has been shown to significantly reduce inflammation in joints. Dosages for MSM should be similar to glucosamine, at around fifteen milligrams per pound of body weight per day.

Polysulfated glycosaminoglycan injections (Adequan, Chondroprotec, Cartrophen, and Ichon are a few of the trade names) have also proven to be highly effective in my opinion. These products contain the building blocks of joint fluid and will help block some of the inflammatory causes of degenerative joint disease. When looking at the joint fluid of an arthritic joint, the fluid will be thin, watery, and possibly bloody. A healthy joint will have a thick, sticky, clear lubricating fluid. Injections of PSGAG's help the body make a better joint fluid.

Injections are given under the skin or in the muscle once or twice weekly for four weeks. In my practice, we continue monthly maintenance injections, which have been very helpful. The only side effect we have encountered may be a decreased clotting time, and some surgeons may want pets taken off the injections prior to any surgical procedures. I used Adequan injections twice weekly on my daughter's retired thirty-five-year-old show pony that was so arthritic he could barely walk from the barn to the paddock. By the time I had given his sixth injection, he actually galloped across the field chasing the other horses!

Omega-3 fatty acids, when given in high doses, have been shown to protect the body from inflammation. I recommend all pets with arthritis should take omega-3 fatty acid supplements. It can be difficult to find a high potency product; commonly, multiple pills need to be given daily. In this case, I do not recommend just buying "fish oil," as the active omega-3 is only a small portion of the oil in the capsule. The active ingredients in the capsule are eicosapentaenoic acid (EPA) and docosahexaenoic acid (DHA). Add the milligrams of these two together to get the milligrams of active omega-3 in the capsule. If the product does not list the actual milligrams and instead gives a percentage of active ingredients, avoid it.

I currently recommend a sixty-pound dog be given about 2,400 milligrams daily; you will find you need to give multiple capsules. Be careful of the source of the fish oil because many products can have high levels of mercury, lead, PCBs, and other contaminants. For pets that do not like the taste of the oils, natural sources like wild caught salmon or sardines can be fed as well. Vitamin E must always be given along with fish oils or omega-3 fatty acids because vitamin E levels in the blood will drop when omega-3s are fed. Most prescription products will have vitamin E added.

Vitamin C has been shown to be beneficial for pets with arthritis by decreasing inflammation, which decreases pain. Dogs must be given a bio-available, buffered vitamin C, not over-the-counter human products. Vitamin C will definitely cause diarrhea if dosed too high. If your pet is prescribed this vitamin and develops diarrhea, decrease the dose to the level the dog can tolerate. Small dogs will usually tolerate 150 to 500 milligrams twice daily, and large dogs can usually take 500 to 1,000 milligrams twice daily. Start low and increase gradually. If the pet develops diarrhea, decrease to the last dosage that caused no side effects.

Herbal anti-inflammatory products have become more popular in the last decade. Herbs that may decrease pain and inflammation include willow bark (do not use in cats as it contains salicylate, the active compound in aspirin), devil's claw, feverfew, yucca, boswellia, turmeric, ashwaganda, arnica, and garlic. There are many products available, but again, these are not regulated by any government agencies.

Herbals can and do have side effects, just like prescription medications. Please consult with a veterinary herbalist prior to using these products. Many herbal products cannot be used along with traditional medications; always ask if products can be used together! I like Dog Gone Pain, which is given at a dosage of one tablet once daily per thirty pounds of body weight. Do not give Dog Gone Pain along with NSAIDS or aspirin because the combination can cause stomach ulceration.

A newer product we have been using, Duralactin, is made from the dried milk protein of hyperimmunized cows. This product blocks the white blood cells responsible for inflammation from migrating, attaching, and participating in reactions that cause pain and inflammation in the body, particularly in the joints. There have been no side effects associated with this product, and it does not cause gastrointestinal upset.

Duralactin is available in vanilla-flavored wafers that smell like cake. (I always know when the technicians are counting these. I have tasted them, and they're not bad!) It is also available in a soft chew that contains glucosamine, MSM, and omega-3 fatty acids. Personally, I do not feel the levels of these additions are high enough for therapeutic value. I like to use the vanilla wafer and supplement the glucosamine, chondroitin, and omega-3 fatty acids separately. For cats, the product is available as a capsule, liquid, or paste.

One big problem for older, arthritic dogs is slipping and sliding on wood, laminate, or tile floors. Many dogs will not walk on slippery surfaces for fear of falling. Not only is the sliding scary, it can also be dangerous, resulting in torn ligaments and muscles and broken bones. "Toe grips" are small, thick, rubber bands that can be placed around the properly trimmed nails of dogs to help them "get a grip" on slippery floors. Charlie was our first pet to wear them, and once he realized he wouldn't fall, he ran everywhere in the house.

Toe grips can be ordered online and are easy to apply, but you may want to ask for help from a veterinarian or technician the first time you try. If you soak the bands in alcohol for a minute, they slip on fairly easily. Once the alcohol dries, they should stay in place if sized correctly. Toe grips will need to be replaced as the nails grow out or the bands wear through. Charlie is not very active, so his bands will stay in place for months.

Another method to decrease slipping is by using rubber boots that can be applied to the paws with Velcro closures. Boots should not be left on for long periods of time, as they will trap moisture and lead to infections between the toes. They are great for use on long walks or for dogs that drag their toes or feet, causing abrasions. Sizing is important; follow directions for the product you choose.

We have rubber floors throughout our clinics to minimize slipping for pets and people. We love them, but most people are not going to put rubber floors in their homes. An inexpensive alternative is the use of rubber "tiles" that can be purchased at home supply stores. They come in multiple sizes and colors and can be locked together like puzzle pieces. Most people use them in children's playrooms. These are much better than throw rugs, unless you get rugs with rubber backing that will not slip.

My favorite arthritis treatments in the past few years have been nontraditional therapies, including acupuncture, acupressure, and chiropractic care. Acupuncture and acupressure can be used to decrease pain and inflammation and help with improved mobility. All pets with arthritic joints will benefit from chiropractic care since the pain in the joints affects mobility and results in improper movement of the spine.

Once animals have a chiropractic adjustment and mobility is restored to the spine, the lower limbs move in a more fluid manner. Think of the spine as a "Slinky" that should be mobile at every joint. When watching people or animals run, the spine should be relaxed, allowing fluid motion of the limbs. A locked or stiff spine will result in a stilted gait, which puts more pressure on the joints. Watching a horse from behind, the tail head should naturally swish side to side during the walk or trot. I love seeing animals move before and after treatment. Clients are continually amazed the first time they see the free movement of their horse or pet after an adjustment.

Massage to loosen tight, contracted, painful muscles in spasm can help immensely. There are many professional massage therapists available to work on pets, but I usually give my clients home massage techniques to perform between visits. Once I am able to release muscle spasms in the office with acupuncture, chiropractic care, or myofascial release, the pet will maintain the benefits of therapy much longer if the owner continues the work at home with daily massage. Generally pets will enjoy gentle massage along both sides of the spine and over the hips. Start with very light pressure, gradually increasing to a level your pet will tolerate. A good reference for home acupressure treatments is *Four Paws, Five Directions* by Cheryl Schwartz.

Cold laser therapy has recently become commonplace, and many traditional veterinarians are starting to perform this treatment. There are many levels of cold-laser available for use, but this is another place where you need to do your homework and be sure the laser being used will be beneficial and not harmful. Some lasers can burn the skin when not used properly. Others have minimal power and are not effective. The FDA only approved high-power class IV lasers for use in 2005. This is the category I recommend using because of its ability to penetrate deep into the tissues and joints.

Wavelength and power are the determinants of strength and effectiveness of the laser. Lasers work using specific wavelengths of light that stimulate blood flow, release oxygen from the red blood cells, release energy to heal tissues, and stimulate acupuncture points. This results in decreased pain, increased wound healing, neurologic repair, and decreased production of scar tissue. Besides arthritis, cold-laser therapy can be used to heal infected wounds, infected ears, chronic lick granulomas, sprains, strains, and fractures, as well as to speed healing after surgery. New uses for cold-laser therapy are constantly being developed.

Treatment using cold-laser therapy usually consists of five to seven treatments performed over two to three weeks, then follow-up treatments as needed. If high-level lasers are being used, the operator, the person holding the animal, and the animal should wear protective goggles to prevent damage if the laser were to be accidentally pointed at the eyes.

Physical therapy has become a prominent specialty in veterinary practice in the past ten years. Specific prescribed exercises, pools, treadmills, and underwater treadmills have helped animals recover from surgery, arthritis, and traumatic injuries much more quickly than they would without therapy. Many owners with dogs used for show, agility, dance, and strength work use physical therapy techniques to keep their pets strong and in great shape. When choosing physical therapy for your pet, use a reputable therapist trained by one of the licensed centers currently in operation. Don't hesitate to ask for credentials and referrals from other clients.

Newer therapies, including stem cell regeneration and enhanced platelet therapies, are more complicated because they involve anesthesia and surgical procedures, but they are showing great promise. My first client to request stem cell therapy owned a giant German shepherd named Roxy. Roxy weighed over 110 pounds and had been born with elbow and hip dysplasia. I had been treating Roxy for over five years with joint supplements, Adequan, herbal supplements, and chiropractic, but her arthritis was progressing—and she was starting to show lameness. The owner reluctantly started using low doses of Rimadyl, which made Roxy more comfortable, but we were both worried about the long-term effects of using an NSAID. When I mentioned stem cell therapy, Roxy's owner was thrilled at the possibility of decreasing pain and increasing mobility for his beloved girl.

When we radiographed Roxy's joints, we found bad elbows, stifles, and hips. The joints were some of the worst I had ever seen on x-ray, and I was actually pretty impressed that Roxy was maintaining her current level of mobility. Roxy was sedated, and multiple vials of fat were removed from under the skin over her chest and behind her shoulder. The fat cells were shipped to California, processed to harvest the stem cells, and shipped back to us. The cells were then injected into Roxy's hips, stifles, and elbows, and one dose was given intravenously. Within two weeks, I received multiple phone calls and text messages proclaiming Roxy was running like a puppy. Since that time, Roxy has had stem cells injected an additional time, and she continues to do well.

I have also performed platelet-rich plasma therapy (PRP). The procedure is much simpler than stem cell therapy in that no harvesting of fat cells is required. A blood sample is processed and filtered to isolate a platelet-rich fraction, and that is injected into the arthritic joints. The first patient I treated with PRP, a young dog with hip dysplasia, did very well, showing a decrease in pain and an increase in mobility.

Orthopedic, heated, or magnetic pet beds can also help relieve pain for many pets. Some arthritic pets are worse in cold weather, and others will actually be worse in hot weather. (Most of us associate cold wet weather with joint pain, but that isn't always the case.) There may be times when pets seem very comfortable even though they have severe arthritis, like Roxy, but there will also be times when you will need every tool in the toolbox to keep the pet moving.

Treatment options for pets with arthritis include the following:

- a healthy, species-appropriate diet free from dyes, chemicals, or preservatives to decrease inflammation (The diet should contain high-quality proteins and be low in carbohydrates.)

- weight loss, if needed

- controlled daily exercise

- omega-3 fatty acids dosed at 30 to 50 milligrams (some holistic veterinarians recommend up to 200 milligrams) per pound of body weight along with vitamin E at 1 to 2 IU per pound of body weight daily

- natural anti-inflammatories like Duralactin given twice daily

- joint supplements containing glucosamine, chondroitin sulfate, and MSM, dosed at 15 milligrams per pound once daily (Cosequin, Glycoflex, Conquer K9 Plus)

- hyaluronic acid dosed at 2 to 20 milligrams per dog once daily (Conquer)

- polysulfated glycosaminoglycan injections (Adequan, Cartophen, Ichon, Chondroprotec) given once or twice weekly for four weeks, then once a month

- vitamin C 150 to 1,000 milligrams twice daily based on size of dog and bowel tolerance
- cold-laser therapy
- chiropractic adjustments or Veterinary Orthopedic Manipulation
- acupuncture or electroacupuncture
- herbal anti-inflammatory medications (Dog Gone Pain, 1 tablet per 30 pounds of body weight daily)
- Chinese herbals for qi, yin, or yang deficiency or Bony Bi (arthritis); check www.tcvm.com to find a veterinary practitioner in your area.
- stem cell therapy
- platelet-rich plasma therapy
- massage
- acupressure (*Four Paws, Five Directions* by Cheryl Schwartz)
- toe grips (www.toegrips.com)
- rubber boots (Ruffwear www.ruffwear.com or Therapaws www.therapaw.com)
- puppy stairs and ramps (www.puppystairs.com)
- hind-end lifts (www.gingerlead.com and www.ruffwear.com)
- carts (www.eddieswheels.com)
- physical therapy, including underwater treadmills
- orthopedic, heated, or magnetic beds
- pain management with NSAIDS, opioids, or other medications
- steroids (as a last resort)

# Just Say No To NSAIDs

B ute, or phenylbutazone, which is commonly used for lame and arthritic horses, falls into a class of medications called nonsteroidal anti-inflammatory drugs or NSAIDS. Other drugs that fall into this category include Rimadyl (carprofen), Previcox (firocoxib), Deramaxx (deracoxib), Metacam (meloxicam), Etogesic (etodolac), Zubrin (tepoxalin), ibuprofen, aspirin, and naproxen, as well as others that are being newly researched and marketed. Some of these have a high toxicity rate, like ibuprofen and naproxen, for pets. Aspirin is toxic to cats unless given in extremely small doses every three to four days. Acetaminophen is toxic to cats in any dose.

Common side effects from these medications include stomach or small bowel ulceration, liver damage, or kidney damage. One study showed up to 80 percent of dogs given aspirin on a routine basis have evidence of bleeding ulcers in their stomachs. In the past, when animals have shown gastrointestinal upset when taking these medications, veterinarians have dispensed anti-ulcer medications like sucralfate and antacids like cimetidine to decrease the side effects. This is a poor way to deal with the problem because the side effects are just being masked. In my opinion, any dog that stops eating, vomits, develops diarrhea, or has bloody or black stools should never be given any medication that falls in the NSAID category.

For instance, when Rimadyl first came on the market, some dogs vomited or showed signs of gastrointestinal distress. Rather than withdrawing the Rimadyl from the patient treatment plan, more drugs were given to mask the symptoms caused by the Rimadyl. Many dogs were given sucralfate to coat the stomach and antacids to decrease stomach acid production. While this helped mask the symptoms caused by the Rimadyl, it did not protect some dogs from the deadly erosion of the lining of the stomach and small intestine, resulting in perforated bowels, sepsis, and death.

For dogs that did not develop bowel perforation, some developed swelling of the stomach wall so that it became so thickened they were unable to eat and vomited nonstop, losing weight and perishing from this deadly combination. This happened to my business manager's Labrador retriever. Another veterinarian had been treating Radar with Rimadyl and an antacid for a long time. When Radar started vomiting, we assumed he had ingested a foreign object (all Labradors seem to eat everything in sight). Luckily, during exploratory surgery, we found the swollen and thickened stomach wall and biopsy revealed the results of this deadly combination of drugs. Withdrawal of both drugs allowed Radar to recover, and we have developed other options for treating his arthritis. I am not saying that Rimadyl is a horrible medication that should never be used, but like any medication, it must be used correctly.

I require any pet being placed on an NSAID to have laboratory testing to monitor liver and kidney function every three months. Some clients feel this is overkill and will leave my practice to seek care from a veterinarian who requires lab work to be repeated once a year or less. I do not want to be responsible for the death of any pet, and I am adamant about this. Any side effects or an increase in liver or kidney enzymes is immediate cause for withdrawal of the medication.

Many of the NSAIDS are sold in chewable tablets or as treats to make them taste better and easier to administer to pets. Unfortunately, many pets view these as treats and will eat the whole bottle of pills if given the chance. These medications must be stored out of reach, in a closed cabinet.

More than one NSAID should never be given at the same time. Many pets have died because the veterinarian dispensed an NSAID and the owner decided to give aspirin along with it. If one NSAID is stopped, there must be at least a one-week waiting period before starting a different NSAID.

I once had a client whose primary veterinarian dispensed Deramaxx. The owner ran out of medication on vacation and started giving ibuprofen. Ibuprofen alone may have been enough to kill the dog, but the deadly combination of starting the ibuprofen without the waiting period after stopping the Deramaxx caused kidney failure and bowel ulceration, resulting in the demise of her beloved pet. My recommendation is that a pet that cannot tolerate one NSAID should never be given a different NSAID. The danger for a bad reaction and possible fatality is just too high.

Pets with arthritis or other painful maladies can be treated with many drugs, alternative medications, and therapies other than NSAIDS. Over the past thirty years, there have been so many advancements in therapies, surgical remedies, and supplements to help pets live longer, more comfortable lives that I see no reason to rely solely on these drugs.

# Another Throwaway:
# Treating Diabetes

W hile I was completely enamored by small spaniels, I was not unwilling to open my heart to dogs of other breeds. When I had Dobermans, I always thought it would be fun to have a miniature pinscher because they look like a smaller version of a Doberman. Unfortunately, many miniature pinschers don't have the nicest personalities and can be a bit nippy or downright nasty. I didn't want to risk having a dog that might bite my children or people coming to the farm.

As usual, a sad case came before me, and I couldn't say no. An older couple had a miniature pinscher that was diabetic (as many of them are). The dog was obese, having been fed carbohydrate-laden dry kibble his entire life, along with whatever handouts he could grab from his well-meaning parents. The owners were reluctant to spend the time or money on treating the diabetes; they were on a fixed income and would have a hard time giving insulin injections twice daily. After six months of trying, the dog's blood sugar was not regulated—and he was drinking gallons of water and urinating all over the house. The owners brought him in for euthanasia. He was the nicest miniature pinscher I had ever met, and he was only six years old. I asked for and received permission to keep the dog as my own.

When I took this new dog home, we were skeptical. Hue had never given injections and wasn't sure he would be able to help with the treatments. It would be imperative that he be able to help because with my work schedule, I wouldn't always be available when the injections needed to be given. Luckily, the new dog was great for his injections and made it easy for everyone involved. The dog came with one of those typical German names, like Fritz or Hans, and we knew we wanted to rename him. For days, when people would enter our house, they would ask, "Who's the new guy?" Finally, his name became "New Guy" because we couldn't come up with anything better, and he seemed to like it.

The first thing I wanted to do for New Guy was to change his diet. Getting him off carbohydrates would be imperative to getting his blood sugar regulated. Carbohydrates basically break down to sugars and require the body to make more insulin to keep them regulated within the body. Pets fed diets high in carbohydrates have to make more insulin in their pancreas to break down the sugars. Most diabetic pets resemble type 2 diabetics in humans. The pancreas can't keep up with the sugars they are being fed or has been damaged by repeated bouts of pancreatitis. By eliminating carbohydrates from New Guy's diet, I could lower his current insulin requirements. He was receiving twenty units of insulin twice a day, which was far above the recommended dosing. He weighed twenty pounds and should have weighed ten.

I immediately started New Guy on the raw meat diet that was being fed to my other dogs. As usual, he didn't recognize it as food and turned his nose up at it for the first few days. Diabetics must eat in order to receive their insulin injections, so I broke down and gave him small amounts of grain free kibble or canned food. Many people think a grain-free kibble means there are no carbohydrates in the diet.

This is not true. In order to make a dry kibble stick together, some form of carbohydrate must be used.

Dry foods that do not have rice, corn, soy, or wheat in them to act as a binder have green pea starch, tapioca starch, or potato starch as the binder. These are still carbohydrates that must be broken down by insulin. Most traditional veterinarians will recommend prescription diets that are low on fat, such as W/D, which is advertised as low-fat glucose-management diet, for diabetic pets. The canned version of W/D contains egg product, whole grain corn, chicken, and cracked barley. The chicken is good, the barley can be cooling and draining which may be beneficial, but the corn? The glycemic (sugar) index of barley is twenty-eight, and corn comes in at sixty. Meats do not have a glycemic index because they do not raise blood glucose levels. This canned diet (since dry food of any kind should not be used for diabetics) contains 52.6 percent carbohydrates. Needless to say, I do not recommend the use of this diet for diabetic patients.

By the third day, New Guy realized the raw meat was delicious, and he started eating ravenously. By the fifth day, we had a new problem. I had lowered New Guy's insulin down to thirteen units from twenty, knowing he would not need as much insulin on the new diet. Unfortunately, I did not realize how much less he would need.

By the fifth night, New Guy's blood sugar had dropped precipitously. His blood sugar was so low that he started to have seizures. I gave him corn syrup under his tongue. He seemed okay for a few minutes, but then he went into another seizure. I gave him more syrup. This was repeated a few times, and we were getting nowhere. We packed up and headed for the clinic at midnight. I started New Guy on an intravenous drip of sugar-laden fluids. His blood sugar was only twenty (normal is eighty to one hundred twenty). We spent a long, cold night huddled in blankets sleeping next to New Guy on the clinic floor, hoping he would survive.

Luckily, by morning, the seizures had stopped—and New Guy was ready to eat. He loved his raw food and couldn't get enough. Over the next few months, New Guy lost half his body weight and got back to a normal weight of ten pounds. Overweight dogs will always lose weight if the carbohydrates are taken out of their diet and they are fed only their required amount of calories. Instead of twenty units of insulin twice a day, New Guy needed only three units twice a day. If New Guy's original owners had been willing to put him on a no-carbohydrate diet, their expenses for insulin and regulation would have been much lower. He didn't drink gallons or urinate in the house when his blood sugar was normal. He was a model citizen.

We kept a glucometer at home so we could test his blood sugar routinely and make sure things were under control. One of the most interesting things that happened with New Guy is that every time his blood sugar would be a little high, his vision would deteriorate. We got to the point where we didn't have to measure his blood sugar on the glucometer to know his blood sugar level. We have an in-ground pool, and when New Guy's blood sugar was high, he would walk out the back door and into the pool. Luckily, he was a good swimmer, and we never let him out without keeping an eye on him. We took many dips into cold water to fish him out!

The spaniels never accepted New Guy as one of their own. They tolerated him, but he was not allowed to sleep in the spaniel pile in the crates or the big dog bed. Funny how they knew the difference, but at least they were never mean to him.

When treating diabetic pets, keep the following things in mind:

- You are going to need to work closely with your veterinarian to regulate and maintain the blood sugar. There is no quick fix. Glucose curves (a series of blood glucose tests performed every two hours for an eight-hour period) will need to be performed periodically to determine how well the pet is responding. If you buy a glucometer, you can monitor blood glucose at home and discuss results with your veterinarian.

⚬ Be alert for signs of low blood sugar, including wobbly gait, staring into space, disorientation, weakness, collapse, tremors, or seizures. Keep maple or karo syrup on hand to smear on the gums if you are suspicious the blood sugar is low. Low blood sugar is an emergency and should not be ignored; brain damage and death can result.

⚬ Diet plays an extremely important role in regulating and maintaining diabetic pets. Without controlling the diet, you will not control the diabetes. Diets high in carbohydrates will cause increased insulin requirements and will make control more difficult. Diets deficient in moisture will add to the problems of increased thirst and urination.

⚬ Different forms of insulin can be used; some pets that do poorly on one type may do well with a change to a different type.

⚬ Some cats may do well on once-daily insulin dosing, but most pets require insulin every twelve hours. Some cats will revert to being non-diabetic. Monitor closely.

⚬ Medications and supplements can interfere with insulin and sugar metabolism, making it difficult to get the pet regulated. Be sure to tell your veterinarian about all supplements you are giving.

⚬ If you are having a difficult time achieving diabetic regulation, have your pet checked for other endocrine diseases, such as Cushing's disease or hypothyroidism. If concurrent disease is left untreated, diabetes can be hard to manage.

⚬ Most diabetic pets will develop cataracts. An ophthalmologist will be able to tell you if removing the cataracts is an option for your pet. If the cataracts cannot be removed, the pet usually adjusts well to life without sight since it is a gradual loss. Be kind to your blind pet—and do not rearrange the furniture. Make sure outdoor areas are safe so the pet cannot wander away from home.

❖ The best prevention for diabetes is proper nutrition and preventing obesity.

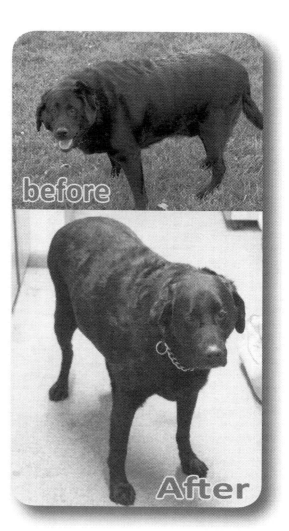

# Me and My Big Mouth: Obesity

I love going to work every day, and I love most of my clients. There are always going to be a few people who are just plain cranky and can't be pleased, but luckily, they are the minority at my practice.

One of my more memorable clients was a blind man with a trained guide dog. His first dog was an awesome German shepherd. She lived a long life of service to him, and when she passed, he had to wait a long time to receive a new trained guide dog. When the time finally arrived, he marched in with his new black Labrador retriever. The beautiful dog proudly wore his service harness and carefully guided his owner around our office. The dog weighed sixty-five pounds and was the picture of health. I enjoyed seeing the dog and his owner for the next few years, but there was trouble brewing on the horizon.

Each year when the owner came in for the dog's annual exam, the dog was getting heavier. I asked what the dog was being fed, and I gave the owner a measuring cup to measure the dry kibble. I admonished the owner that overfeeding was going to cause many problems over the life of his dog. This dog was not only his companion; it was also his lifeline to freedom.

By the third year, when the dog came in for his annual exam, he was not wearing his working harness. The dog weighed 128 pounds. He was *double* his ideal weight, no longer fit into his working harness, and was not able to work as a guide dog. The owner was truly broken up about the problem and promised he would do whatever it took to get the dog back to his normal weight. This was about the time a new drug came onto the veterinary market. It was a diet drug that was supposed to make dogs lose weight. The owner wanted to try the drug. We ordered it, against my wishes.

The owner brought the dog in faithfully every month to be weighed and to get a new prescription of the drug. The dog did not lose *any* weight. I talked about measuring food and not giving treats and snacks. I talked about the importance of exercise and walking to burn calories. After five months, we were all depressed—and the dog was fat as ever. In my frustration, I told the owner that if this dog lived with me, I guaranteed he could lose weight and get back into his working harness. This was ridiculous, and the owner was just being noncompliant. I was tired of hearing his complaints about the dog being overweight if he was unwilling to feed appropriately. I understood the owner was on a fixed income and couldn't afford the best-quality food, but at least he could feed the right amounts. Or so I thought.

The owner got quiet. Then he said, "Really, Doc? Would you do that for me? Could you take my dog, get him to lose weight, and then give him back to me? The guide dog people who trained him are going to take him away from me if he can't lose weight. I can't afford to lose him. Please take him home with you."

Oh boy. Me and my big mouth. I called home and asked Hue if it would be okay if I brought home another dog to feed. This would be number nine in our house at the time. I couldn't even fit the dog in my little sports car to get him home. I had to ask Hue to drive to the office to pick him up. I was sure I was crazy.

Thus began the biggest loser challenge in our house. The dog's owner was sure I could get the weight off in one month. He didn't get it when I said that it would be unhealthy for the dog to lose the weight that fast. This would take months. What had I gotten into?

The owner was on a fixed income and was certain he could not afford to feed the raw meat diet I loved so much. I decided that feeding a high-quality grain-free kibble would be the next best choice. If the owner fed the correct amount instead of overfeeding, I was sure it would be affordable for him. I started this obese 128-pound dog on one and a half cups of kibble twice daily. The rule of thumb is that an adult dog needs approximately one cup of food per twenty pounds of body weight each day. So, by feeding this large dog only three cups of food daily, I was only giving him the nutrients for a sixty-pound dog. That's what he was supposed to weigh; I figured if I wanted a sixty-pound dog, I was going to have to feed a sixty-pound dog.

We started the big guy on an exercise regimen of daily walking. By the end of the first week, he could only get to the end of the driveway without collapsing. I was afraid it was going to take forever.

I was so excited for the first weigh-in. With a lot of pushing, pulling, grunting, and lifting, we got him in the car to go to the office. Everyone crowded around to see how much weight he had lost. The owner was on the phone waiting to hear. And the answer was … *zero*. How could it be? We were all very sad.

The next week, I dropped him to one cup of food twice daily, with a vitamin supplement because I was sure he wasn't getting enough nutrition. He was walking a little farther; surely, he would lose weight this week. Once again, we pushed, pulled, grunted, and lifted him into the car for his weekly weigh-in. We all crowded around the scale, and the owner was waiting on the phone. Only a few tenths of a pound. Better than zero, but not by much. The owner was smart enough not to say, "I told you so," but he was also disheartened that I wasn't going to be able to do this in a month.

By the fifth week with minimal weight loss, I finally decided to throw caution to the wind and start the big oaf on the raw meat diet. I was sure he couldn't handle any carbohydrates—and that was the problem. I started feeding him twelve ounces of a frozen raw dog food twice daily. Normally, dogs should be fed 2–3 percent of their body weight daily. I fed him one and a half pounds of meat, which was 2.5 percent of the sixty pounds I wanted him to weigh.

The next week, we pushed, pulled, grunted, and lifted him back into the car for his trip to the clinic for his weekly weigh-in. We all crowded around the scale and held our breath. The owner waited on the phone for the final reading on the scale. Lo and behold ... ... a 3.4 pound loss!! We were on the right track, but it was still going to take a lot longer than a month to get rid of sixty-five extra pounds.

We were doing the biggest loser challenge with this dog during the summer. We owned a house at the shore, and every weekend, we would pack up the nine dogs and head for our small place at the beach. We had an upstairs condo and no yard, which meant taking nine dogs for a lot of walks for potty breaks. Everywhere we went, people would stop us and ask if we were dog walkers. They pointed and stared and laughed at the eight small dogs and one huge blimp. It was crazy.

As the big dog was losing weight, he was able to walk a little farther. We decided he needed to walk more to burn more calories. By the end of the second month, he was walking three or four times a day—a mile or two at each walk. Sometimes when people would stop us to talk about our large group, he would plop down on the sidewalk and fall fast asleep. He was exhausted from his diet and exercise plan, which included walking up to thirty miles per week.

By the end of the summer, the big guy had lost twenty-eight pounds and was down to an even hundred. Things were going well. The owner really wanted his dog to come home, but I didn't want to see the dog gain back all the weight. I was very, very stern with the owner. I told him that I would supply him with the tube of frozen raw patties that the dog needed to get through the week, along with one small bag of healthy, low-calorie treats. Each week he would have to bring the dog in for a weight check. For every week the dog lost weight, I would supply the next week's food. If he gained weight, the owner would have to buy the food.

Now, for someone on a fixed income, he would have to have been an idiot to turn down that kind of offer. He took me up on the offer, and I waited to see how it would play out. I was certain the dog would gain weight by the first weigh-in.

To my surprise and delight, the dog lost two more pounds his first week home with his owner. The owner lit up like a Christmas tree. He was so happy! He lived in an apartment complex and wasn't able to walk the dog very much. In order to keep up with the exercise plan, he had gone around to people in other apartments and asked if they would be willing to walk his dog to help him continue losing weight. He had a line of helpers at his door!

I'm happy to say that the last time I saw the dog, he was below ninety pounds, back into his harness, and back to work. Unfortunately, the owners moved away to another state, and I don't know how the big guy is doing. I can only hope the owner understands the needs of the pet and keeps going in the right direction so they can have many more happy years together.

# Hormones: Treating Endocrine Diseases

Diabetes and obesity are categorized as endocrine diseases. Endocrine glands secrete hormones that affect the body in various ways, regulating metabolism, hair growth, muscle strength, digestion, reproduction, and pretty much everything the body does. Yes, I did say obesity is an endocrine disease. Fat cells produce hormones that can contribute to other diseases like diabetes and hypertension.

The most common endocrine disorders seen in veterinary practice include diabetes mellitus, obesity, hypothyroidism (dogs), hyperthyroidism (cats), Cushing's disease (dogs), and Addison's disease (dogs, not as common). Improved diagnostic capabilities have allowed more cases of these disorders to come to light. However, I think we also see more endocrine disorders in pets and people due to the horrible diets of fast food, processed food, and chemicals in our environment. Many of the meats we eat come from animals that have been fed antibiotics and hormones to increase growth rates. Our endocrine systems are overloaded and working hard all the time, which leads to imbalances and disease.

Most of these diseases have symptoms that overlap. One of the earliest and most common symptoms is increased thirst. The body tells the pet to drink more, which means there is internal heat and inflammation. There seems to be some genetic predilection as well. Some diseases are associated with weight gain, such as hypothyroidism (underactive thyroid) and Cushing's disease (overactive adrenal and/ or pituitary gland). Others can be associated with weight loss, like diabetes and Addison's disease (underactive adrenal gland). Many times, pets will have more than one endocrine disease at the same time. Hypothyroidism, diabetes, and Cushing's disease commonly occur together.

*Hypothyroid disease,* or an underactive thyroid gland, is the most common hormone imbalance treated by veterinarians. The thyroid gland is responsible for metabolism; when it doesn't function properly, the body slows down. Pets become sluggish and gain weight. The cycle of hair growth and shedding is interrupted, and many dogs develop bald patches, particularly along the flanks. The hair will become dry and brittle and lack shine. Skin and ear infections are commonplace. Some dogs become anxious, depressed, aggressive, or develop seizures. These dogs seek warmth.

Primary hypothyroidism is caused by autoimmune thyroiditis; the immune system attacks the thyroid gland. Decreased production of thyroid hormone may also occur with age. Some pets will drink and urinate more often. Large breeds seem to be affected more often; Dobermans, Labradors, and greyhounds lead the list. Environmental and food toxins, vaccinations, and medications contribute to the constant attack on the thyroid gland.

Older dogs with untreated thyroid disease may also develop laryngeal paralysis as a complication. Laryngeal paralysis may be related to the autoimmune disease that affects the thyroid gland. The folds that close over the larynx, or airway, do not open and close properly due to decreased nerve function. The dogs make a loud roaring noise when breathing heavily and may cough and choke when drinking water since water gets into the airway. These dogs are at a high risk for swelling of the laryngeal tissues and difficulty breathing secondary to environmental factors like high heat and humidity, and stress factors like obesity and exercise. They have increased incidence of aspiration pneumonia. Treatment with thyroid supplementation does not correct the laryngeal paralysis.

Diagnosis of hypothyroidism requires blood testing for different thyroid hormones and antibodies against the thyroid gland (T3, T4, freeT4, AAT3, AAT4). Cholesterol and triglycerides are commonly elevated in hypothyroid dogs.

Treatment usually consists of:

- supplemental synthetic thyroid hormone, starting at 0.1 milligrams per ten to fifteen pounds optimal body weight (Synthroid is the gold standard medication)

- a healthy species-appropriate whole food diet (more protein, less carbs) that is minimally processed

- decreasing (or stopping) vaccine usage

- supporting the immune system with vitamin D (found in cod liver oil, sardines, eggs, kefir, and beef liver)

- kelp as a source of iodine, which is required for thyroid function (¼ teaspoon for small dogs, ½ teaspoon for medium dogs, 1 teaspoon for large dogs)

- omega-3 fatty acids (give 20 to 30 milligrams per pound of body weight daily)

- Licorice root, Rehmannia, and Ashwaganda are commonly included in herbal thyroid supplements.

- vitamin A (50 to 100 IU per pound of body weight daily), ester-C (100 to 500 milligrams daily, dosed to bowel tolerance; lower dose if diarrhea develops), and vitamin E (400 to 1,000 IU per day) are also important to support endocrine function

- ❧ some supplements contain ground thyroid gland, which can add thyroid hormone without synthetic supplementation (Standard Process and Animal Nutrition Technologies)

- ❧ thyroid hormone levels should be closely monitored, as over or under-supplementation can have dire consequences

*Hyperthyroidism,* an overactive thyroid gland, is a disease of cats. When seen in dogs, it is almost always related to a malignant functional thyroid tumor. Cats rarely have malignant thyroid tumors. Thyroid hormone is responsible for metabolism, and increased levels will effectively "rev the engine." Symptoms may include hyperactivity, increased thirst and urination, vomiting, diarrhea, increased appetite with weight loss, excessive vocalization, racing heart rate, high blood pressure, and possibly a palpably enlarged thyroid gland on the neck. Testing to confirm suspected thyroid disease in cats may include a blood test for T3, T4, and free T4. Liver and cardiac enzymes will often be elevated on routine chemistry screens. The average age at time of diagnosis is eight to thirteen.

The causes of hyperthyroidism are still not completely known. A relationship has been theorized between this disease and PBDEs (polybrominated diphenyl ethers), which is a chemical flame retardant used in many industries and BPA (bisphenol-A), which is a chemical used to coat the inside of pet food cans. The BPA may not be the cause of the problem, as PBDE is found in ocean fish from pollution; the association may be the chemicals in the fish, not the can. The amount of iodine in cat foods may also play a role, as well as the addition of soy, which can disrupt thyroid function.

Treatment for hyperthyroidism consists of four options. A daily medication called methimazole can be given as a pill, liquid, or transdermal gel. Methimazole will stop production of thyroid hormone, but it will not shrink the thyroid tumor. Side effects include suppression of the bone marrow with low red and white blood cell production, liver failure, vomiting, and allergic dermatitis. Cats taking this medication need to be monitored with blood work every few months. This is probably the most common form of treatment. Many cats with thyroid disease have underlying kidney disease, which will become apparent when the thyroid disease is treated.

Surgery is a less commonly used option for treatment. *Removal of the thyroid gland should only be performed by a highly skilled surgeon in a specialty center.* Accidental removal of the parathyroid glands, which are very small and are found next to the thyroid gland, can have devastating results, including death. If the entire thyroid gland is removed, the cat will need to be given thyroid supplements for life. Many hyperthyroid cats have cardiac disease and are not good candidates for surgery.

Radioactive iodine therapy has become more popular as the primary form of treatment for this disease. While the initial cost may run well over a thousand dollars, this cost may be less than the money that will be spent on medications and monitoring when treating with drugs. Treatment consists of an injection of radioactive iodine under the skin. The iodine is concentrated in the thyroid gland, causing selective destruction of the gland tissue. A small percentage of cats may become hypothyroid after treatment, requiring thyroid hormone supplementation. An equally small percentage may need a second injection of radioactive iodine if the tumor was particularly large or malignant (only 2 to 3 percent of tumors in cats are malignant). The cats must stay in a lead-lined room for three days after treatment so owners are not exposed to any radioactive particles.

The fourth method of treatment is relatively new. Hill's food company has added Y/D to the alphabet soup. This diet is severely deficient in iodine, decreasing the availability of iodine to the thyroid gland and resulting in decreased production of thyroid hormone. While decreasing hormone production will help diminish symptoms, the diet does nothing to actually diminish the size of the thyroid tumor, which can continue to grow and potentially become malignant over time. The diet may actually cause the tumor to enlarge, as hormones such as thyroid-stimulating hormone will detect decreased levels of iodine and cause the thyroid to work even harder. Iodine-deficient diets in people cause goiter, which is benign enlargement of the thyroid gland. Could cat foods actually be causing this disease by providing too little iodine? And by restricting iodine levels further, are we adding to the problem? The entire body is also being deprived of iodine, which may have unknown repercussions.

The diet comes in canned and dry formulations. I never recommend feeding dry food to cats, which will be covered in a later chapter. The ingredients of the canned food include liver, unspecified meat byproducts (which meats?), chicken, whole grain corn, and rice flour. Cats are carnivores and do not need carbohydrates. Canned Y/D contains 24 percent carbohydrates; the dry formulation is closer to 29 percent. They need high-protein diets when they are in a muscle-wasted state, which occurs with this disease. The dry product does not contain any meat. It is made with corn, pork fat, and soybean run meal. Cats should not be fed corn, soy, and rice, which are cheap fillers. This diet cannot be fed to healthy cats without thyroid disease, so owners of multiple cats will have to separate cats at feeding. I do not recommend feeding prescription diet Y/D for treatment of hyperthyroidism in cats.

Alternative treatments for hyperthyroidism in cats can be helpful.

- ❧ A high-quality, high-moisture diet (canned, frozen raw, home-cooked, or rehydrated freeze-dried raw) should be the basis for treatment.

- ❧ Yin-tonifying (cooling) meats—see "Energetics" chapter—are needed (rabbit, duck, grass-fed beef, liver, and clams are good protein sources).

- ❧ Liver support is essential because liver enzymes are commonly elevated with this disease. Milk thistle (5 to 10 milligrams per pound twice daily) and/or SAM-e (90 milligrams daily) may be helpful.

- Foods high in vitamin A like carrots, kale, spinach, and barley grass should be added in small amounts if the cat will eat them. They can be cooked and minced or fed raw.

- L-Carnitine (250–500 milligrams twice daily) should be added for cardiac support (found in high quantities in red meats).

- Taurine (250–500 milligrams two to three times daily) should be added for cardiac support (also found in high quantities in red meats, poultry, eggs, dairy products, and fish).

- Home-cooked diets for cats are hard to balance and must include sufficient carnitine and taurine.

- Herbs to balance thyroid function should be added. Bugleweed has been shown to decrease output of thyroid hormone by the thyroid gland. Dosage will depend on product used. Hawthorn can help lower blood pressure and decrease work of the heart. Many cats will be too sick at the time of diagnosis to be treated with herbal therapy alone.

- Acupuncture can help balance the immune system, lower blood pressure, and support the kidneys and liver.

- Hyperthyroid cats should no longer be vaccinated.

The hardest thing about using alternative treatments is getting them into the cat. Most cats do not enjoy being medicated. While I do not like the ingredients used to make Pill Pockets, they can be a lifesaver for medicating cats.

*Hyperadrenocorticism or Cushing's disease,* caused by overproduction of hormones by the adrenal gland, is being diagnosed in dogs with increasing frequency. Symptoms include increased thirst and urination, excessive panting, hair loss, muscle weakness, pot belly, liver enlargement, and chronic skin or urinary tract infections. The adrenal gland is ruled by the pituitary gland, and the disease can stem from either gland. Hormones released from the adrenal gland include cortisols similar to prednisone as well as lesser estrogen, progesterone, and testosterone types of hormones.

One of the earliest indicators of adrenal gland dysfunction is an elevation in serum alkaline phosphatase (SAP or AlkP) on the chemistry panel. The best test of adrenal gland function is performed at the University of Tennessee endocrinology lab, and I recommend sending all samples to that lab. They will test for an array of hormones—and not just cortisol. By performing a Dexamethasone suppression/ACTH stimulation combination test, it is usually possible to discern whether the excess hormone production is originating in the pituitary or the adrenal glands.

This disease can be caused by a tumor in the adrenal gland (may be more common in large breeds), a tumor in the pituitary gland (may be more common in small breeds), or by over-administration of steroids. If testing reveals primary adrenal production, an abdominal ultrasound is recommended to rule out an adrenal gland tumor. Adrenal gland tumors can be highly malignant, aggressive, and difficult to remove surgically. Pituitary gland tumors are much more common, occurring in about 85 percent of dogs with Cushing's disease. These benign, slow-growing tumors usually do not spread to other areas of the body.

Dogs with Cushing's disease commonly have high blood pressure; this should be monitored and treated if needed. Blood pressure can be lowered with herbal medications containing hawthorn, acupuncture, or traditional medications. These dogs may also have elevated calcium levels, which can lead to production of bladder and kidney stones. Dogs with high calcium levels should be x-rayed to check for the presence of stones.

Traditional treatments for hyperadrenocorticism include harsh medications including mitotane (Lysodren), ketoconazole (Nizoral), selegiline or L-Deprenyl (Anipryl), and trilostane (Vetoryl). Dogs taking these medications must be monitored closely for reactions. The medications work by stopping production of hormones by the adrenal gland cells. Side effects are common, including vomiting, diarrhea, anorexia, liver failure, kidney failure, and diminished hearing (I had one patient become deaf on selegiline; luckily, hearing returned on discontinuation of the drug). Considering most dogs with this disease have significant liver dysfunction, it seems odd to use medications that can cause liver failure. I rarely use these drugs in my practice (I can remember two dogs treated with these drugs, and I was not the one who prescribed them).

Luckily there are quite a few alternative treatments available for this disease, particularly if caught early:

- melatonin (3 milligrams twice daily for small dogs, up to 6 milligrams twice daily for large dogs); decrease dose if pet is too sleepy or lethargic

- flax seed lignans (20 to 40 milligrams once daily)

- glandular products, including ground adrenal and thymus glands (Animal Nutrition Technologies and Standard Process are two good companies)

- antioxidant vitamins A (50 to 100 IU per pound of body weight daily), Ester C (100 to 500 milligrams daily dosed to bowel tolerance—decrease dose if diarrhea develops), and E (400 to 1,000 IU per day)

- CoQ10 (30 to 100 milligrams daily as an antioxidant)

- Si Maio San (Chinese herbal formula at 0.5 gram per ten to twenty pounds body weight, twice daily)

- acupuncture to lower blood pressure and increase energy and muscle strength

- hawthorn berry to lower blood pressure; feed one teaspoon of ground berry per one pound of food fed or ½ teaspoon of hawthorn tincture daily

- diet issues must be handled with quality protein sources, minimal or no carbohydrates, and plenty of leafy green vegetables (barley can be used, as it is cooling and draining)

❧ discontinue vaccines (and stress should be kept to a minimum)

❧ support liver function with milk thistle (five to ten milligrams per pound of body weight, twice daily) and SAM-e (90 milligrams for small dogs, 225 milligrams for medium dogs, and 400 milligrams for large dogs)

*Hypoadrenocorticism or Addison's disease* is the opposite of Cushing's disease. The adrenal gland does not produce enough cortisol and/or mineralocorticoids (hormones that regulate salt and water balance). Middle-aged female poodles are the most commonly affected, although it can be seen in almost any breed. Symptoms include vomiting, diarrhea, lethargy, anorexia, dehydration, kidney failure, muscle weakness, tremors, and collapse. When in crisis, these dogs need to be treated immediately or face certain death. Electrolyte imbalances, including high potassium levels, will slow the heart rate and can cause heart function to cease.

Diagnosis of this disease can be elusive. Dogs are commonly presented for vague, repeated episodes of vomiting and diarrhea. Commonly, symptoms occur during times of stress or increased activity. Normally, the adrenal gland is responsible for the fight-or-flight response that increases heart rate and metabolism when the body is stressed. Without those hormones, the body is no longer able to fight or flee.

Blood work may show low sodium and high potassium levels, elevated BUN or creatinine (kidney enzymes), and low red blood cell count. These tests are not diagnostic but may be early indicators warranting further diagnostics. The definitive test for diagnosis is the ACTH stimulation test. ACTH is a gel that is injected to stimulate the adrenal gland to produce hormones. A blood sample is taken before and after giving the injection to determine how well the adrenal glands respond. A dog with Addison's disease will have no response to the ACTH gel, confirming the diagnosis.

Causes of Addison's disease include autoimmune disease, in

which the body attacks the adrenal glands or the overuse of steroids for treatment of other diseases. Constant stress and bombardment with dietary and environmental toxins can cause the adrenal glands to shut down. When steroids, particularly long-acting injections, are used for treatment, they suppress the normal production of steroids by the adrenal glands. When used for prolonged periods of time and then suddenly withdrawn, the body does not have time to respond— and the animal can crash in Addisonian crisis. Overuse of long-acting injections of steroids can permanently shut down the adrenal glands.

Treatment of Addison's disease consists of replacing the hormones the adrenal gland is not producing. Low doses of prednisone are usually given daily to replace cortisone. If mineralocorticoid supplementation is necessary, fludrocortisone (Florinef), a tablet that is given daily, or desoxycorticosterone pivolate (Percorten-V), can be given as a monthly injection to replace the mineralocorticoids. Not all dogs with Addison's disease will require mineralocorticoid supplementation.

During times of stress (boarding, holidays, dog shows, veterinary appointments, etc.) additional or increased dosing of prednisone may be required. Kidney and liver function, along with electrolytes, must be monitored frequently to ensure proper dosing of the medications. I recommend at least every three months once the pet is stabilized and more often during the initial treatment period. There are no herbal or homeopathic supplements that will treat Addison's disease without concurrent use of drugs.

In some cases, Addison's disease is caused by genetics. Dogs diagnosed with this disease should be removed from breeding programs, and the parents may also need to be removed.

❧ The best way to prevent Addison's disease is by avoiding stresses on the immune system. Avoid stressful situations like boarding or crowded events.

❧ Feed a healthy, species-appropriate diet with no artificial preservatives, dyes, or chemicals.

❧ Minimize vaccinations, medications, and parasiticides, which will stress the immune system.

❧ Once diagnosed, support with glandular products (Animal Nutrition Technologies or Standard Process), antioxidant vitamins (A, C, and E), and herbals will help keep the immune system in the best shape possible.

# Dalilah's Dilemma

Our wonderful little Dalilah, who started us on our journey of rescuing dogs and our love for spaniels, developed a problem after Gwen had owned her for a few years. I picked her up one day and realized I could feel her heart pounding against her chest wall—and there was a fluttering under my fingertips. That flutter could only mean one thing. Dalilah's heart had a leaky valve. I grabbed my stethoscope and listened. Dalilah had a grade four heart murmur. A heart murmur is a noise heard when listening to the heart. It means there is turbulence in the blood flow. Murmurs are graded on a scale of one to six. Four is significant.

Dalilah had no symptoms of heart disease, which is why we were unaware of her problem. Dogs with failing hearts will usually show signs of fatigue, coughing after exercise, or coughing after sleeping. They may lose their appetites, vomit more often, or lose muscle mass. Dalilah had none of those symptoms, which was a good sign.

I took an x-ray of Dalilah's chest to determine if she had an enlarged heart. Sadly, her heart was greatly enlarged on the x-ray, which was not good news. I made an appointment for Dalilah to see a cardiologist immediately. We needed an echocardiogram to determine how far her heart had deteriorated.

The cardiologist gave us grim news. The heart disease was very advanced. Cavalier King Charles spaniels have a predisposition toward heart failure. The original three cavalier stud dogs all carried the gene for heart disease, and good breeders have spent decades trying to breed this trait out of their lines. Unfortunately, Dalilah was a puppy mill rescue, and her lineage was sketchy, at best.

The cardiologist recommended starting Dalilah on a long list of cardiac drugs. She would take Enalapril to keep her blood pressure low and make it easier for her heart to pump. We added Furosemide as a diuretic to keep her from building up fluid in her lungs. Pimobendan would help her heart pump with more strength to keep her blood flowing in the right direction. The cardiologist shook his head and added that anything I could do with my "voodoo medicine" probably wouldn't hurt either. He gave her a guarded prognosis of three to six months to live. We left with broken hearts of our own.

Dalilah was the only one who was unaware of her grave prognosis. She still ran, played, and acted as if life was perfectly normal. She still followed Gwen and went everywhere with her. She went for walks, ran in the yard, and played with the other dogs. She didn't have any symptoms. I decided I would find everything I could to make Dalilah as healthy as possible and keep her going strong for as long as possible.

I added a long list of supplements to her regimen. She took 30 milligrams of CoQ10 as an antioxidant, 300 milligrams of omega-3 fatty acids twice daily for their anti-inflammatory action, an herbal that contained hawthorn and dandelion leaf to help her heart muscle strength and help drain fluid, a glandular product containing heart muscle, vitamin E, magnesium, potassium, L-Carnitine, and taurine to strengthen heart muscle. I fed her a diet rich in blood tonics, which included beef, cold-water fish like sardines (which are also high in omega-3s), heart, liver, and eggs. She needed qi tonics like pumpkin and sweet potato, which are energy tonics, to help her heart move the blood, and supplements like garlic and turmeric to resolve stagnation and keep her blood moving. Dalilah continued to do well, but after five months, she started to cough. It was time to return to the cardiologist.

When the cardiologist saw us in his office, his first comment was that he was surprised we were back. He had expected Dalilah to have passed away by then, given the severity of her heart disease. When he repeated the echocardiogram, he saw that Dalilah's disease had advanced a bit, and some of the internal heart muscles had ruptured since our last visit. The cough was not due to fluid in Dalilah's lungs; the problem was that her heart was so enlarged it was pushing on her trachea, or airway, causing it to compress so that she had trouble getting air when she was lying in certain positions. He added Spironolactone to her list of drugs, another diuretic. Overall, that was good news, since her heart was still pumping blood effectively.

We continued treating Dalilah with the same supplements and diet. We restricted her exercise to leash walks and quiet time in the yard, not allowing her to be crazy with the rest of the pack. Four months later, Gwen left for college, leaving Dalilah in our care. We felt so sorry for that sad little creature. She sat on the top stair outside Gwen's bedroom, awaiting her return. When Gwen came home on the occasional weekend or for a holiday, Dalilah ran and spun and barked and held her own little celebration. She would cling to Gwen until she left again, returning to her vigil on the top step.

After six months, it was time to check in again with the cardiologist. Again, he was shocked Dalilah was still alive. She had surpassed the three-to-six-month prediction by a year. Her echocardiogram was awful, showing an extremely weak heart muscle, but Dalilah was still going strong. We took Dalilah to college and to Gwen's horse shows almost every weekend so that she could see Gwen. She was everyone's darling, but she only had eyes for Gwen. Gwen came home for spring break, and Dalilah spent ten glorious days following her and sleeping next to her. This was her own little bit of heaven.

Dalilah continued to show no symptoms, wanting to run and play with the other dogs. We were limiting her to short walks and trying everything we could to keep her stress level to a minimum. One day in April, I received a frantic phone call at work. Dalilah had eaten dinner and taken a nap. Suddenly, she ran into the kitchen, looked up at Hue, and collapsed on the kitchen floor. The closest emergency hospital was fifteen minutes from home, and I agreed to meet Hue there as quickly as possible.

When I arrived to the emergency hospital, Dalilah was on oxygen and had monitor wires everywhere. Her oxygen level was low, her heart was barely moving, and she was comatose. I called Gwen and told her we needed to let her go. It was one of the saddest moments of our lives. Dalilah passed on her own.

Dalilah was a trooper. She survived for more than a year past what had been predicted. I have no way of knowing if the supplements and diet made a difference in her longevity, but I have to believe they did because she beat the odds by a long shot. There will never be another dog that will win our hearts like Dalilah. She taught us so much about unconditional love, rescue work, and survival.

# Broken Hearted:
# Treating Heart Disease

C ertain breeds are more prone to heart disease, including Maine
Coon cats, Ragdoll cats, cavalier King Charles spaniels,
Doberman pinschers, boxers, and others. Early warning signs of heart
disease can include shortness of breath, exercise intolerance, fainting,
coughing, and fatigue. All pets should have a professional veterinary
examination at least once per year, but once these breeds reach the
age of five or signs listed above are noticed, the examinations should
be performed at least twice per year.

A chest x-ray should be taken at five years of age or earlier if a heart
murmur is detected on auscultation with the stethoscope. The x-ray
should be repeated every six months to monitor heart size. A vertebral
heart score (a measurement comparing the size of the heart to the
vertebrae) helps show progression of disease. Unfortunately, many cats
with severe heart disease will not have a murmur or heart enlargement
on x-ray. Cats commonly develop a different form of heart disease
than dogs, in which the heart muscle becomes thickened, restricting
the flow of blood as it passes through the heart chambers. Cats fed

vegetarian, vegan, or unbalanced home-cooked meals are much more likely to succumb to heart disease. Cats are obligate carnivores and need whole meats to supply the right balance of amino acids to support heart function. The most common symptoms of heart disease in cats are vomiting, rapid or labored breathing, blood clots causing hind-end paralysis, lack of appetite, restlessness, and sudden death. One of my cats died suddenly from heart disease while walking up the stairs at the age of ten. He had no murmur and no symptoms that I noticed prior to his demise.

An EKG should be performed every six to twelve months to look for signs of abnormal heart rhythm or heart enlargement once a pet has been diagnosed with heart disease or a murmur. Once heart disease is noted, these pets should be evaluated by a board certified cardiologist and have an echocardiogram. The echocardiogram is an ultrasound that will show the movement of the heart muscle and heart valves. Strength of muscle contraction, systemic blood pressure, and pulmonary blood pressure can be measured. Increases in blood pressure need to be managed to avoid secondary problems like kidney failure and glaucoma. Blood pressure should be monitored periodically.

I like treating heart disease with a combination of traditional and alternative therapies:

* Acupuncture can be extremely helpful to increase heart qi or energy, decrease blood pressure, and regulate blood flow.

* A meat-based diet, including heart muscle (beef or chicken hearts are easy to find) can be helpful too (include ground bone or allow dogs to chew on raw bones).

* Hawthorn can help widen the coronary arteries to boost blood circulation and help regulate abnormal rhythms. Give 1 teaspoon of ground hawthorn berry powder per pound of food fed or ¼ to ½ teaspoon of hawthorn tincture. Many herbal supplements contain hawthorn as one of many ingredients.

- Gingko can facilitate blood flow and lower blood pressure. Cayenne pepper, rosemary, bilberry, and gotu kola have similar effects.

- CoQ10 is an antioxidant. Give one milligram per pound of body weight daily, which may need to be split into two doses. Round up or down to easiest dosage available.

- L-arginine is an amino acid that improves endothelial cell (cells lining the heart chambers) function and cardiac output in congestive heart failure; give up to 100 milligrams per pound of body weight daily.

- L-carnitine is abundant in red meat and may be deficient in many diets. It increases heart function, particularly in dilated cardiomyopathy; give 500 to 2,000 milligrams twice daily (depending on size of the pet).

- Taurine is an amino acid abundant in raw meat, particularly heart muscle. It may be destroyed in cooking and is deficient in many dry food formulations; give 250 to 750 milligrams twice daily (depending on size of the pet).

- Chromium aids metabolism, decreases cholesterol, and improves heart health. It is found in many trace-mineral supplements (Rx Vitamins, Standard Process, and Wysong are three companies that have supplements that contain chromium).

- Omega-3 fatty acids (EPA and DHA) decrease cardiac inflammation and decrease muscle wasting; give 30 milligrams per pound of body weight daily (must be given with vitamin E at 1 to 2 IU per pound of body weight daily). The best source in this case is fish oil. Vegetable oils may not be as well absorbed.

- Calcium works with magnesium to regulate contraction and relaxation of the heart muscle. Pets fed a raw diet with ground bone will get plenty of calcium.

- Magnesium works with calcium to regulate contraction and relaxation of the heart muscle.

- Selenium may reduce inflammation and decrease risk of forming blood clots (found in organ meats like hearts).

- Vitamin A (50 to 100 IU per pound of body weight daily), Ester-C (100 to 1,000 milligrams daily dosed to bowel tolerance—decrease dose if diarrhea develops), E (400 to 1,000 IU daily), and B complex (25 to 50 milligrams daily, also found in eggs, heart, and liver) can all strengthen the heart.

There are good supplements in the veterinary market that combine a lot of these ingredients, making them easier to administer. I like Animal Nutrition Technologies' Cardiac Support formula.

In pets that are progressing to congestive heart failure, attention should be given to protect the liver since it will become congested and swollen. Milk thistle is protective for liver cells (dosed at five to ten milligrams per pound of body weight daily), and dandelion leaf (uva ursi) will help drain excess fluid like a diuretic pill.

Old and new traditional medications for congestive heart failure include medications to lower blood pressure (enalapril, benazepril, lisinopril, atenolol, diltiazem, amlodipine, and others), increase heart muscle strength (pimobendan, digoxin), and decrease fluid build-up (furosemide, spironolactone, chlorthiazide, hydrochlorthiazide). Many times, alternative therapies can be combined with these medications, but be sure to check with your veterinarian before combining treatments. Always inform your veterinarian if you are giving supplements since there could be an adverse reaction when combined with prescription medications.

Pets with heart disease should be fed a diet that will promote heart health and spare the liver and kidneys. I am a strong proponent of "like cures like," so all dogs and cats with heart disease should be fed hearts. Chicken hearts are easy to find and easy to feed. They can be fed raw or cooked and can be added to a commercial diet. Adding small amounts of beef or chicken liver will also help support the liver. Be careful not to overdo the liver, feeding only two to three times per week, since the liver is the detoxification center in the body and can store heavy metals and other wastes. Try to find free-range or grass-fed, antibiotic-free liver.

Qi or energy tonic foods can help the blood move more easily through the body. Feeding things like beef, chicken (I like dark meat better), rabbit, or tripe as the meat source will keep blood flowing freely. Good vegetable sources are pumpkin, squash, sweet potato, yams, and shiitake mushrooms. Foods that promote diuresis (elimination of excess fluid) include celery, watermelon, dandelion greens, and parsley. These can be added to a commercial diet—or you can prepare a home-cooked stew with the ingredients. If you are going to cook for your pet, you must add vitamins and minerals to balance the diet, particularly calcium. This will be addressed in a later chapter.

# Spats: Raising Healthy Cats

I've talked a lot about the dogs that have come and gone through our lives, but I haven't mentioned much about our cats. Over the years, I've had many cats, even though I grew up in a family where it was said the only good cat was a dead cat (that old book *101 Uses for a Dead Cat* given to me by my grandfather way back when). When I became an adult and moved out on my own, I decided I would someday have a cat.

As luck would have it, on my first day back at work after my honeymoon in 1985, an old farmer walked into the veterinary office where I was working. He held a small buff-colored male kitten in his hands. A Doberman had attacked the kitten, and his hind end was a mess. The farmer asked if we could put him to sleep and end his suffering. I asked if I could keep the kitten if I could fix him up, and the farmer said he didn't care—as long as it didn't cost him any money. I called home and asked my new husband if I could bring home a kitten. He said no. I called again and received the same answer. I'm pretty sure he said no at least ten times that day.

When my new husband walked into our apartment at the end of the day, a small buff-colored male kitten sat on our sofa with eyes as big as saucers and both hind legs in a cast. Our Doberman was watching the kitten intently, and I'm sure the kitten thought he was going to be eaten all over again. My new husband looked at the kitten, looked at me, and said, "Oh, now I see how this is going to go for the rest of my life."

The new kitten was named Puff and later shortened to Mr. P because everyone thought Puff was too feminine. Mr. P went back and forth to work with me every day. I was commuting over an hour each way, and Mr. P became the best car-riding cat ever. I had to change his little casts every two weeks because he kept outgrowing them. He became best friends with our Doberman, and they played and ran through the house all the time. Mr. P was an indoor kitty, but he did manage to escape one time and was missing for three days. When he returned home, he was covered with bite and scratch marks, and I knew he had paid a visit to a nearby farm where there were a lot of stray cats. Mr. P recovered with the help of antibiotics and seemed fine.

Nine years later, I had a sick cat at the hospital that needed a blood transfusion. I volunteered to take blood from Mr. P. The first thing we always do before transfusing is test both the donor and the recipient for feline leukemia and feline immunodeficiency virus (FIV). To my surprise, Mr. P came up positive for FIV. There was only one way he could have become infected: the bite wounds nine years earlier. He had been an asymptomatic carrier all those years.

Three years following the test, Mr. P became symptomatic. He developed lymphoma in his throat and couldn't eat. This was prior to my foray into holistic medicine, so we took Mr. P to a surgeon and had a feeding tube placed in his stomach. We started him on Prednisone and chemotherapy drugs. Once he started taking the drugs, he started eating—and the feeding tube came out within a month. Mr. P lived for another year before the lymphoma spread to his kidneys. At that point, there was nothing more I could do for him and had to let him go. My first kitty lived with me for almost fourteen years.

Over the years, I managed to collect quite a few cats. They usually arrived when we were least expecting them. I took in one with a broken leg and no owner. I scraped a feral cat off the road that had been hit by a car and nursed her back to health. I took in a small kitten to give to my son when I was expecting my daughter so he would have a best buddy all his own. A friend closed down her barn and gave me one of her barn kittens with a hurt leg and a million fleas. When we moved to a farm years later, we adopted more cats to live in the barn. There were usually at least four cats in the house and a few more in the barn.

When the last farm was finally sold and I moved into a neighborhood, I was down to two cats. That number was much more manageable, especially since we seemed to be adding more dogs. But my daughter had different plans for us. My kids both grew up hanging out at the veterinary hospital and helping with the animals. Gwen took on the job of bottle-feeding kittens when they didn't have a mother. One year, she raised twenty-one kittens and found homes for all of them.

The summer after Gwen graduated from high school, she took a full-time job at the veterinary clinic. She took on more bottle baby kittens and raised a litter of five. When the next litter came along, she said she was too sleep-deprived to take them too. She pawned them off on Hue and me. I really don't like taking care of bottle baby kittens. They take a lot of time and need to be fed every few hours— even all night long. Bottle baby kittens usually do well for a week or two, but then many of them develop fading kitten syndrome and just die. It can be heartbreaking.

We were spending a lot of time at the shore on the weekends and would have to take kittens back and forth with us. They had to be on a heating pad and had to be fed and cleaned frequently. This was no vacation. Hue had never participated in one of these projects and thought it would be a good experience. I warned him, but he insisted we should take this on. The older I get, the more I hate being deprived of sleep.

So we took on a litter of five kittens. The first few days, things went pretty well. We were feeling good about it. Then a kitten died. Hue was devastated, and I said something about the circle of life. We forged onward with our four babies. Things were going well, until the end of the second week, and we lost another kitten. It just stopped eating and died. It's always frustrating. Hue was upset, and I probably repeated my circle of life statement that was met with a cold stare.

We were determined to keep the remaining three kittens alive. Gwen's kittens were two weeks older than ours, and she had lost one from her litter as well. But her kittens had opened their eyes and were starting to crawl and were the cutest things. We couldn't wait to get ours to the same point. We persevered and were rewarded with three huge, potbellied, crawling babies two weeks later. We managed to talk Hue's daughter into taking one kitten, and we decided we were going to keep the other two. Since Gwen was keeping one from her group, our house was about to have five cats instead of two.

The kittens grew up in a house full of spaniels. They spent a lot of time at the shore house with the dogs and didn't see the housecats until they were a few months old. The kittens followed the spaniels and played with them. They curled up and slept in the spaniel pile at naptime. When it was time to learn how to eat real food, they tried to eat from the spaniel bowls.

I was determined that the kittens would grow up on a healthy diet. Cats are carnivores and should be fed a meat-based diet. Cats in the wild eat small prey like rabbits, rodents, and birds. They will eat all the meat and bones and some of the organs, usually leaving the fur and intestines behind. Cats fed this way will live long, active, healthy lives. For years, cats have been fed commercial dry food that is loaded with corn and other grains—and overloaded with carbohydrates. In my practice, I have seen many cats with illnesses that can be attributed to poor diet, including diabetes, kidney failure, arthritis, and dental disease.

Cats do not process carbohydrates very well. Carbohydrates break down to sugars, and the pancreas produces insulin to process those sugars. For cats, eating a diet laden with carbohydrates is like a person eating candy bars all day. When a cat eats carbohydrate-laden dry food, their blood sugar goes up; the pancreas produces insulin, which lowers the blood sugar, making the cat hungry again, and it eats more dry food. This cycle is repeated many times throughout the day. For most indoor cats, the only exercise they get is walking back and forth to the food bowl. They eventually become obese, and they eventually become diabetic, requiring insulin injections when the pancreas is no longer capable of producing insulin. Caring for a diabetic pet is an expensive and time-consuming endeavor—not to mention, a challenge for a lot of owners that may not be comfortable giving injections. Many times, if I can get an owner to stop feeding dry food and start feeding a meat-based diet, cats can avoid having to receive insulin injections, reversing the diabetic state.

The other problem with feeding dry food to cats involves urinary issues. Dry food is highly processed to remove as much moisture as possible, leaving 10 percent or less moisture in the food. Canned or home-cooked diets, on the other hand, contain around 85 percent moisture. Most cats are not big drinkers, so those fed only dry foods are constantly in a state of dehydration. Their urine is highly concentrated and is more likely to contain crystals, which can lead to urinary tract disease and obstructions. Cats fed moist food have much more diluted urine and urinate more often, helping to flush the kidneys and bladder. Again, I have "cured" many cats with urinary tract disease with the simple change from feeding dry food to feeding moist food. Obese cats are more prone to urinary tract infections because they are unable to groom themselves well. By feeding a diet lower in carbohydrates, obese cats can lose weight, enabling them to reach around and groom themselves better.

The biggest problem with feeding cats is that they have extreme preferences. Some cats absolutely will not eat wet foods. They will walk away and starve themselves to death. A cat that doesn't eat for four or five days will develop fatty liver syndrome, and die, if not force-fed.

My older cats were raised on dry foods since I didn't know then what I know now. The new, young cats, needed to be started out correctly so they would never become addicted to carbohydrates. My older cats had to be transitioned to a moist diet, which took six months of perseverance, offering many brands and flavors of wet foods and slowly decreasing the dry food available.

Luckily, the kittens were raised with the spaniels and thought they were dogs. Hence, we called them our little spaniel cats, or spats. The spats wanted to share the spaniel food, stealing raw meat at any chance they got. So it was easy to get them started correctly. We introduced canned foods, home-cooked stews, and frozen raw meat patties. They loved them all.

Recently, freeze-dried raw foods have become readily available, and they are generally highly palatable to cats. They can be sprinkled over the dry food to get the cats to try them, and then water can be added to rehydrate the food once they fall in love. This is an extremely healthy diet.

Luckily, our kittens loved everything we offered, which made feeding them healthy food extremely easy. The kittens are the healthiest cats I have ever had the pleasure of owning. We live in a safe neighborhood, so the spats get to run and play in the yard with the spaniels. Sometimes a dog is chasing a cat, and sometimes a cat is chasing a dog. It's absolutely comical to watch seven dogs and three cats play outside. It's a little less comical when they race through the house and knock over lamps.

# How to Grow Hair Using Food

In an earlier chapter, I referred to myself as a pet food salesman. But over the years, I have become less satisfied with commercial pet food products. In the first decade of this century, we started hearing about pets dying from tainted pet foods. There were scares about foods contaminated with salmonella, aflatoxins, melamine, and euthanasia solutions. Once tainted foods started killing pets, owners were desperate to find alternative food sources. Home cooking became very popular with owners because they felt they had a lot more control over what was being fed to their furry kids. Unfortunately, pets started becoming ill due to vitamin and mineral deficiencies from improperly prepared diets. Personally, I love home-cooked diets, but they have to be done correctly. They need to be balanced and have the proper minerals added because pets require high levels of calcium in their diets.

The more I heard, the more I shied away from commercial pet food products. I started doing research and found a large contingency of natural pet owners leaning toward feeding raw meat diets. I resisted feeding raw meats for years, believing all the scare tactics about bacterial contamination and illnesses in pets and people. Unable to find a commercial pet food I could really get behind at the time, I started having frozen raw meat patties formulated for pets shipped to my house. My dogs absolutely loved the food. They ate that product like it was going out of style.

The previous summer, I had adopted an English toy spaniel with a long list of health issues—and no hair. Lora Lu was improving slowly just by being out of the puppy mill and getting proper care, but she just couldn't grow a good coat. It was patchy, dull, and lifeless. Once I started her on the raw diet, it seemed like her hair was growing in leaps and bounds. Six years later, she grows so much coat that I have to shave her down every six weeks to keep up with it. Her foster parents didn't recognize her when we went to visit!

I loved the frozen raw product, but it had to be shipped on dry ice, and each delivery carried a high price tag just for shipping. I needed to find a better source. Fortunately, frozen raw diets have started to become a little more mainstream. They are now available in many small, high-quality pet stores and a few veterinary offices (like mine!). My favorite frozen raw diet is Stella N Chewy's, but Primal, Nature's Variety, Oma's Pride, Darwin's, and a host of other good products are available.

Many clients come to my practice to learn how to use raw diets or to cook for their pets. I help them plan a balanced diet, and I help them feed the appropriate protein sources based on the pet's personality, lifestyle, and health issues. That is probably the part of practice that I currently enjoy most.

# Label Reading for Life

I am not allowed to walk down the pet food aisle in the grocery store. When I see the aisle, Hue quickly steers me away before I can get started reading labels on popular pet foods while loudly proclaiming how horrible they are. I can be an embarrassment, and someday I will probably be kicked out of our grocery store and told never to return. It takes a lot of restraint to keep me from chasing down people who have large bags of awful foods or boxes of chemical-laden treats in their carts.

When I take my mother to the big box store to buy groceries in bulk, she has learned to just allow me to pick out the treats for her dog. She's too afraid to pick something herself and have to listen to my tirade. All I want to do is educate people so they will feed their pets healthier diets. And don't even get me started on the crap food they have in their carts for their kids and themselves.

In order to choose the right pet food, you must be able to read the labels on the bags and cans of food that you buy. Ingredients are listed on the label in decreasing quantities, meaning the first ingredient listed is found in the highest quantity. Cats are carnivores, meaning they need to eat meat. Dogs are either carnivores or omnivores, depending on who you ask. Either way, they should all be eating a meat-based diet. So it stands to reason that the main ingredients in their foods should be meats. If you read a food label and the first ingredient is not meat, do not buy the food.

I have some vegan clients who will not feed meats to their pets. Dogs can adapt fairly well to a vegan diet (although it is not ideal). In my opinion, cats should never be fed a vegetarian or vegan diet. I have lost many feline patients to heart disease because their owners refused to feed them meat. No matter how many vitamins you add to the diet, you cannot achieve the amino acid and vitamin profile that an obligate carnivore needs without feeding meat.

I prefer the first ingredient to be a whole meat source, not a meat or fish meal. Others argue that a meat or fish meal is a more concentrated protein source that will add more protein to the diet. In the first five ingredients in a dry food, I want two—and preferably three—to be meats (unless you are using a grain-free product, in which case there may be more meat products listed). In Orijen Regional Red dry dog food, the first *sixteen* ingredients are meats. I love this company. When adding up the percentages each of the first five ingredients contributes to the ingredient list, remember that three grains will outweigh two meats, so you are feeding a high grain product.

I never want to see meat byproducts in the ingredient list, only whole meats. Byproducts are the parts of the animal that are not fit for human consumption and do not include muscle meat. If organ meats are used, which are fine, they should be listed as the whole organ, not as a byproduct. I want the meat protein source listed as chicken, beef, lamb, sardines, etc., not just as "meat" (mystery meat?).

Things like animal digest, animal fat, dried egg product, meat and bone meal, beef tallow, generic fish meal, fish oil, or byproduct meal will never appear on the label of a good quality food. Animal digest is a slurry made from enzymatic or *chemical* hydrolysis of rendered animals and animal parts. FDA studies have found detectable levels of euthanasia solution in meat and bone meal, beef and bone meal, animal digest, and animal fat, meaning euthanized animals were used to make the product. Our pets are consuming euthanasia solution on a daily basis.

Bone meal is a poor-quality product used to increase the protein content in foods. "Animal fat" is sometimes added as a cheap, unspecified fat source and can contain high quantities of chemicals that can be found in diseased animals. Ol' Roy, Pedigree, Big Heart Pet brands, Kibbles N Bits, Purina, Beneful, Chef Michael, Cesar, Alpo, Whiskas, and Special Kitty are some of the foods that commonly contain these ingredients.

The only grains I like to see listed are healthy grains like barley, brown rice, or quinoa. I don't like to see wheat in any form, white rice, brewer's rice (which is cheap, non-nutritive filler), brewer's yeast extract, corn in any form, dried beet pulp, rice hulls, ground psyllium husks, or soy in the food. These are less expensive grains used as fillers and as a way to increase the protein level in the food. Many pets have allergies to these grains and fillers.

I never like to see any kind of glutens added to a diet. Commonly, wheat, corn, or rice glutens are used as a binder in canned foods. Sugar and high-fructose corn syrup are commonly added to make food taste better. These have no place in pet food. Dyes are added to color the bits of food and make them more pleasing to the eye of the consumer (not the pet—they really don't care about the color of the food). Some of these dyes have been incriminated as causing cancer and ADHD in children.

Preservatives like Ethoxyquin, Glyceryl Monostearate, BHA, BHT, and propylene glycol have been linked to cancers and illness in pets and people. Pet food manufacturers do not have to list Ethoxyquin on the label if it was added to preserve meat or fish meal by another company before manufacturing of the food. Fish meal is the product most likely to be preserved using these chemicals.

In general, I have found that smaller pet food companies tend to use higher-quality ingredients. Larger companies often outsource to a food-processing facility, which may substitute lower-quality products that can be purchased more cheaply. When a contaminated grain product is used in one of the processing facilities, many brands of pet food will be recalled because they were all processed in the same plant. The FDA maintains a website that shows pet food recalls. I recommend looking at the site occasionally to see which brands have been recalled. There are quite a few repeat offenders on the list. Pay attention to whether the recalls were mandatory or voluntary. Good pet food companies will pull a product if there is any suspicion that there may be a contaminant present. They don't wait for pets to become ill if they are aware of a problem. If you want to get an idea of the quality of the food you currently feed your pets, check out www. dogfoodadvisor.com. This website does a good job of rating foods based on the ingredients.

The other thing to consider when choosing the right product to feed your pets is the form in which the food will be fed: canned, dry, raw, or home-cooked. The worst form is the packaged plastic pouches that contain semi-moist food. Here is a partial list of ingredients of one of the more popular semi-moist foods: beef byproduct, soy grits, soy flour, high-fructose corn syrup, wheat flour, corn syrup, animal fat, yellow 6, red 40, yellow 5, and Ethoxyquin. That's a whole list of things I just listed that should never be found in pet food! When I tried to look up the ingredients in semi-moist foods, I had to go to the store to read the package label. The ingredients are so awful they aren't listed on the company website. I see many pets with chronic skin disease, allergies, cancer, and diabetes that have been fed these semi-moist products for long periods of time.

I do not recommend prescription veterinary diets very often in my practice because I feel many companies use low-quality ingredients to formulate the diets. I do appreciate that the prescription diet companies spend a lot of money on research and support of the veterinary community, but I cannot support the use of poor-quality ingredients. Here is a list of the first five ingredients in a dry feline prescription diet: corn gluten meal, animal fat, whole grain corn, soybean mill run, and dried egg product. Every one of those ingredients is on our do-not-feed list! Here is a partial list of ingredients for a canned canine prescription diet: water, corn flour, pork liver, rice flour, beef byproducts, and dried beet pulp. Awful!

Many clients bring pets for a consultation because they realize the ingredients in the food that has been prescribed for them are subpar, at best. How do I get around using the prescription diets? I formulate a home-prepared raw or cooked diet or a combination of home-cooked and high-quality canned, raw, or dry food. Most owners are very happy to be able to feed a high-quality diet that meets the nutritional needs of the pets, and the pets are much happier eating something that tastes great.

Each diet must be tailored to the needs of the individual pet. Great websites, like www.balanceit.com, help owners and veterinarians balance diets to ensure nutritional completeness, and there is now a veterinary nutrition specialty. Most veterinary colleges have a nutritionist on staff, and many are willing to work with owners and referring veterinarians to formulate home-cooked diets.

For ideas on home cooking, check out my YouTube videos at:

- http://www.youtube.com/watch?v=bB3bd84gwmA
- http://www.youtube.com/watch?v=a0tBgV7xU8k
- http://www.youtube.com/watch?v=krNU_6mOT9I
- http://www.youtube.com/watch?v=xWJGT646OBg

In summary, when shopping for pet food:

- Look for high-quality meat proteins.
- Avoid meat byproducts.
- Avoid animal digest, animal fat, meat and bone meal.
- Avoid preservatives like BHA, BHT, Ethoxyquin, Glycerol Monostearate, and Propylene Glycol.
- Avoid corn, wheat, brewer's rice, soy, rice hulls, and dried beet pulp.

- Avoid wheat, corn, rice glutens, and gluten meals.
- Avoid dyes and colorings.
- Avoid sugar and high-fructose corn syrup.
- Avoid all semi-moist foods in cellophane pouches.
- Check www.dogfoodadvisor.com to find ratings on foods.
- Check for recalls on pet foods at http://www.fda.gov/animalVeterinary/safetyhealth/recallswithdrawals/default.htm.

# Dry and Brittle versus Moist and Messy

D ry food is the most common formulation fed to pets today. It is convenient, easy to feed, easy to store, and is usually palatable to most pets. Dry food has a long shelf life, but that can have its own problems. Dry food may be stored on the shelf at the manufacturing plant for a few months, shipped and stored at the sales location for a few more months, and then stored at your house for months (depending on how quickly you use the product). Most expiration dates on bags of dry food are at least one year out from the manufacturing date. It would be more useful for the consumer if the pet food manufacturing company put the manufacturing date on the bag so consumers would be sure they were buying fresh product.

One of the biggest problems with food that has been stored for long periods of time is storage mites. Over 80 percent of dry food stored for more than a few months will test positive for storage mites. Storage mites are a common cause of skin allergies and itching in dogs and cats. If you feel you absolutely must feed dry food to your pets, please buy a small bag that you will use completely within one month. Store the bag in an airtight container. If you empty the bag into another container, make sure you empty all food particles and clean the container well between bags. Old kibble that remains in the container will become stale, rancid, and loaded with storage mites.

I recommend always keeping the label from the bag—even if you empty it into another container. That way, you will have a list of ingredients and the lot number and expiration date in case there is a recall.

Dry pet foods are processed using high heats, which denature many of the vitamins and enzymes that our pets need. Vitamin/mineral mixes are added to the dry food formulations to bring them up to AAFCO standards (Association of American Feed Control Officials), but those standards are not regulated and may not be ideal. They only set minimum recommendations. When feeding only dry food, it would be a good idea to add a high-quality probiotic at the time of feeding and possibly digestive enzymes to help digest the food. Avoid probiotics that contain animal digest.

Dry foods are always loaded with carbohydrates. The newest fad to feed grain-free dry foods has created a lot of confusion. Grain-free dry diets still have 40 to 50 percent carbohydrates in them. Pea, potato, or tapioca starches are commonly used to make the kibble stick together. Without adding a starch, the meats will not form a kibble. Feeding dry food to diabetic pets is never going to work. These pets need to have low- or no-carbohydrate diets. And not all grains are bad. I really like barley, quinoa, millet, and brown rice. Corn, wheat, and soy have been used for years as cheap fillers for pet food, leading many pets to become allergic to these grain sources.

Signs of allergy can range from itching, vomiting, and diarrhea to skin and ear infections. A huge percentage of yeasty ear infections are secondary to food allergies. Pets with chronically yeasty ears or skin should always have a diet change. That may or may not mean eliminating grains from the diet. In my opinion, the problem is related to feeding dry food and foods with poor-quality ingredients more than the grains alone.

Dry food requires moisture from the pet's body to rehydrate it for digestion. Pets fed dry food for long periods of time are in a constant state of dehydration, leading to a moisture deficit in their bodies. This is manifested as a dry, brittle coat, dry nose and footpads, early graying, and loss of pigment in the nose and footpads. When I look at the tongue of an older pet fed only dry food, I commonly see a sticky white phlegm coating the tongue. Phlegm is produced when there is not enough moisture in the body, and bodily fluids like saliva become thick and sticky.

Early kidney disease may also be linked to chronic ingestion of foods with little to no moisture. It is not physically possible for your pet to ingest enough water to make up for this deficit. Just adding water to the dry food when feeding will not make up the difference your pet needs. Remember, this is a diet with 3 percent to 6 percent moisture, whereas a canned food will contain 85 percent to 90 percent moisture. Pets fed a high-moisture diet will drink very little, whereas pets fed a dry diet will consistently drink more, trying to catch up.

As stated earlier, cats should never be fed dry food since they are prone to obesity and diabetes from carbohydrates—and urinary and kidney disease from lack of moisture. Many dry cat food products have dl-methionine added to lower the pH of the urine in an attempt to decrease production of crystals and stones in the urine. This is something you should avoid. A healthy, high-moisture, high-meat diet will automatically decrease production of urinary crystals.

The idea that pets need dry food to keep their teeth and gums healthy is a fallacy. The carbohydrates in dry pet food, which break down to sugars, actually contribute to dental disease. Most pets do not chew the dry food; they swallow it whole or almost whole. Notice when they vomit after eating that it comes up whole and undigested!

The only way a dry food will help clean the teeth and gums is to feed a dry food specifically formulated in very large pieces with a large matrix that the pets actually have to chew in order to break it down to swallow. The pieces of the special food are too large to be swallowed whole; the fiber in the food helps scrub tartar off the exposed tooth surfaces during the chewing action. Only the exposed surface area is affected; any tartar or plaque under the gumline will not be impacted while chewing. I do not recommend these diets, however, because they are made with poor ingredients. Ingredients in one of these products include brewer's rice (waste product of milling rice), whole grain corn (including the indigestible parts of the grain), chicken byproduct meal (byproducts, no real meat), powdered cellulose (fiber filler), soybean mill run (leftovers from processing soybeans), and flavoring. This is a very expensive product, made from cheap leftovers not fit for human (or pet) consumption.

The best way to prevent tartar and plaque on the teeth is by brushing, twice a day, every day, using toothpaste specifically formulated for pets or no salt chicken or beef broth. The action of the brushing is the most important part of the procedure. Some pets will not allow brushing, and some owners cannot commit to brushing. Natural ways to work the teeth and gums include feeding raw marrowbones a few times a week (throwing them away after an hour or two of gnawing to avoid brittleness from drying and bacterial contamination). Raw chicken or turkey gizzards also work well because they are lined by epichitin, which is gritty and hard, removing plaque from the teeth when chewed. Some natural gels containing zinc and vitamin C (MaxiGuard Gel) can be spread daily on the teeth and gums to help prevent plaque buildup. Professional dental cleaning should be performed at the first signs of plaque or tartar buildup.

Dry food pros:

- can be less expensive
- easy storage
- long shelf life
- convenience
- pet preference (those darn cats)

Dry food cons:

🐾 high heat processing

🐾 carbohydrate laden (bad for diabetes, obesity, allergies, ear infections, and dental disease)

🐾 storage mites

🐾 dehydration (bad for kidney disease, lower urinary tract disease, and dry skin)

🐾 should not be fed to cats

The second most commonly fed form of pet food is a canned diet. Canned food is cooked and processed at lower heat than dry food, so it retains more of the vitamins that naturally occur in the food. It has a long shelf life, usually for years, however it would be nice to know the manufacturing date.

Canned food has a high moisture content, which is much healthier, and therefore makes it preferable to dry food. Most pets love canned foods and will eat them readily. However, when choosing a canned food, you should be very picky! Most canned foods will contain some sort of binder or gluten. The glutens are usually corn, rice, or wheat. Other common binders are guar gum and carrageenan. If at all possible, buy foods without these additives. They can be highly inflammatory and will contribute to inflammatory bowel disease and allergies.

Vary flavors so that proteins are rotated. Use food manufactured by a small, high-quality company with their own production plant. Once a company grows big and outsources the production, the quality of the ingredients will usually fall, based on the past history of the pet food industry.

Canned food pros:

🐾 convenient

🐾 long shelf life

- high moisture content
- pets usually like them
- usually cooked at lower temperatures

Canned food cons:

- expensive
- does not work teeth and gums
- may contain binders and gums
- processed product
- packaging may not be environmentally friendly (recycle!)

Refrigerated rolls are one of the newer forms of pet food available. They are convenient and easy to feed. They are also cooked at lower temperatures so the food retains a higher nutritive value. They have high moisture content, and pets usually like them. Again, this is a case of having to read labels carefully. Look for whole meats, whole vegetables, and no fillers. These commonly contain binders like rice bran and carrageenan. They do have an added vitamin and mineral mix, so they fulfill the requirements for a complete diet. Watch for freshness—and be sure to keep them refrigerated. They are only available in a few varieties. I like to rotate proteins, which may be limited here.

Refrigerated rolls pros:

- convenience
- cooked at lower temperatures
- higher moisture than dry food
- pets usually like them
- consumer feels like they are feeding a higher-quality product

Refrigerated rolls cons:

* expensive
* does not work teeth and gums
* processed product
* protein sources may be limited
* may include fillers and binders like rice bran, soy flour, and carrageenan

Semi-moist foods are the kinds that are sold in cellophane wrapping. These are the worst foods on the market. Consumers like the looks of the food and get fooled into thinking they are feeding a high-quality product containing real meat. In actuality, these are made using meat byproducts, sugar, corn syrup, wheat, soy, and food coloring dyes. The ingredients are actually so bad they are not listed on the manufacturer's website. Semi-moist "bits" are also found mixed in with some dry foods. These products should never be fed. They cause diabetes, dental decay, skin disease, allergies, and death. I will not even donate these foods to animal shelters.

Included in this semi-moist category are many of the treats and snacks found in the grocery store aisles. Treats that look like soft bones or small steaks are actually dyed wheat and sugar formed into enticing shapes. Of course pets like them—just as children like candy and chips. If the bag, box, or can lists something as "flavored," there is none of that actual ingredient in the product. It means a chemical flavoring has been added. If the label says "with," there is anywhere from 3 to 24 percent of that ingredient in the product. I love reading labels that say "with real beef," knowing that in actuality there may be only 3 percent beef in the product (and probably is).

Semi-moist pros:

* appealing to consumers
* pets usually like them because they are filled with sugar

- ☙ convenience

- ☙ minimal packaging

Semi-moist cons:

- ☙ horrendous ingredients (byproducts, wheat, soy, dyes, sugars, and high-fructose corn syrup)

- ☙ cause diabetes, cancer, allergies, skin disease, obesity, dental decay, and death

Raw feeding for pets has only recently become more mainstream. Many holistic and open-minded veterinarians are starting to push for raw feeding. The old school veterinarians still abhor raw feeding, and the American Veterinary Medical Association recently passed a policy against raw feeding. The Centers for Disease Control provided a statement to the AVMA recommending against feeding raw food to dogs and cats because of the risk of illness to the pet as well as to people living in the household, going so far as to say, "Do not feed your pet a raw diet" (emphasis is theirs, not mine.) The American Animal Hospital Association approved a policy in August 2012 that discourages feeding raw meat to pets. The National Association of State Public Health Veterinarians and the American Association of Feline Practitioners also supported this policy. These are pretty harsh statements.

When reading the website discussing these statements, they also say that to date, there have been *no* reports of human illness associated with raw food diets. However, in 2006 to 2008, there was a multistate outbreak of salmonella infections in people traced back to dry dog food. And in 2012, another forty-nine people were infected with salmonella from dry dog food. There are documented outbreaks of salmonella in people from processed pet treats like pig ears, rawhides, and cow hooves. Personally, I don't understand the negativity about raw feeding when the data point solidly toward processed foods causing more human illness than feeding raw products to pets.

With that said, pets can be fed a raw diet that has been cold pasteurized to minimize potential bacterial threat to humans and pets. Many of the commercial raw food processors use state-of-the-art technology to avoid bacterial contamination. I have done raw feeding with my own dogs for almost a decade, with no problems, and improved health for every one of them.

For anyone deciding to feed raw meats, care must be taken in handling and cleaning the areas where the meat is handled. This is not any different than cleaning the kitchen after preparing raw meats for human consumption. Also, be sure the source of the meats you feed is reputable. Raw chicken and ground meats bought in the grocery store will commonly have positive bacterial cultures when tested. If I am going to feed ground meat, I buy whole meats and grind them in my own kitchen for feeding immediately.

Many clients buy raw meats like poultry necks, backs, and wings in bulk, freeze them, and thaw them out to feed. This gives the dogs a high-quality meal with bones for calcium. Probably the biggest problem I see related to this kind of raw feeding is constipation if dogs are not used to eating raw bones. Always start gradually before using this as a whole meal.

Raw meat fed without bones will lead to a calcium/phosphorous imbalance. Meat is high in phosphorous and low in calcium. Dogs have a fairly high calcium requirement and must have a calcium supplement if not being fed whole or ground bone with the raw meat. Animals fed meat without bones will eventually develop rickets, which is a softening and bending of the bones.

When I first started in practice in the 1980s, Mighty Dog was a popular canned all-meat diet. It was meant to be used as a top-dress on dry food, but people saw how much their small dogs enjoyed the meat and stopped feeding the dry food along with the cans. Many small dogs would be presented to the clinic in kidney failure—with no lower jaws because that seemed to be the first bone that would disappear. When the phosphorous level is too high, the body will draw calcium from the bones to keep the calcium-phosphorous ratio normal. Now this pet food has an added mineral mix to make it a complete diet. Unfortunately, it is no longer a whole meat product and is filled with meat-byproducts, wheat gluten, soy flour, and artificial colors and flavors, making it a low-quality food.

However, now I see clients who make the mistake of deciding they want to feed a raw diet so they buy ground hamburger and feed that as a whole diet. This is so far from balanced; these dogs will develop many deficiencies, weakness, and rickets—and they will eventually die. On the other end of the spectrum, newer studies are showing that young dogs fed too much calcium may be at higher risk for developmental bone diseases like hypertrophic osteodystrophy, osteochondritis dissecans, and hip dysplasia.

An adult dog needs approximately 120 milligrams of calcium per kilogram (2.2 pounds) of body weight per day. So a twenty-two-pound dog needs around 1,200 milligrams of calcium. A growing puppy would need around 320 milligrams of calcium per kilogram of body weight. Phosphorous requirements are lower, around 90 milligrams per kilogram of body weight in adults and 240 milligrams per kilogram of body weight in growing puppies. Tables on the Internet show the milligrams of calcium and phosphorous in certain foods, but you might be figuring out that it is very difficult to know exactly what you are feeding. This is why a veterinary nutritionist or sites like www.BalanceIt.com come in pretty handy!

If you want the easy way to feed raw food, use a product specifically formulated by reputable pet food companies that have already figured out how to balance the diet. Many companies provide raw food diets for pets, and new ones are showing up every day. You should research the food you want to feed to make sure the company is reputable. Try to talk to others who are using the diet to see if they are satisfied. Now that social media has taken over our lives, this task is much easier than the old word-of-mouth approach!

Raw feeding pros:

❧ species-appropriate diet

- less incidence of allergies, ear infections, and skin disease

- can be convenient (pre-packaged frozen raw patties or freeze-dried raw)

- balanced diet (if you buy one already prepared)

- high moisture content

- long shelf life (frozen or freeze dried raw)

Raw feeding cons:

- can be expensive

- will not work teeth and gums (unless you include some whole raw bones in the diet)

- can be less convenient and more labor intensive (if you are making your own meals)

- may have a short shelf life (if you are feeding fresh raw meat)

- need to add vitamins and minerals (if bones are not included in diet)

Home-cooked diets have surged in popularity in the past decade. I love cooking for my dogs, and they certainly love to eat the finished product. Veterinary nutritionists and pet food companies have a lot of negative things to say about home-cooked diets. They spend a lot of time analyzing published recipes, finding flaws and deficiencies in every one. They feel that every meal needs to be balanced and complete. I strongly disagree with this sentiment. I do not balance every meal I eat, and I do not take a daily vitamin supplement. However, over the course of a few days or weeks, I consume a healthy diet that contains the complete nutrition I need.

When making a home-cooked diet, I usually include about 70 percent meat and 30 percent vegetables and grains. Up to 30 percent of the meat portion of the diet can be made using organs like liver, kidney, heart, and gizzard. This will cut down on cost and add some extra nutrients that are not found in muscle meat. Home-cooked diets can be made in a crockpot, as a meatloaf, or cooked individually for each meal. If I want to supplement with sardines, pumpkin, or other ingredients, they can be added at the time of feeding. Probiotics, digestive enzymes, and supplements should be added at the time of feeding. Probiotic bacteria will be killed if mixed with hot ingredients, so make sure food is room temperature when adding the supplement. All meals should be fed at body temperature; always warm any diet that has been refrigerated or frozen.

Home-cooked diet pros:

- owner has control over ingredients (easy to avoid foods to which pet may be allergic)
- can be less expensive
- high moisture content
- usually not cooked at high temperatures
- not processed (no preservatives or chemicals)

Home-cooked diet cons:

- can be expensive
- can be time consuming
- does not work teeth and gums (unless diet includes whole raw bones)
- short shelf life
- need to add minerals (and possibly vitamins)
- may need to work with a nutritionist

If I found a dry cereal that contained all the added vitamins and minerals some nutritional council deemed necessary for a complete diet, I still would not eat that cereal twice daily every day. This is essentially what the nutritional councils are telling us we need to do with our pets. Poor-quality ingredients are dehydrated and cooked until very little nutrient quality remains; a vitamin and mineral mix (which may or may not be contaminated with substances like melamine) is added to bring the nutrient label up to the "required" levels.

My dogs' meals alternate between home-cooked stews, home-cooked meatloaf (puploaf), frozen raw patties, and home-ground raw foods. When they are fed home-cooked diets, I add a mineral mix, like Rx Minerals made by Rx Vitamins (unless I use a product like Honest Kitchen, which already has a vitamin and mineral mix added) to ensure proper levels of calcium and trace minerals. I have fed my dogs in this manner for over a decade with superb results.

Treats for pets are not a necessary part of the diet, but owners enjoy being able to give rewards and special goodies as a way to strengthen the human-animal bond. Treats should not make up more than a small percentage of the total daily caloric intake—unless they are nutritious and the extra calories are subtracted from the daily meals.

Store-bought treats containing wheat, soy, artificial colors and flavorings, sugar, toxic preservatives, or high-fructose syrup should never be fed. Use whole foods like fresh or frozen berries and bananas (no grapes or raisins). Make your own dehydrated pieces of meat, liver, or sweet potato by putting pieces on a tray in the oven on the lowest heat overnight. Store them in sealed containers in the refrigerator or freezer.

Do *not* purchase dehydrated chicken jerky treats, no matter which country is the origination point. Jerky treats from China have been responsible for the illness and death of thousands of dogs in the past few years. The FDA has not been able, as of this writing, to identify the toxic principle in these treats, but they did finally publish a statement urging pet owners to avoid feeding them. More recently, people have become ill and some have died from eating chicken jerky treats made for pets.

Beware of packaging that says "processed" or "packaged" or

"distributed by" an American company. That does not mean the ingredients came from the United States. The ingredients may have been sourced overseas. There are many recipes available to make your own biscuits and treats using simple ingredients. If your pet has a specific food intolerance, you can control what goes into the treats. If at all possible, use organic, locally sourced, fresh whole ingredients. For a list of good and bad diets—and to check out thoughts on the food you are currently serving—go to www.dogfoodadvisor.com or check out the *Whole Dog Journal*. These sources are generally fairly up to date.

# Dr. Morgan's Puploaf

2 pounds ground meat (beef, bison, turkey, chicken, or whatever you want)

½ pound ground organ meat (liver, hearts, gizzards)—not essential but decreases cost and these have good nutrients

3 to 4 eggs

½ cup Honest Kitchen Preference or similar dehydrated vegetable base rehydrated with ¾ cut hot water. If preferred, you can use a cup of fresh finely chopped vegetables

½ cup cooked barley or quinoa—not essential, can be eliminated if grain-free is your preference

Mix all ingredients in a bowl. Place in meatloaf pan (may require two pans, depending on size) and bake at 350 degrees for 40–60 minutes. Should be firm, but not dry.

If you are not using a dehydrated vegetable base with added mineral mix, you will have to add a commercial calcium/mineral supplement or very finely ground eggshells.

At our house, we make 35 pounds per week, to feed seven small dogs. Most dogs will eat 2 to 3 percent of their body weight per day (about 8–12 ounces daily for a twenty-pound dog).

# Hot Dog: The Energetics of Food

The foods we eat can help change the dynamics within our bodies. Some foods will warm us and make us sweat; others will cool our bodies on hot days. Think about what you would want to eat on a sweltering summer day. Usually, watermelon, ice cream, and ice-cold lemonade would come to mind because those foods have cooling effects on our bodies. We can use these qualities to our advantage to treat our pets and ourselves.

In Chinese medicine, yin and yang are the two main characteristics used to describe life. Yin stands for cool or cold, female, dark, and down. Yang stands for warm or hot, male, light, and up. So animals that are too hot have too much yang or have too little yin (yin deficient). Animals that are too cold have too much yin or have too little yang (yang deficient).

All animals (and people) can be classified as "hot/yang" or "cold/yin" or "neutral" based on a few characteristics. For instance, I am a "cold/yin" person. I could spend every day basking in ninety-degree heat and loving every minute because I am always cold. I have friends that are extremely happy when the snow falls because they are "hot/yang" people and love the coolness of the winter season.

If you think about your pet's preferences, you will be able to discern whether he or she is cold or hot. Does your pet enjoy romping through the snow and sitting outside on cold days? Does your pet constantly lie on the cold tile floors, sprawled with as much body contact with the cold floor as possible? Does your pet pant a lot? The pet displaying these characteristics is a "hot" pet that is trying to cool off. Generally young, active puppies and kittens tend to be hotter, as well as certain breeds of dogs like Jack Russell terriers. They are hyperactive and always in motion. These animals are displaying "yang" characteristics; yang means warm, sunny, and hot. They either have too much yang or not enough yin.

Older animals that pant a lot or seem hot have lost the ability to cool from within. This is the same process that causes hot flashes in women as we age. We become "yin" deficient, lacking the ability to cool and moisturize our bodies. Yin deficiencies can be exaggerated in animals that have eaten dry food their entire lives or animals that have been bombarded with too many vaccines, drugs, or chemicals, which cause chronic inflammation in the body. Inflammation is hot and requires constant cooling from within, using up too much yin.

Animals that are yin deficient commonly have dry, brittle hair, noses, and footpads. They want to drink a lot and tend to have dry, flaky, itchy skin. The tongue of these animals will tend to be dark or red and dry; sometimes there will be white sticky phlegm on the tongue.

On the contrary, "cold" animals look for the warm, sunny places to lie in the house. These are the dogs that want to sit in the sun outside on a ninety-degree day. Many times these animals are sluggish, overweight, and more laid back. They want to snuggle by the fireplace under the covers. They hate going out in the snow or on cold windy days, and they don't drink very much. They prefer dry food and can get diarrhea if there is too much moisture or oil in their diets. They are prone to gooey ears and skin infections. Their tongues will usually be a paler pink and very wet. They may drool a lot. These animals are "yang" deficient—and they don't have enough energy in their bodies to maintain warmth.

Since no animal is completely "hot" or completely "cold," you need to assess the majority of symptoms. Symptoms may change based on the season or climate. Your pet may be very comfortable all winter—and suddenly be miserable in the heat of the summer. By adding certain foods to the diet, you can help your pets deal with problems of being too hot or too cold.

Whether you feed dry, canned, raw, or home-cooked food, you can change ingredients or add to the diet to manipulate the energy of the food. For instance, if you feed dry food and your pet is too hot, a switch from a lamb-based diet (which is yang) to a fish-based diet (which is yin) will help cool and balance the pet. While it is pretty impossible, and actually undesirable, to feed a food that is all hot or all cold, you can try to match the energy of the first few ingredients to what you are trying to accomplish.

Hot animals need to be fed cooling foods, which are "yin tonics," to treat their yin deficiencies. Most cold-water fish fall into this category. Clams, herring, oysters, sardines, scallops, shark, tuna, and whitefish would all be cooling in nature. There are dry foods on the market that are made with herring and whitefish, and many "hot" dogs do well on these diets (although I do not recommend feeding dry food as the sole diet, particularly not to dogs that are already dry).

Barley and brown rice would be the best "cooling" grains to look for in the dry or canned diets. The meat base could include grass-fed beef, duck, buffalo, pork, or rabbit. Dogs with itchy dry skin should be fed fish-based diets or use the meats just listed. Melons, cucumbers, pears, bananas, and most berries are cooling and make great treats or additions to the meal. I like to freeze pureed watermelon in ice cube trays for summer treats. A little fresh or dried ginger can be mixed in for dogs with any digestive upset or inflammatory condition like arthritis.

Cold animals need warming foods that will be "yang tonics" to treat their yang deficiencies. Lamb, venison, chicken, grain-fed, feedlot-raised beef, pheasant, liver, and kidney are warming meats. Lamb is energetically the hottest, and venison is close behind. Oats and sorghum are warming and would be the grains of choice. Brussels sprouts, kale, pumpkin, winter squash, white potato, and black beans are also warming. Dried pieces of liver or chicken make good treats. Pumpkin works well for dogs with diarrhea because it is warming and is loaded with fiber to help dry the diarrhea and soothe the bowel. Animals with greasy, smelly skin may do well on warming foods, but dogs with itchy, dry skin should not be fed energetically hot foods as the majority of their diets.

I do not recommend feeding foods with corn, soy, wheat, or white rice in general, but white rice is a good warming food with lots of energy. It can be soothing to the digestive tract and is easily digestible when using long-cooked rice.

The energetics of food can also be used to help deal with behavior issues. Hyperactive, overbearing pets are showing too much "yang" energy. They need "yin tonics" to balance and tone down the yang energy. Everything in life is about balance. Hyperactive young Jack Russell terriers or Labrador retrievers will be difficult to train when they are being fed warming foods like lamb or white rice. They need diets of fish or rabbit with barley or brown rice to balance the energy.

Animals with yang excess that are fed yang-based diets (lamb, venison, white rice) will eventually burn out their cooling systems, using up their yin, which cools and moisturizes. These animals are being set up to have yin-deficient diseases in the future (hypothyroidism, diabetes, and kidney disease). Conversely, old, slow, cold animals with no energy will continue to decline in health with decreased mobility and muscle wasting if they are not given foods to warm them. These pets need to be fed yang tonics.

In addition to being classified as yin or yang tonics, foods can also be used to increase blood supply, decrease phlegm or mucous, increase qi or energy, resolve stagnation (lumps, bumps, tumors), and to replace kidney "Jing," which is the life essence. George's Dry Eye Diet, discussed earlier, included ingredients to dissolve phlegm, like clams, peppermint, almonds, and pears. Foods to resolve stagnation will be discussed further in the chapter on treating cancer. Jing tonics will be discussed in more depth in the chapter on kidney disease. Pets with low energy will benefit from qi or energy tonic foods.

Using food as therapy is one of the most rewarding parts of practice for me. I have developed a series of food webinars that you can access on YouTube by typing in "Dr. Judy Morgan food webinars." I also have a few videos on how to make your own pet stews.

Blood Tonic Stew: http://www.youtube.com/watch?v=xWJGT6 46OBg

Qi (Energy) Tonic Stew: http://www.youtube.com/watch?v=krNU_ 6mOT9I

# Energetics of Food

## Qi (Energy) Tonics

Use qi tonics for animals that need energy like weak, older animals or animals recovering from surgery or illness.

- Meats: beef, chicken, rabbit, lamb, and tripe
- Fish: eel, carp, trout, herring, and mackerel
- Grains: millet, corn, oats, glutinous rice, and brown rice
- Vegetables: pumpkin, squash, sweet potato, yam, and shiitake mushrooms
- Fruit: cherry and figs
- Nuts and Seeds: peanuts, chestnuts, and lotus seeds

## Yang (Warming) Tonics

Use yang tonics for animals that are cold and need to be warmed. This includes sluggish animals that like to sleep under blankets or lie by the fireplace. These foods can be useful in winter.

- Meats: venison, lamb, and kidney
- Fish: shrimp, lobster, and prawns
- Grains: oats
- Herbs: chives, cinnamon bark, cloves, nutmeg, dried ginger, garlic, dill seed, fennel seed, basil, rosemary, thyme, and raspberry

## Yin (Cooling) Tonics

Use yin tonics for animals that are hot and need to be cooled. This includes animals that like to sleep on the cold tile floors and pant a lot. These foods are also useful in summer.

- ❖ Meats: duck, rabbit, clams, mussels, and pork
- ❖ Vegetables: black beans, kidney beans, string beans, asparagus, spinach, tomatoes, and peas
- ❖ Grains: wheat and barley
- ❖ Fruits: apples, lemons, mangos, pears, and melons
- ❖ Nuts and Seeds: black sesame seed
- ❖ Miscellaneous: tofu, cheese, honey, and eggs

## Blood Tonics

Use blood tonics to nourish blood. These animals may be weak, anemic, and have pale tongues. They may have dry, flaky, itchy skin.

- ❖ Meats: beef, liver, and heart
- ❖ Fish: sardines
- ❖ Vegetables: carrots and kidney beans
- ❖ Fruit: apricots, dates, and longan
- ❖ Herbs: parsley
- ❖ Miscellaneous: eggs

## Resolve Stagnation (Move Lumps, Move Blood)

Use foods that resolve stagnation to help move masses. Use when tumors are present.

- Meats: lamb and venison
- Fish: crab and shrimp
- Vegetables: radish and chili pepper
- Fruits: orange peel
- Herbs: ginger, garlic, chives, cloves, coriander, dill seed, mustard, turmeric, hawthorn
- Nuts: chestnuts
- Miscellaneous: vinegar

## Transform Phlegm (Decrease Mucous)

These foods should be used any time secretions are thick and dry, like mucous from the eyes or nose. Fat is also a type of Phlegm, so these foods may help dissolve lipomas (fatty tumors).

- Fish: clams
- Vegetables: radish
- Fruits: pears, oranges, and apples
- Nuts: almonds
- Herbs: garlic, mustard, pepper, marjoram, and peppermint
- Miscellaneous: seaweed, kelp, lemon peel, and grapefruit peel

## Drain Damp (Drain Fluid)

Use these foods when there is edema or swelling of the legs or feet. They will help drain fluid in cases of heart failure or liver failure.

- Fish: mackerel
- Grains: rye, barley, and corn

- Vegetables: radish, turnips, alfalfa, aduki bean, celery, kidney beans, and mushrooms
- Herbs: garlic, green tea, horseradish, jasmine tea, job's tears, marjoram, and mustard
- Fruits: lemon

## Jing (Birth Essence) Tonics

Use these foods for pets with bone deformities, orthopedic diseases, kidney disease, or dental disease like poor enamel or loose teeth.

- Meat: liver and kidney
- Fish: sardines and small fish
- Vegetables: barley sprouts, alfalfa sprouts, barley grass, and wheatgrass
- Seeds: black sesame seeds, almonds, and walnuts
- Miscellaneous: eggs, royal jelly (comes from honeybees), bone marrow, algae (chlorella, spirulina), and seaweed

# To Spay or Not to Spay

Before I became involved with holistic medicine, I would have said that all pets should be spayed or neutered at six months of age before the females have their first heat cycle. This is a popularly held belief in the United States; however, in some European and Asian nations, it is a very unpopular notion.

The single biggest reason to spay or neuter is population control. Thousands and thousands of animals are euthanized at shelters every year due to unwanted production of puppies and kittens. However, if we could all be responsible pet owners and keep our young pets from being accidentally bred, our pets would be healthier by allowing them to reach full maturity before considering spaying or neutering.

I do not support pediatric spaying and neutering, but I do understand the usefulness when adoption agencies and shelters want to get puppies and kittens adopted and know they will not be able to breed. Many shelters are spaying and neutering by eight weeks of age. There have been many studies showing long-term health problems related to early spaying and neutering. Obesity, some cancers, hypothyroidism and other endocrine diseases, musculoskeletal disorders like hip dysplasia, incontinence, and urinary tract infections may occur more frequently in pets undergoing early spaying or neutering.

Recent retrospective studies have shown higher incidence of some cancers in dogs that have undergone spaying or neutering prior to maturation. In particular, hemangiosarcoma of the spleen or heart, osteosarcoma of the bones, prostate cancer, and lower urinary tract cancers may have a higher incidence of occurrence in animals that are spayed or neutered early. The estrogen and testosterone hormones seem to have some protective effects.

On the other hand, mammary cancer dramatically increases in unspayed older females. Current studies show that spaying between twenty-four and thirty months of age will allow females to reach maturity and may have some beneficial protective effects against certain cancers, while still having a low incidence of mammary cancer. The incidence of uterine infection, which is life threatening, also increases with age. Currently, I think allowing our pets to undergo two or three heat cycles and develop to maturity is probably the best answer. Sterilization without removal of the gonads (ovaries and testes) may be a good solution. Although these techniques in animals are not commonly used, there does seem to be some movement toward using these procedures. Again, being a responsible pet owner and not allowing a pet to be accidentally bred is paramount.

Studies of intact males, particularly large breed dogs, have shown there may be beneficial protection against cancers like prostate cancer, hemangiosarcoma, and osteosarcoma. Testicular cancers can occur, but they have a low mortality rate. Benign prostatic enlargement is common in older unneutered males, but it is usually treatable. Perineal hernias occur much more commonly in unneutered males than neutered males and can be life-threatening conditions if the bladder becomes entrapped in the hernia.

Neutering males can help decrease unwanted behaviors such as aggression, urine marking, and desire to roam. Prostate cancer is much higher in neutered males and is difficult to treat. The number of health problems associated with neutering may outweigh the benefits of leaving males intact—as long as owners are responsible and do not allow their intact males to wander and produce unwanted litters. The one contradiction is the case of a retained testicle that has not descended into the scrotum. Retained testicles have a very high rate of developing into cancerous tumors as the temperature inside the body is higher than the temperature in the scrotum. Retained testicles should always be removed if they have not descended into the scrotum by one year of age. Some acupuncturists have had success in getting the testicles to descend using herbals and acupuncture.

A new product has recently been introduced to the market that will allow males to be chemically neutered without surgery. Zinc gluconate is injected into each testicle, which will kill sperm and cause fibrosis of the tubules through which sperm normally pass. Since the cells that produce testosterone are spared, the dogs will still have about half the normal testosterone level of an intact male. This could be beneficial, as new studies have shown testosterone may help prevent some cancers. However, unwanted male behaviors such as aggression, territorial marking, and chasing and mounting females in heat may still occur.

The pharmaceutical company is targeting use of the product in shelters across the country. Currently, they are training veterinarians to give the injections, and the company admits there is a learning curve to performing the procedure properly. It is recommended for use in dogs three to ten months of age, whereas most shelter dogs are much older. The dogs can still impregnate females for up to twenty-one days after the injection, meaning dogs will need to be housed without adoption for an additional three weeks, whereas dogs undergoing surgical castration are often released to adoptive parents the same day. While they are touting that shelters will save money by not paying veterinarians for surgery, I question whether they have factored in housing for longer periods.

The procedure is painful, and in my opinion, qualified personnel should sedate the dogs. The company literature states 76 percent of dogs were injected without sedation. I may be a bleeding heart, but any time we inflict pain, I feel it is our responsibility to minimize that as much as possible. Some dogs will chew their painful, swollen scrotum, resulting in ulceration and infection. Infection rates were higher in dogs housed on wet concrete, which is exactly how most shelter dogs are housed. Studies performed in rural Mexico showed a high rate of dermatitis, ulceration, and infection due to the unsanitary conditions where dogs were housed. Unfortunately, many nonprofit shelters in the United States do not have good sanitation. Dogs with severe inflammation and infections will need treatment and may need to undergo surgical castration to remove the infected scrotum and testes, which will increase costs to shelters.

Once a dog is "zeutered," they need to be microchipped—and the database needs to be consistently updated (microchipping is a good idea anyway). Not all shelters implant microchips. Anyone finding a stray dog needs to have the dog scanned for a microchip, but not all scanners read all chips. I worry some dogs will be "zeutered" more than once or subjected to unnecessary surgical castration if picked up as strays. This product is new, and long-term studies have not been performed. The company literature states that forty dogs were followed for two years. I question what side effects or cancers we may see in ten or twelve years after large-scale use of this product. For now, I decline to use the product.

# Vaccination?

When I was in veterinary college, parvovirus in dogs was just starting to be recognized. There was no vaccine available for use in dogs, so a cat vaccine for panleukopenia, which is 98 percent identical to parvovirus, was being used in dogs. We had hundreds of cases of puppies dying from bloody vomiting and diarrhea. Caring for them was hard work, and watching them die was gut wrenching. Even if they survived, they were commonly plagued by cardiac disease and stunted growth.

By the time I graduated, the first vaccinations for parvovirus were being introduced. We pushed hard to vaccinate every dog we could to protect them from this horrific disease. For another ten years, we routinely lost unvaccinated puppies to this disease. Luckily, thanks to use of the vaccine, we now see many fewer cases of parvovirus. Similar stories could be heard years earlier involving dogs with distemper and animals with rabies. My mother's favorite farm dog, a collie, died of distemper when she was young. The old name for distemper was "Hardpad Disease," and I remember my mother talking about the heart-wrenching loss she suffered. Vaccinations have been a wonderful addition to the health of animals and people everywhere. With that said, the overuse and misuse of vaccinations has also become a problem.

Typically, dogs and cats are vaccinated against rabies when they are four to six months old, then again one year later, and every three years after that. Beginning in 1987, Pennsylvania required cats to be vaccinated annually for rabies. Rabies is transmitted through bite wounds from infected animals. Since this is a zoonotic disease (can be spread from animals to people) with no treatment once infected, it was important to vaccinate as many pets as possible to stop the transmission of disease from wildlife. The biggest flaw with the system was that stray cats and barn cats were the animals that needed protection, but they were not the animals being vaccinated. House cats that were being presented annually to the veterinarian were being over-immunized.

In 1985, the first feline leukemia vaccine became available for use, and many veterinarians recommended vaccinating every cat. Feline leukemia is a virus that is transmitted from one infected cat to another through bodily secretions, and there is no effective treatment for the disease, once infected. Once again, the wrong cats were being immunized. Feral, stray, and barn cats that should have been immunized were rarely caught and taken to the veterinarian, but house cats were being immunized for a disease for which they would not have exposure.

Suddenly, in the early 1990s, the University of Pennsylvania and the University of California at Davis pathology laboratories had more tissue samples than ever before from tumors in cats. Through years of research, it was determined that cats were making sarcoma tumors related to products in vaccines. Rabies and feline leukemia vaccines were incriminated. Heavy metals and preservatives in the vaccines were seen as foreign materials by the body. The immune systems of the cats tried to wall off the offending foreign material and extrude it from the body, leaving large, open, cancerous wounds that were impossible to heal. Most of the tumors were located between the shoulder blades on the backs of cats—the most common site for injecting the vaccines.

Since the discovery of the vaccine-related sarcoma problem, recommendations have been made to give the rabies vaccination as low as possible on the right hind leg and the feline leukemia vaccination as low as possible on the left hind leg. The reasoning is that if a vaccine-related sarcoma occurs, the leg can be amputated, which I find pretty offensive.

Fast-forward a decade. More owners started keeping cats inside, often declawing them, eliminating any outdoor time and exposure to viruses. Pets were being treated more like family members and children, not being allowed to roam the countryside. Yet, these cats and dogs were still being vaccinated annually for diseases to which they had no exposure. This, I consider, is misuse of vaccines.

For years, just as we were taught in veterinary school, veterinarians advocated annual vaccination of dogs with a five-in-one vaccine covering distemper, parainfluenza, leptospirosis, parvovirus, and hepatitis. Some veterinarians add coronavirus to this list. Lyme, influenza, kennel cough, porphyromonas, and giardia vaccines are also available. Cats have been routinely immunized against panleukopenia (distemper), calicivirus, viral rhinotracheitis (herpes virus 1), chlamydia, feline leukemia, and rabies. More recently, vaccines for feline infectious peritonitis, feline giardia, feline immunodeficiency virus, feline ringworm, and feline bordetella have been added to this list.

For years, dogs and cats have been bombarded with anywhere from five to ten disease antigens in one vaccination visit, and this has been repeated annually. Slowly, we have begun to see more cases of hypothyroidism, hyperthyroidism, tumors, Cushing's disease (adrenal gland disease), immune-mediated diseases, cancers, and long-term illnesses. Researchers are starting to link overuse of vaccinations to these diseases.

My current recommendations for vaccinations vary with each pet. No two pets have the same lifestyle and exposure to disease. Indoor cats are not going to be exposed to viral diseases spread by other cats—unless an unknown stray is brought into the mix or the indoor cat escapes to the great outdoors. Small dogs that use indoor piddle pads and never go outside certainly do not have the same exposure to disease that hunting dogs or show dogs would have. Dogs in large kennel situations or that spend time around shelter dogs will have much higher rates of disease exposure.

Vaccine manufacturers are becoming more aware of client desires to vaccinate less often. Vaccinations with three-year duration of immunity have been developed for the core diseases like distemper and parvovirus. Blood titers that determine whether a dog has immunity to distemper or parvovirus have also been developed. I recommend vaccinating only if a dog has a low titer and is at risk of exposure to the disease. Cats can be tested for immunity to panleukopenia, or feline distemper, as well. Governments requiring vaccination against rabies usually have the final say in whether pets need to be vaccinated, although exemptions can be written in most states for animals with diseases that would make them poor candidates for vaccination.

I do not recommend vaccinating any animal that has ever had an allergic reaction to a vaccine. Most veterinarians will give a dose of an antihistamine or a steroid injection at the time of vaccination to deter a reaction from occurring, but I do not feel that offers enough protection to the pet. The administration of a steroid along with the vaccine may render the vaccine useless; the immune system needs to respond to the vaccine to make immunity to the disease, and the steroid suppresses the immune system's response. Pets with cancer or immune-mediated diseases should not have their immune systems bombarded with vaccine antigens. Each pet should be evaluated as an individual to determine which, if any, vaccinations are needed.

I will give my personal feelings on vaccinations, but please take into consideration the lifestyle and exposure for your pet before making decisions for which vaccinations your pet should receive.

## Canine Distemper and Feline Panleukopenia (Distemper) Virus Vaccines

This is a core vaccine that most dogs and cats should receive at some point, usually as a puppy or kitten. It takes a series of at least two vaccinations at least two weeks apart to get optimum immunity. I like to give the first vaccine at ten to twelve weeks of age and the second vaccine at fourteen to sixteen weeks of age. I like individual vaccines to be given one month apart.

During the first four months of life, the puppy or kitten will not have good immunity against disease and should be kept away from areas where pets with unknown health statuses may congregate. This includes pet stores, dog parks, fundraising events, groomers, dog and cat shows, daycare, and boarding kennels. Perform a blood titer at six months of age and annually thereafter. If the titer level is protective, no additional vaccination is necessary (and for many dogs and cats, these two vaccines will confer lifelong immunity). Current research has shown these vaccines to protect against infection for four to seven years in most cases, depending on the vaccine product that is used.

## Canine Adenovirus Type 2 or Hepatitis Vaccine

Luckily, this is a disease that is not seen very often. It is closely related to canine adenovirus type 1, which causes upper respiratory symptoms and is included in the kennel cough vaccine. This disease often affects the eyes of the dogs, causing swelling and a blue haze in the cornea. This is a disease that is most dangerous for dogs less than one year of age and is included in the core puppy vaccination, DAP or DAPP. Currently, I do not perform annual titers for adenovirus. I do include this vaccination in the core puppy vaccines as described under "Canine Distemper Virus." Since immunity probably lasts for seven years or longer, I do not repeat this vaccine in adult dogs.

## Parvovirus Vaccine

This virus is most lethal in puppies and certain breeds that seem to be predisposed, possibly due to genetics, including Doberman pinschers, pit bulls, and rottweilers. Other black and tan breeds may also be more susceptible to the virus. The virus itself is not necessarily the cause of death. Death occurs due to dehydration and sepsis by bacteria entering the bloodstream from the damaged intestines. Environmental stress, parasite infestation, and concurrent bacterial or viral infections also contribute to a high mortality rate.

There is a cardiac form of the disease that will leave recovered puppies with long-term heart damage. For this disease, I recommend two vaccinations given about four weeks apart in puppies at the same time as the distemper vaccination. There are individual vaccines available that contain only the parvovirus, but currently there are no individual distemper vaccinations available. As with distemper and hepatitis, puppies under four months of age have not developed good protection and should not be exposed to group situations. A parvovirus blood titer should be run at six months to confirm immunity and be repeated annually. If the parvo titer is low, an individual vaccination for parvovirus can be given.

## Leptospirosis Vaccine

This is one of the most reactive vaccines on the market. Many dogs will have allergic reactions, including hives, facial swelling, vomiting, diarrhea, and difficulty breathing. These reactions are seen most commonly in small breeds of dogs. For that reason, I never recommend this vaccine for dogs weighing less than ten pounds.

Leptospirosis is a disease caused by a spirochete, a type of bacterium. It is spread through the urine of infected animals, most commonly rats, raccoons, foxes, skunks, and dairy cattle. It can be found in contaminated stagnant water and streams, and it survives well in hot, humid environments. Leptospirosis is also zoonotic, meaning the disease can be transmitted from animals to humans.

Leptospirosis is treatable with antibiotics and intravenous fluids, if diagnosed in time. Most common symptoms are related to kidney and liver failure. The old name for this disease was "Red Water disease" because of the bloody urine that is often seen with this disease. Currently, there are seven sub-varieties of leptospirosis that can be diagnosed in dogs. The old vaccines protected against two of the serovars, and the newer vaccines protect against four of the serovars.

There is no good reason to perform annual titers for leptospirosis once the pet is vaccinated because the vaccine only confers immunity for nine to twelve months. If a pet is at high risk for exposure to leptospirosis, vaccination should be performed annually. High-risk pets include hunting dogs, dogs in urban areas with high rat populations, and dogs that go camping or hiking with their owners in wilderness areas. During my thirty years in practice, I have diagnosed leptospirosis three times.

## Canine Parainfluenza Virus and Bordetella (Canine or Feline) Vaccine

These upper respiratory diseases are highly contagious and are spread through nasal secretions. Symptoms of disease include sneezing, coughing, lethargy, fever, and lack of appetite. These are two of the causes of tracheobronchitis or kennel cough. This illness does not cause death and is roughly equivalent to the human cold.

While kennel cough can be irritating and inconvenient, it is not lethal. I do not recommend routinely vaccinating for this. However, dogs or cats that are taken to boarding kennels, groomers, shows, and other high-pet-population events will most likely be required to have this vaccine. It is not highly reactive, but it does stimulate the immune system; some dogs and cats will have adverse reactions. Many pets will develop symptoms of kennel cough, lasting three to ten days, when given the vaccine and can shed the organisms for one to seven weeks after vaccination.

Giving this vaccine does not guarantee that your pet will not get kennel cough, but it may lessen the symptoms. I recommend finding groomers who do not require the vaccine, do not house large numbers of pets in a confined space, or who will come to your house. Find a boarding kennel that is clean, has good ventilation, and does not require the vaccine. Leave your pets with friends or find a good house sitter to stay with your pets.

## Canine Coronavirus Vaccine

This is a highly contagious intestinal virus that causes vomiting, diarrhea, fever, lethargy, and loss of appetite. This disease is not as lethal as parvovirus, but it is commonly found in pets that are also infected with parvovirus. When not associated with parvovirus, disease caused by coronavirus is generally self-limiting. Coronavirus is not considered a core vaccine, and it is not recommended that dogs be routinely given this vaccine. I do not recommend this vaccine.

## Canine or Feline Giardia Vaccine

Giardia is a parasite that is transmitted through infested water or food contaminated with feces. It is impossible to know, without testing, if giardia organisms are present in the water. Water becomes infested when it is contaminated with feces from an infected animal. It is found most commonly in large kennel situations, multiple-pet households, or dirty environments. The most common cause of infection outside of kennel situations is drinking from a contaminated lake, pond, or stream. Many people are infected when hiking, by drinking from contaminated streams. Infection with giardia can cause chronic vomiting, diarrhea, loss of appetite, and weight loss.

Giardia is treatable with anti-parasitics like Metronidazole and Fenbendazole. The key to preventing giardia is diagnosis, treatment, and cleanliness, as well as having a healthy immune system. Most cases of giardia that I see are pet store puppies with weak immune systems, multi-pet households, and dogs exposed to stagnant water.

Giardia can also infect humans, so pets should have stool samples run twice annually to detect any issues. My son had giardia when he was two years old, and treatment lasted four weeks. I'm pretty sure they have better ways to treat this now, but twenty years ago, he had to drink liquid Furazolidone, which has now been shown to be carcinogenic and is no longer available in the United States. Since I have never had a pet infected with giardia, my son had to have picked it up in the environment. I guess we should have been better about the hand washing!

I do not recommend using the giardia vaccine. It can be reactive, and the easiest way to prevent giardia is to test and treat any new animal coming into the household. Test stool samples twice a year, making sure giardia testing is included. Normal fecal flotation testing may not pick up giardia. Keep water bowls clean—and avoid stagnant water in the environment.

## Canine Influenza Vaccine

The canine influenza virus is not the same as the parainfluenza virus related to hepatitis (the adenovirus). Influenza virus was originally diagnosed in greyhounds in Florida in 2004, and the first vaccine was released in 2009. The influenza virus jumped from horses to dogs when the animals were housed together at racetracks. This virus does not transmit to humans. Because greyhounds are shipped all over the country, this virus can now be found in most states.

Just as with any illness, most dogs with good immune systems will either remain healthy or have a short illness with flulike symptoms. A small percentage of dogs will develop pneumonia with a high fever and may succumb to the disease. The severe outbreaks that have occurred have been in high-population, high-stress facilities like pet stores that sell puppies, puppy mills, boarding kennels, and veterinary hospitals with many sick animals. Many groomers, kennels, and high-density pet centers have started to require this vaccine for admission. I do not recommend giving this vaccine. Again, a small, clean kennel, a groomer with good ventilation, or someone who will come to your home are better choices.

## Canine Lyme Disease

Lyme disease is transmitted by ticks. The Borrelia bacteria that cause Lyme disease are commonly found in field mice and deer, and the most common vectors for transmission are the deer tick and other closely related ticks. The ticks are most active from early spring to late fall, but symptoms may take two to five months to show up after infection, so disease can be diagnosed any time during the year. Up to 95 percent of infected dogs will never show any symptoms of disease. This has caused great controversy over whether dogs with positive tests should be treated with antibiotics if they are asymptomatic. Dogs that have positive tests may have protective antibodies and never need treatment. I only like to treat dogs that are symptomatic with a positive test. Symptoms generally include loss of appetite, lethargy, mild fever, swollen joints, lameness, painful muscles, and occasionally digestive upset. More severe cases result in kidney failure and heart disease.

My mother's first Doberman had the cardiac form of the disease. It was early in my veterinary career, and Lyme disease was new to the veterinary world. I wanted to sedate the dog for a dental cleaning. During the pre-operative workup I performed an EKG, which revealed an abnormal heartbeat. Lab work revealed she was positive for Lyme disease, even though she had no other symptoms. I treated her with Doxycycline for a month, and her arrhythmia cleared. Her dental work was performed with no complications.

There have also been reported cases of seizures and other neurologic symptoms secondary to Borrelia infection, which I have seen and treated successfully.

I do not recommend vaccinating against Lyme disease. Most of the dogs exposed to ticks carrying Lyme disease do not develop symptoms (although there are isolated pockets in the United States where a high percentage of exposed dogs will become symptomatic). The tick must be attached and feeding on the dog for at least twelve hours—and more likely twenty-four to forty-eight hours—in order to transmit the infective Borrelia organisms.

The most effective way to avoid Lyme disease is to avoid tick infestation. Keeping grass cut, bushes trimmed, and checking daily for ticks during tick season can be your best defense. There are many chemical and natural products available to keep ticks off pets. Obviously, I prefer the natural products. No product is 100 percent guaranteed to keep your pets free of ticks, and daily tick checks are essential if you live in a high-tick area.

Lyme disease is very treatable when diagnosed early; don't ignore symptoms. The symptoms of Lyme disease are associated with the immune system's reaction to the Borrelia organism. Antigen-antibody complexes are deposited in the joints and kidneys, causing much of the problem. Vaccination may actually contribute to this problem. Vaccination is not 100 percent effective and is only helpful in dogs that have not already been exposed to Borrelia. If you really want to vaccinate, a negative test showing no antibodies in the system would be a good idea, and vaccination should be started when the dog is less than four months old. Many times, I get results showing good immunity due to vaccination when the pet has never been vaccinated. That means they have essentially vaccinated themselves by having a proper response to exposure to the natural organism.

There are at least ten tick-borne diseases that can affect dogs, including anaplasmosis, Rocky Mountain spotted fever, ehrlichiosis, babesiosis, bartonellosis, tularemia, hepatozoonosis, rickettsiosis, and tick paralysis. While Lyme disease seems to be the most commonly diagnosed infection, vaccinations do not exist for any tick-borne disease except Lyme disease. The obvious answer is to keep your pet from becoming infested with ticks—not to prevent only one disease of many.

## Porphyromonas Vaccine

This is a fairly new vaccine that is supposed to prevent serious periodontal disease in dogs. Dogs must be healthy and have clean teeth when the vaccine is given. Adverse reactions to the vaccine include fever, lethargy, allergic reaction, soreness, and autoimmune disease. There is no reason, in my mind, that any dog should ever receive this vaccine. The key to good dental health is good diet, good dental hygiene, and a good immune system. Vaccinations will only damage the immune system even more.

## Feline Viral Rhinotracheitis Vaccine (Herpes Virus 1)

Herpes virus 1 causes upper respiratory disease and conjunctivitis in cats. Once infected, the cat will always be a carrier of the virus, just like herpes virus infections in humans. When cats are subjected to stresses like vaccination, overcrowding, travel, or concurrent illnesses, the herpes virus will become active, bringing out symptoms of disease and/or shedding of the virus.

The most common chronic symptoms seen in practice are conjunctivitis and corneal ulceration. This can be very painful and can lead to blindness or perforation and loss of the eye if not treated aggressively. The FVRCP vaccine includes herpes virus 1 (FVR) and is given in the nose or by injection under the skin. Kittens have the highest risk of infection.

Vaccination will not prevent shedding of the virus, and vaccinated cats can still become ill with a mild form of the disease. I generally include this vaccination in a series of two kitten vaccines when they are vaccinated for panleukopenia, but I do not give it to adult cats.

## Feline Calicivirus Vaccine

Calicivirus causes upper respiratory infection, stomatitis, and gingivitis (inflammation and ulceration of the mouth and gums) in cats. Fever, lethargy, and loss of appetite are common symptoms.

There are multiple strains of the virus, including a new severe strain that is commonly fatal. There is a new vaccination for the severe strain, but it should only be used for cats in shelters or very high-population situations. Kittens are most susceptible to this disease, and infected animals will most likely remain carriers for life. Rarely is the milder form of this virus life threatening, and immunity, once vaccinated, probably lasts for years. This is included in the series of kitten vaccines given in the first few months of life, along with the distemper (panleukopenia) and feline viral rhinotracheitis vaccination. I do not recommend vaccination of adult cats. This virus is resistant to most disinfectants and can remain in the environment for days to weeks. The key to prevention is vaccination of young kittens, keeping a clean environment, and isolating any new cats coming into a colony for a minimum of three weeks to make sure they do not develop any symptoms.

## Feline Chlamydia Vaccine

Chlamydia is a bacterium that causes coughing, sneezing, runny eyes and nose, conjunctivitis, and upper respiratory symptoms. Occasionally, kittens will develop pneumonia. This infection is seen most commonly in kittens, shelters, and high-stress living environments.

The chlamydia vaccination will not prevent infection, but it may reduce symptoms of disease. Side effects from the vaccination are common, including fever, loss of appetite, lameness, and lethargy. This bacterium does have zoonotic potential (can be transmitted to humans). It is uncomfortable and annoying, but it is rarely life threatening. Using this vaccine is not recommended.

## Feline Leukemia Vaccine

The feline leukemia virus is spread through nasal secretions and saliva. Kittens can contract the virus in utero from the queen. Some kittens will convert to negative status within three months of birth, others will still test positive, and some will die shortly after birth. The average life expectancy after contracting the disease is less than three years.

Cats usually develop anemia (low red blood cell count), cancer, and secondary infections due to immune deficiency. Cats must be in fairly direct or intimate contact to contract the disease. Indoor cats in a closed colony that test negative for the disease do not have opportunities to be exposed to the virus. Indoor cats should not be vaccinated for feline leukemia unless the owner is likely to bring in untested stray cats. Owners should have all new cats tested for feline leukemia and feline immunodeficiency virus before exposing them to cats already in the household. If a stray cat is brought into a closed colony, the cat should be isolated; testing should be performed immediately and repeated in three months since any recent exposure may not show up before that period of time.

The length of duration of immunity from this vaccine is currently unknown, and the recommendation is to repeat the vaccination annually. I believe the duration of immunity is much longer, but there is no proof of that. Not all cats will achieve protection even when given the vaccine. For outdoor cats with exposure to stray animals, I recommend testing and vaccinating kittens less than four months of age with a series of two vaccinations three weeks apart.

## Feline Infectious Peritonitis Vaccine

There are still many questions about the transmission of this disease and why some cats exposed to the virus do not become ill, some become carriers that shed the virus, and others become sick and die (a small percentage). This disease is commonly associated with large cat colonies, stressful conditions, or cats suffering from concurrent diseases. The intranasal vaccine should only be used in cats that have never been exposed to coronavirus, which limits the use of the vaccine. This vaccine is of minimal, if any, benefit and is currently not recommended for use.

## Feline Immunodeficiency Virus Vaccine

FIV is transmitted primarily through bite wounds and is seen mostly in outdoor male cats that fight with other cats. FIV is not necessarily a death sentence, as many cats can be carriers of the virus for years with no signs of illness. There are five strains of virus that cause FIV, but the vaccine protects against only two strains and does not protect against the most common strain found in the United States.

Once a cat is vaccinated with this product, the cat will always test positive for the FIV virus. If a cat is picked up as a stray and tested at a shelter facility, there is no way to know if the cat has been vaccinated or infected. This could result in cats being euthanized as infected cats when, in reality, they are not infected. This vaccine also contains adjuvants, which are the material incriminated in causing vaccine-related tumors. It is not recommended that this vaccine be given.

## Feline Ringworm Vaccine

Ringworm is a fungal skin infection seen commonly in cats and kittens living in crowded, unsanitary conditions. Like any fungus, ringworm species grow best in dark, damp conditions and are sensitive to sunlight and drying. Cats with compromised immune systems, like young kittens or those infected with feline leukemia or feline immunodeficiency virus, are more likely to contract ringworm (named for the ring-like lesions on the skin).

Cats can be asymptomatic carriers of the fungal organisms, particularly longhaired cats. This vaccine should only be given to healthy cats over four months of age and consists of a series of three injections over two months. The vaccine only protects against one strain of ringworm fungus. Field studies have shown only two-week duration of immunity when the vaccine is used for prevention or treatment. I do not recommend ever using this vaccine.

## Rabies Vaccine

Rabies virus is deadly to any pet or person contracting the disease. Because of the zoonotic potential threat to humans and the almost certain death from the disease, most municipalities and states in the

United States require vaccination and licensing of pets with required proof of current vaccination. People in the United States rarely die of rabies because of the vaccination requirements. In third world countries where vaccination is done less commonly, thousands of people die from rabies every year.

The most common transmission to humans in the United States comes from exposure to bats. Rabies virus is transmitted from saliva to blood through open wounds (most specifically bite wounds), but it has been transmitted through mucous membranes like the gums and conjunctiva. Rabies virus travels from the wound along nerve pathways to the brain where infection and inflammation eventually kill the host.

Pets are vaccinated for rabies beginning any time after three months of age. The first vaccine is valid for one year, and pets must receive a booster vaccination at the end of that one-year period. The second vaccination will be good for three years, as long as a product approved for three-year duration is used. (There are some one-year vaccinations on the market.) Even if more than one year has elapsed from the initial vaccination, the second vaccination is still valid for three years.

There has been an ongoing discussion regarding the actual duration of immunity for rabies vaccination. A rabies vaccination study spearheaded by Dr. Jean Dodds has shown the vaccination definitely gives protection from disease for three years, but immunologic testing showed declining titers in the fourth and fifth years (Rabies Challenge Fund). (http://www.rabieschallengefund.org/) It is currently unknown if the dogs actually have immunologic memory if challenged with the virus. Unfortunately, because of the zoonotic threat of this disease, changes in vaccination protocol may never happen.

One of the worst problems I have seen with the three-year vaccination protocol has been veterinarians signing vaccination certificates stating two-year duration of immunity when a three-year vaccine has been administered. This is just another way to get pets back into the office more frequently, giving unnecessary vaccines. Always ask for a vaccine with three-year duration of immunity—and make certain that the certificate states three-year duration as well. There are no two-year vaccines in existence. This vaccination should never be given at the same time as other vaccines. Make the effort to wait at least one month between vaccinations if multiple vaccines need to be given.

The rabies virus is introduced into the body through a bite wound and travels along nerve pathways until it reaches the brain, causing encephalitis, brain swelling, and death. Because the rabies vaccine targets nerve pathways, I never recommend that this vaccine be given to pets with seizure or nerve disorders. One disorder that I think is related to rabies vaccination is eosinophilic myositis of the masseter and temporalis muscles (the chewing muscles on the head). Dogs with this disease will develop pain and inflammation in those muscles, and the muscles will atrophy (shrink) until the top of the head has the appearance of a skull covered with skin. I see this most commonly in Golden retrievers, but it can occur in any breed and is reported commonly in Doberman pinschers, German shepherds, Labrador retrievers, and cavalier King Charles spaniels.

Symptoms are usually seen ten days to two months after the rabies vaccine is given. (Think how long it takes for the virus to travel along nerve pathways from the hind end of the pet, where the vaccine is given, to the head.) Treatment for this disease in the past has included high doses of steroids to decrease inflammation. I have never seen this cure the disease, but it does make the dogs more comfortable while the process of muscle atrophy is taking place. Affected dogs have shown a greater response to acupuncture and herbal therapy, in my hands, than to steroids.

My recommended vaccination protocol (under ideal circumstances in a closed colony, home environment):

For dogs:

* DAP (distemper, adenovirus, parvovirus) for puppies at twelve and sixteen weeks, if the puppies are in a clean, healthy environment with no exposure to sick dogs.

🐾 Draw blood for distemper and parvo titers at six months of age and annually thereafter. Give booster vaccine for parvo if titer is low. I continue running titers for life because dogs are constantly exposed to other dogs outside.

🐾 Rabies at six months to one year of age; repeat one year later with a vaccine good for three year duration, then every three years provided the pet is healthy enough to be vaccinated (based on state requirements).

For cats:

🐾 FVRCP at twelve and sixteen weeks of age if the kittens are in a clean, healthy environment with no exposure to sick cats.

🐾 Draw blood for panleukopenia (distemper) titer at six months of age and annually thereafter. May not be necessary for adult cats housed indoors in a closed colony where no new cats will be introduced, provided the titers at six and eighteen months of age show good immunity.

🐾 Rabies at six months to one year of age; repeat one year later with a vaccine good for a three-year duration, then every three years provided the pet is healthy enough to be vaccinated (based on state requirements). I do not vaccinate indoor cats after the second vaccine provided the owners are responsible and do not allow their cats outside at all.

Even though the focus of this chapter has been on vaccination of pets, I feel I must give my opinion on vaccinating horses. Over-vaccination is just as much an issue in horses as it is in small animals. In New Jersey, people commonly vaccinate their horses twice a year, in the spring and the fall. We generally vaccinate for rabies, Eastern and Western encephalitis, West Nile virus, tetanus, and influenza. Vaccines are also available for equine herpes virus, botulism, strangles, Venezuelan encephalitis, Potomac horse fever, rotavirus, equine viral arteritis, and equine protozoal myeloencephalitis, but these diseases are not a big problem in the area where I practice.

I have stopped vaccinating twice a year. The influenza vaccine has duration of immunity of one year (depending on product used), and the tetanus vaccine has duration of immunity of two years or more. Rabies vaccination lasts fourteen months to three years, maybe more. Eastern and Western encephalitis vaccines are labeled with one-year duration of immunity. Encephalitis is a mosquito-borne disease, so vaccinating in the late fall or winter, when mosquitoes are not active, makes no sense at all. Vaccines for mosquito-borne disease should be given in the late spring when the weather becomes warm enough for mosquitoes to become active. Some holistic practitioners are recommending use of this vaccine every three years instead of annually.

Ideally, vaccines should be given only when a horse has an actual risk of exposure to the disease. Unfortunately, groups like 4-H, some horse shows, and some farms have requirements for vaccinations that do not allow for individual tailoring of vaccination protocols. Older horses that have been vaccinated many times in their lives probably have long-lasting immunity to many of the diseases for which they continue to be vaccinated annually. Blood tests for titers are available for Eastern, Venezuelan, and Western encephalitis, West Nile virus, rabies, equine herpes, Potomac horse fever, equine viral arteritis, equine influenza, strangles, and Lyme disease, but they are still fairly expensive—and availability is limited.

Horse owners should have frank discussions with their equine veterinarians to determine actual risk to horses under their current living conditions. Blindly giving vaccines for every possible disease can result in laminitis, behavior problems, cardiac dysfunction, lameness, arthritis, muscle disease, and inflammation in the eyes (uveitis). Unless your horse has great risk of exposure, limit vaccination to what is required by your barn or events you attend.

# Poop Happens: Treating Gastrointestinal Disease

One of our cavalier King Charles spaniel foster dogs, Madison, a six-year-old, was very special. She had been the gift the couple who owned her had given to each other for their wedding. They loved her as much as they would love a child. In fact, she was their only child for many years because it took them a long time to be able to have a child. They were wonderful parents and had Madison vaccinated for everything their veterinarians recommended. They fed the popular dry dog food recommended by their veterinarians. Everything seemed to be going well, until one day when Madison became ill.

She started with vague symptoms of diarrhea and was treated with all the usual medications. Then she started vomiting. Then she stopped eating. Then she lost weight. Her parents kept giving all the medications that were prescribed, but Madison was losing ground. Finally, Madison was admitted into a veterinary critical care center where she received transfusions of protein and a long list of medications for two weeks. When Madison's bills topped $10,000, her owners were at a loss. They couldn't go forward. They brought

Madison home (along with their new human baby!) in the hopes they would be able to treat her with all the medications, which included drugs that required wearing gloves because they were potentially toxic to people. That didn't work out very well.

Madison refused to eat and continued to vomit and have liquid diarrhea. Her owners were concerned about having a dog with intractable vomiting and diarrhea that was being treated with chemotherapy drugs that could be harmful to the baby. Their only hope was that a rescue group would be willing to take her and try to find a cure. Some of you may be wondering how they could give her up. The answer is that they loved her so much that they didn't want to put her to sleep—and they were willing to give her a second chance.

When we received the phone call about Madison, we of course said we would try to help. Her medical records were over three hundred pages long. Her white blood cell count and liver enzymes were through the roof. Her protein levels were so low they hardly registered. She had been treated for pneumonia, sepsis (overwhelming infection), and fluid build-up in her chest and abdomen. She had gone from sixteen pounds down to eleven. It was a miracle she was alive.

When we first met her, she seemed happy but very dull. She would eat small bites of kibble on occasion, but she generally had no appetite. I performed every gastrointestinal diagnostic test I could think of, and I had an abdominal ultrasound performed. The working diagnosis was protein-losing enteropathy and lymphangiectasia. Both of these diseases are difficult to treat and are really just descriptions of the disease process. The underlying cause can be difficult to find, but it may include bowel inflammation, stress to the immune system, cancer, and an inability to digest fats. An intestinal biopsy probably would have provided an answer, but Madison was too sick to be sedated for the procedure. I already had proof of an over-reactive, stressed immune system since Madison had been over-vaccinated and over-medicated. The other thing I discovered was that the food Madison had been eating when her problem began had been recalled for salmonella contamination.

I began treatment by starting Madison on a home-cooked diet and decreasing her medications. She was being given fifteen medications twice daily. I cut them out one by one, every few days. I added probiotics and digestive enzymes when I could get her to take them. Poor Madison was so tired of taking drugs, and it was a struggle. I discovered she loved sour cream, which may not have been the best food in the world, but it was great for coating pills. Within two weeks, Madison was eating ravenously and gaining weight. Her blood tests were all normal, which was incredible. I was sure a miracle had occurred.

Unfortunately, the miracle only lasted for one month. Suddenly the diarrhea returned with a vengeance. It was a foul-smelling, bloody liquid. Her appetite started to decline, and her lab values were as bad as when we started. I tried different foods, different medications, herbal supplements, acupuncture, subcutaneous fluids, and complicated herbal soups. Nothing worked.

I finally had to admit Madison into the local veterinary specialty center for protein transfusions. This time, her ultrasound showed dark spots in her liver and spleen. Madison was diagnosed with cancer. We decided to let Madison cross the Rainbow Bridge, but losing her affected us more than any loss to date. She was just very, very special. (You can check out her Facebook page, Madison's Miracle, for more of her story.) Since we were unable to perform biopsies earlier when she was ill, we will never know if the cancer was there all along or if it was caused by the inflammatory process in her bowel.

Gastrointestinal disease in pets ranges from minor to life threatening. Pets are a bit like children in that they like to taste and chew things they shouldn't, resulting in poisoning and ingestion of foreign bodies. Commonly treated diseases include infection with bacteria, viruses, or parasites, and foreign bodies with or without obstruction. Symptoms of gastrointestinal disease can include vomiting, diarrhea, bloody stools, constipation, anorexia, weight loss, drooling, and abdominal pain. Other diseases seen include pancreatitis, exocrine pancreatic insufficiency, cancer, and inflammatory bowel disease. Inflammatory bowel disease is probably one of the most commonly diagnosed (and misdiagnosed) problems in veterinary practice. Any nonspecific case of chronic vomiting and diarrhea without a specific diagnosis will always be classified as "inflammatory bowel disease."

Most bouts of vomiting or diarrhea are short lived, just as they are in people. Withholding food for eight to twelve hours, which allows the bowel to rest and heal itself, will commonly solve the problem. However, if the pet is vomiting repeatedly or many times within a few hours, it can be a symptom of something more serious like a foreign body obstruction or pancreatitis. If blood is noticed in the vomit or stool, the pet should be seen by a veterinarian. Any vomit or stool that is dark black or has a coffee-ground appearance is an indication of bleeding in the stomach or small intestine and warrants a veterinary visit as soon as possible. Pets that are given any anti-inflammatory medications like aspirin or NSAIDS are particularly at risk for ulceration or bleeding in the bowel.

For the occasional bout of upset tummy, my favorite cure includes withholding food for six to eight hours and then offering a bland soup called congee. Congee is a type of rice porridge or gruel popular in many Asian countries.

How to make congee:

- Cook a chicken breast by boiling. When finished cooking, mince into small pieces. If your pet has a sensitivity or allergy to chicken, you may substitute a very lean pork chop.

- Place one cup of long grain white or brown rice in a pot with eight cups of water and simmer over low heat.

- Mince one teaspoon of fresh ginger root.

- Add the minced chicken and the minced ginger to the simmering rice and cook for six to eight hours, adding water as needed.

The finished product should look like a thin gruel. All ingredients should be dissolved. The soothing mixture should be fed in small quantities every few hours until your pet is feeling better.

Slippery Elm Sludge can also be given to settle an upset tummy. Mix one teaspoon slippery elm powder in ½ cup boiling water; let cool. Feed one to four teaspoons, based on size of pet, four times daily. Start introducing the normal diet in small amounts once there has been no vomiting for twenty-four hours.

Once the pet is no longer vomiting, the following can be used to treat diarrhea:

- probiotics (I like Synacore by Van Beek and Rx Biotic by Rx Vitamins)

- powdered clay to absorb toxins and fluid (I like Rx Clay by Rx Vitamins)

- a bland diet that is easily digestible

- You can boil low-fat hamburger and rice or chicken and rice, using one part meat to three parts rice. Use long cook rice, not quick rice. Cook until very well done. Feed small portions three to four times daily. In a pinch, white rice from a Chinese restaurant works well (especially for those who don't cook). Baby food meat (no onion powder) can be substituted for cooked meat if you don't cook. A tablespoon of canned pumpkin (no spices) can be added to each cup of food to provide fiber. Gradually mix in normal diet over a few days once diarrhea resolves.

Causes of more chronic diarrhea and vomiting can include:

- intestinal parasites

- exocrine pancreatic insufficiency

- bacterial overgrowth

- lymphangiectasia

- cancer

- inflammatory bowel disease

- 🐾 immune system dysfunction

- 🐾 overuse of steroids and antibiotics

- 🐾 stress

- 🐾 excess dietary sugar

- 🐾 inadequate dietary fiber

- 🐾 excessive dietary fiber

- 🐾 decreased production of stomach acid

- 🐾 decreased production of pancreatic enzymes

Diagnostic testing to determine the cause of chronic diarrhea or vomiting may include testing a stool sample for intestinal parasites, performing an ELISA test for giardia (see chapters on parasites and giardia vaccine for further discussions), performing an abdominal ultrasound, and blood chemistry screening to look for signs of systemic disease.

Performing bacterial cultures or a test called PCR can be helpful for determining bacterial infection. Testing for folate and cobalamin may be helpful in diagnosing bacterial overgrowth and TLI levels will help diagnose exocrine pancreatic insufficiency (EPI). An intestinal biopsy may be needed to obtain a final diagnosis.

Normally, the bowels are filled with billions of healthy bacteria that help break down nutrients and synthesize vitamins for the body. When antibiotics are given or the pet has a bout of diarrhea, the good bacteria are killed or washed out of the system. When the numbers of the healthy bacteria are diminished, the "bad" bacteria can take over, causing bacterial overgrowth.

Many pets with chronic diarrhea are treated with long courses of antibiotics (tylosin or metronidazole), steroids, and antacid medications. Since antibiotics also kill the beneficial bacteria, steroids suppress the immune system, and decreased stomach acid can contribute to chronic diarrhea, it seems like we are treating bowel disease the wrong way. Pets may need initial antibiotic therapy to kill bad bacteria, but long-term healing will require a change of thinking.

Probiotics need to be fed to put the beneficial bacteria back into the bowel. Prebiotics, which are food for the good bacteria, should be added to the diet. Digestive enzymes to decrease the work of digestion are essential. And a healthy, species-appropriate, protein-based diet low in simple carbohydrates and sugars should be fed.

Functions of the good bacteria in the bowel include digestion, absorption of nutrients, and elimination of toxins from the body. More than a thousand different strains of healthy bacteria reside in the bowel to form a protective barrier against absorption of toxins, prevent overgrowth of harmful bacteria, and synthesize vitamins B and K. Studies have shown that the microbial species population can shift dramatically within three to four days of changing from a plant-based to a meat-based diet.

Inflammation in the bowel leads to invasion of the intestinal lining by harmful bacteria and absorption of toxins produced by those bacteria. In order to have a healthy gut, inflammation in the body needs to be kept to a minimum. Chronic inflammation in the body is a sign that the immune system is under attack and has run amok, which sends out cells to attack the body, causing disease and degradation.

The immune system is under constant attack from pollution in the environment, inflammatory hormones released by fat cells in obesity, overstimulation with vaccinations, and chemicals in processed food. Signs of chronic inflammation and an overworked immune system include inflammatory bowel disease, arthritis, allergies, and chronic infections anywhere in the body.

While treating with steroids and antibiotics may stop or decrease the signs of inflammation, they are not correcting the underlying problem, which is a distressed immune system; 70 percent of the cells involved in a healthy immune system reside in the gut. Keeping the bowel healthy is the most important thing that can be done to ensure good health.

A pet diagnosed with one of the more chronic diseases of the bowel needs to get the immune system functioning properly in order to heal.

❧ Take the pet off commercial, processed pet food.

❧ Feed a home-cooked or raw diet comprised of at least 70 percent meat and organ meat proteins. Add healthy vegetables for fiber and vitamins. Some pets may be able to tolerate small amounts of good carbohydrates like cooked quinoa or barley.

❧ Use novel proteins like rabbit, venison, very lean pork, or duck if you suspect allergies or food sensitivities. Red meats may be too rich. Avoid chicken (commonly used in low-quality pet foods, causing many allergies and food sensitivities) and lamb (energetically very hot and may increase inflammation and heat in the body).

❧ Feed fresh cooked, chopped, or ground, brightly colored vegetables.

❧ Canned or fresh cooked pumpkin is a great source of fiber that can help with diarrhea or constipation.

❧ Feed small meals three to four times daily instead of one or two large meals.

❧ Add high-quality probiotics to every meal. I like Synacore by Van Beek and Rx Biotic or Nutrigest by Rx Vitamins. Do not use probiotics with animal digest as the base.

❧ Add prebiotics to every meal. I like Synacore by Van Beek and Nutrigest by Rx Vitamins.

❧ Add digestive enzymes to every meal. I like Synacore by Van Beek and Rx Zyme by Rx Vitamins.

❧ Add clay to absorb toxins and moisture if soft stools are an issue. I like Rx Clay by Rx Vitamins.

❧ Add L-glutamine (500 milligrams per 25 pounds of body weight) daily. This increases absorption of nutrients, decreases bowel inflammation, and decreases cramping and bloating.

❧ Chinese herbal combinations may be helpful based on tongue and pulse diagnostics. Find a veterinary practitioner at www. tcvm.com.

❧ Acupuncture supports digestion, bowel function, and the immune system.

❧ Minimize or stop using vaccines to decrease chronic inflammation and over-stimulation of the immune system.

❧ If your pet is taking steroids or Atopica, do not stop abruptly. Follow a slow weaning course as prescribed by your veterinarian or holistic practitioner.

❧ Subcutaneous injections of vitamin B12 given at ¼ to ½ ml once or twice a week until symptoms are resolved and pet is gaining weight. Then give every two weeks for a few months; then drop to monthly injections for pets with chronic inflammatory bowel disease, exocrine pancreatic insufficiency, or bacterial overgrowth.

❧ Dried or fresh grated ginger at ¼ to ½ teaspoon twice daily can soothe digestion (also found in Nutrigest by Rx Vitamins.)

❧ Slippery Elm Sludge can soothe an inflamed bowel, has prebiotics to feed the good bacteria, and feeds the cells lining the bowel. Mix 1 teaspoon of powder (or open capsules equal to about 1 teaspoon) and mix in ½ cup boiling water. Let cool and feed 1 to 4 teaspoons four times daily, depending on size of the pet. Can be fed directly or mixed with food or broth. Will remain usable for about five days if refrigerated.

Many of these supplements can be discontinued once bowel healing has taken place. I add probiotics every day for maintenance for my dogs.

# Itching, Scratching, and Chewing: Treating Skin and Ear Disease

O ur second wonderful foster failure, Abby, another cavalier King Charles spaniel, was given up by her family because her medical bills were more than they could afford. For years she had repeated skin and bladder infections that were treated with multiple antibiotics. The family could not afford to have cultures performed and only gave antibiotics for a few days at each treatment. Achieving a cure was close to impossible. They also fed one of the worst dry pet foods on the market because it was cheap.

Abby was a hot mess, to say the least. She was obese. My son nicknamed her "Flabs" for "Flabby Abby." Her skin smelled and was covered with oozing sores and crusts. She scratched, licked, and chewed every part of her body all day and night. She urinated in the house every five minutes because of the burning sensation in her bladder. No wonder the family gave her away!

However, her issues were treatable, and she just needed to be given a chance. I immediately changed her from the awful dry dog food to a raw meat diet. I cultured her skin and urine and found an appropriate antibiotic that would heal both bacterial infections. I bathed and scrubbed the crusts off her skin every other day with a medicated tea tree oil shampoo to release the bacteria from the hair follicles. Her diet was supplemented with probiotics and digestive enzymes.

Slowly she started to show improvement. Not only did her skin and urinary tract infections improve; she smelled better, lost weight, and started to become more playful. Her nickname wasn't quite as fitting after she lost ten pounds. It took six weeks to get negative cultures on her skin and urine, but she has not had one infection in the past two years.

Some of the more common complaints we hear in practice are those related to allergies, skin disease, and ear infections. The most commonly used medications to treat allergies are steroids and antihistamines. It has become all too easy for veterinarians to prescribe oral steroids or long-acting steroid injections to treat itchy pets.

Unfortunately, steroids have many long-term undesirable side effects, including excess thirst and urination, diabetes, liver disease, Cushing's disease, blood clots, pancreatitis, stomach ulceration, and suppression of the immune system (allowing secondary infections). Steroids should not be used in patients with diabetes, seizures, congestive heart failure, high blood pressure, kidney failure, stomach ulcers, or if infected with the herpes virus (cats).

Side effects from antihistamine usage include dry mouth, dizziness, restlessness, lethargy, and nausea. In rare instances, they can cause trouble with urination. They should not be used in patients with heart disease, high blood pressure, thyroid disease, kidney disease, liver disease, or glaucoma. These lists rule out the use of steroids and antihistamines in at least half the patients seen, yet they are still prescribed daily to pets suffering from these conditions.

Stronger immune system suppressants like cyclosporine (Atopica) and oclacitinib (Apoquel) have started replacing the use of steroids in some cases, but these medications are extremely strong. Side effects include vomiting, diarrhea, and infection (how do you fight off infection with a suppressed immune system?). There has to be a better way.

I will admit that I do use steroids and antihistamines in my practice, but they are reserved for short-term use or as a last-ditch rescue effort. The solution to avoiding the drugs is curing the underlying problem, which is often not sought out or is overlooked. Itching, scratching, and chewing are symptoms. Itching is not a diagnosis.

*We must start treating the underlying problem and stop treating the symptoms.*

In my opinion, an extremely large percentage of the itchy pets presented to my clinic suffer from a poor diet, over-medication, and over-vaccination, leading to compromised immune systems. Many pets are fed diets high in carbohydrates, which are filled with dyes and preservatives. If I can convince the owners to try a high-quality canned, raw, or home-cooked diet with novel proteins (proteins to which the pet has not previously been exposed), most pets will show immediate improvement.

This is particularly true with bulldogs. I hired a new office manager who is heavily involved with bulldog rescue. Every week, we see a new rescued dog come through the clinic with horrible, smelly skin disease. This breed seems particularly prone to allergy, infection, and mange. I have never seen a bulldog with good skin when being fed dry dog food. (Of course, I don't think I've ever seen a bulldog being fed a high-quality dry food, either.) When fed a raw meat diet, most of these dogs will miraculously improve.

Dry pet food, in general, tends to cause pets to become dry and itchy over time. There is not enough moisture present in the diet for the pet to have a shiny, healthy coat. There are a few fish-based, no grain, dry foods available (Orijen) that are better for the coat, but I always recommend itchy pets be taken off dry food.

Pets with dry, flaky skin are suffering from a blood deficiency from a Chinese medicine perspective. Good blood tonic foods include eggs, sardines, heart, liver, carrots, beef, and parsley. Pets with greasy, thickened, blackened skin suffer more from phlegm and stagnation and need foods like clams, pears, apples, garlic, and ginger. Unless the pet has an allergy to one of these foods, I recommend adding them to the diet. The meals should include raw or home-cooked foods and stews with plenty of moisture. For clients who do not cook, there are some high-quality canned foods (Merrick, Castor and Pollux, Wellness Core, Evanger's, Tiki, Fromm Gold, Evo, Weruva, to name a few) that can be used as the base meal, and some of the foods listed above can be added to supplement the canned food.

Along with a new healthy diet, I recommend supplements to improve the health of the skin and coat. Omega-3 fatty acids are particularly important additions for healthy skin and coat (as well as heart health and joint health). Dosages of EPA and DHA should approach fifty milligrams per pound of body weight (3,000 milligrams for a sixty-pound dog). Decrease the dose if the pet develops loose stools or vomits. Pets with greasy, hot skin may have more problems with diarrhea when given omega-3 fatty acids, so dosages may need to be kept low. Vitamin E should always be given along with omega-3 fatty acids, as omega-3 fatty acids will bind vitamin E in the body and cause deficiencies that can lead to muscle weakness. Some products have vitamin E added; if not, add 1 to 2 IU of vitamin E per pound of body weight, daily.

Licorice is an herb that acts as an anti-inflammatory and can be used short-term to cut down the amount of scratching. Herbal extracts of licorice are available and can be given orally at one drop per pound of body weight two to three times daily. Herbal licorice salves and teas can also be used topically to soothe irritated skin. Obviously, if fleas or external parasites are present, they need to be dealt with as well.

Every pet with skin disease should have an impression slide taken of its skin to perform cytology (looking under the microscope to see if bacteria, yeast, or mites are present). If there are a lot of bacteria seen on the slide, a sterile cotton swab should be rubbed on the skin and sent to the lab to perform a culture and sensitivity test. This will tell the doctor what kind of bacteria is growing on the skin and which antibiotics will kill the bacteria. Without knowing the type of bacteria present and which antibiotics will solve the problem, the doctor is guessing which antibiotics to use. If the first antibiotic chosen does not solve the problem, doctors will commonly choose a second antibiotic, which may also be ineffective. Use of multiple antibiotics leads to antibiotic-resistance by the bacteria. I am amazed how many pets are presented that have been treated with multiple courses of steroids and antibiotics that have developed resistant bacterial infections like MRSA. Once a resistant infection develops, it is much harder to achieve a cure, although it is still possible.

It is only possible to achieve a cure by strengthening the immune system; 70 percent of the body's immune system is found in the cells lining the intestines. Without healthy digestion, good health cannot be achieved. The intestines are filled with trillions of healthy bacteria that help break down food and release vitamins needed by the body. Those good bacteria are also responsible for preventing overgrowth of the bad bacteria in the gut. The species of bacteria in the gut will vary, depending on the diet that is fed.

When antibiotics are given to kill the bad bacteria that cause infection, they also kill the beneficial bacteria responsible for good digestion and immunity. The immune systems of many pets will crash after being given antibiotics. This is why infections of the skin and other organs continue to reoccur. Any time a pet is given antibiotics, it must also be fed probiotic supplements to replace the good bacteria in the bowel.

One of my favorite patients, Lucy, was given Metronidazole, an antibiotic, for an extended period of time by her regular veterinarian for diarrhea and colitis. Metronidazole is commonly used to treat those conditions. Unfortunately, Lucy had an unusual reaction, and her bone marrow stopped making red blood cells. Lucy was treated by the specialists at the local veterinary college with high doses of steroids and chemotherapeutic immunosuppressive drugs.

Lucy's mom was beside herself because the side effects were awful. Lucy developed atrophy of the muscles of her head from the steroids. She was drinking and urinating gallons every day, and her weight ballooned. She was feeding the dry prescription diet she was instructed to use, and Lucy had already received multiple blood transfusions.

Lucy could not maintain her red blood cell count in the normal range, and her owner was told there was nothing else that could be done.

Luckily, Lucy's mom sought alternative care. We started with a change of diet. No more dry food—just lots of home-cooked healthy blood tonic foods like beef, sardines, eggs, and sweet potatoes. We added spinach and green beans to soothe her liver. She had acupuncture twice weekly to stimulate blood production and rebalance her immune system. Best of all, she was taken off all the drugs, started taking herbs to stimulate blood production (Si Wu Tang), and probiotics to replace the good bacteria in her gut. She was able to lose the weight she had gained on the steroids, and the muscles on her head returned to normal. Needless to say, Lucy cannot tolerate antibiotics.

Many pet foods state on the label they have added prebiotics (substances that feed the good bacteria in the gut) and probiotics (the good bacteria needed in the gut) to keep the gut and immune system healthy. Probiotics are live bacteria. Unless they are added after production, heating will kill them. Probiotic supplements need to be refrigerated after opening and kept in a sealed container. Products that are shipped and stored in high heat will not be viable. I recommend adding a probiotic supplement to the daily diet of all pets, and I recommend increasing the dose fourfold when the pet must take antibiotics.

Human probiotics are not the same species as animal probiotics and should not be used. Probiotic and prebiotic supplements fall into the class of supplements called nutraceuticals and are not regulated. Studies comparing label claims to actual number of bacteria grown in culture show huge variations. Some products did not grow any bacteria at all. If you use one product and do not feel you are seeing results, try another. Look for scientific literature supporting the product, not testimonials.

The list of ingredients in the probiotics should include specific bacterial species and strains, number of guaranteed CFU or colony forming units, an expiration date, storage instructions, and a customer service phone number. Also pay attention to the inactive ingredients in the product. Animal digest is produced by chemical or enzyme decomposition of animal tissues. I would avoid products containing this ingredient.

Natural kefir, a type of super yogurt, is a great way to supplement your pet's diet with calcium, magnesium, probiotics, B vitamins, and tryptophan, which is a calming amino acid. Dogs with tear staining below the eyes will benefit greatly from the addition of probiotics or kefir to their diets.

Along with a healthy bacterial population, the bowels must also have a good quantity of digestive enzymes to digest the food that is eaten. Digestive enzymes are produced in the saliva, the stomach, the intestinal cells, and the pancreas. Without them, it is impossible to digest and absorb nutrients from food. Inflammatory bowel disease, decreased stomach acid production, chronic stress, pancreatitis, and medications may cause a decrease in digestive enzyme production. Any time I see a pet with chronic disease and poor immune function, I immediately recommend supplementing digestive enzymes along with probiotics. I do not recommend giving antacids, like famotidine, to pets because they need stomach acid for healthy digestion and good immunity.

In addition to a good diet and healthy immune system, it is imperative to rule out any other imbalances in the body that may contribute to chronic skin disease. Pets with endocrine or hormonal diseases like hypothyroidism, diabetes, and Cushing's disease will commonly have skin disease as well. A complete blood panel should always be performed to rule out underlying disease in any animal with chronic skin disease.

The keys to healthy skin and elimination of allergies include:

- a species-appropriate diet high in protein and low in carbohydrates
- novel proteins to which pet has not been previously exposed
- addition of probiotics to daily meals (I like Rx Biotic by Rx Vitamins and Synacore by Van Beek)

- addition of digestive enzymes (I like Synacore by Van Beek and Rx Zyme by Rx Vitamins)

- elimination of known food intolerances

- omega-3 fatty acids (EPA and DHA) dosed at 50 milligrams per pound of body weight daily

- vitamin E given at a dosage of 1 to 2 IU daily with omega-3 fatty acids

- licorice (given orally at one drop of extract per pound of body weight two to three times daily or applied topically as a salve or tea for itching)

- blood tonic foods for itchy dry skin (beef, liver, eggs, sardines, and spinach)

- phlegm-draining foods and foods to resolve stagnation for dark, greasy skin, including clams, pears, apples, garlic (fresh, crushed, ½ to 1 clove twice daily depending on size of dog), ginger (fresh ground root or dried powder, ¼ to ½ teaspoon twice daily, depending on size of dog)

- natural kefir to decrease tear staining and itching (one to three tablespoons daily, depending on size of dog)

- elimination of fleas, mites, or any external parasites

- bathing with tea tree, mint, or lavender shampoo (Vet Organics, Healing Tree) or an enzymatic shampoo (Zymox) up to three times per week if infection is present (if no infection is present, do not bathe more than once every few weeks because the coat will become too dry)

- avoid shampoos with sulfates, propylene glycol, BHA or BHT preservatives, artificial fragrances, coal tar, triclosan, and artificial colors or dyes

- have lab work performed to rule out any underlying disease not previously diagnosed, and treat any underlying diseases

Chronic ear infections in dogs and cats are simply the effect of poor diet, a poor immune system that is incapable of fighting off infection, and chronic overuse of the wrong medications and antibiotics. Commonly, these pets have an allergy or intolerance for an ingredient in their diets. Finding the offensive ingredient can be time consuming and may (probably) require preparation of a home-prepared diet with novel ingredients that the pet has never been fed. The most common offenders (in my experience) seem to be chicken, soy, and corn. These are probably the most problematic because they are the most commonly used ingredients in poor-quality pet foods.

Ear infections are extremely painful as a result of the swelling and ulceration in the ear canals. You should never use cotton swabs to clean the ear canals. The skin lining the canals is extremely sensitive and easily abraded. You should never use water or hydrogen peroxide to clean the ears since these will always leave moisture in the canals. The ears need a dry, clean environment for good health. Yeast and bacteria like to grow in moist, dark, damp environments. In general, black or dark brown smelly ear discharge that is very itchy is caused by yeast. Nine times out of ten, this is due to food intolerance. Once the infection is cleared, finding and eliminating the offensive food and improving the health of the immune system should prevent further infections from occurring.

Yellow, green, white, or thick smelly discharge more commonly represents a bacterial infection that may require antibiotic treatment. Always have cytology performed on the ear discharge—and a culture and antibiotic sensitivity—if bacteria are present in the ear canal. Topical antibiotics must be applied in the ear canals; oral medications are rarely warranted because they do not achieve high levels in the cells in the external ear canals. Oral antibiotics should only be dispensed in cases of otitis media, or infection of the middle, or inner, ear.

Unfortunately, many dogs have so much scar tissue that the ear canals are almost completely closed and unable to drain. Some of these dogs may require surgery to open the ear canals. Do not have this procedure done until you have cleaned up the diet and the immune system because many of these pets will heal enough to avoid surgery.

My dogs and cats do not require regular cleaning of their ears. Ear infections should not occur if the pet is eating an appropriate diet and has good immunity. Exceptions may include long-eared dogs that swim and constantly get water into the canals and dogs with excessive scar tissue in the canals. Drying agents are available to help dry the ears after swimming and should be used in these cases. A few drops of alcohol, witch hazel, or white vinegar applied in the ear canals will commonly solve the problem. Dogs with excessive scarring may be candidates for surgery or chronic medication use (*not* antibiotic use) to decrease swelling and pain in the canals.

Two of my favorite products to help keep ears healthy when mild infections occur, without the use of antibiotics and antifungals, are Zymox and HydroB-1020. Zymox is an enzymatic agent, and HydroB-1020 contains a drying agent and low dose of steroid for inflammation.

For treatment of infected ears, I recommend the following:

- Follow all suggestions listed above for treatment of skin disease and allergies. Eliminate foods that may be causing allergic ear disease.

- Keep ear canals dry and clean. Use a few drops of alcohol, witch hazel, or white vinegar in canals after swimming.

- Zymox enzyme solution can be used to treat mild yeast or bacterial ear infections. Apply once daily for seven to fourteen days. Do not use with any cleaning solutions.

- HydroB-1020 can be used once or twice daily. For swelling and inflammation, five or ten drops in the ear canals will help clear mild infections. Try this before committing to surgery.

The anal glands, or anal sacs, should be considered along with skin health. These glands can be found on either side of the anus.

Normally, a liquid is expressed from the glands each time the pet has a bowel movement, leaving a specific scent as a marker for other animals. Problems with the glands can include impaction, infection, and leakage. Impaction can occur if the secretions are too thick or the stools are too soft to cause the glands to express during defecation. Infection generally occurs secondary to impaction. Leakage generally occurs secondary to infection. Some dogs will express the glands when they are really excited or scared, resulting in a strong, foul, fishy odor.

Healthy pets will never need their anal sacs manually expressed. A pet being fed a proper diet should have well-formed, firm stools that will apply enough pressure to cause the glands to release at each bowel movement. A diet high in moisture should allow the secretion from the glands to be thin enough to be easily excreted. Phlegm-draining foods like clams, pears, and almond milk may help decrease the thickness of the secretions. The addition of pumpkin as a source of fiber may help with bowel consistency.

One of the best ways to detect the overall health of your pet is by taking a good look at the nose and footpads, as well as the skin and coat. Hair should be soft and silky, not dry and brittle. There should be some shine in the coat. The ears should be clean and free of odor. The nose and footpads should look like black patent leather. People argue with me all the time that their dogs walk on rough pavement or stones, causing their footpads to look rough. This is simply not the case. Dogs with plenty of moisture and a healthy diet will have patent leather shoes.

When I see loss of pigment in the nose, I know the pet is struggling internally. If you are not sure if your dog has always had a pink nose, go back and look at photos of your pet as a puppy. If the color was there and has been lost, something is brewing. Dogs that lose the pigment in their noses are commonly the same pets that show early graying of the muzzle and face. This can be due to thyroid disease, lack of B vitamins, excess vitamin E, anemia, Cushing's disease, and kidney yin or Jing deficiency (among other things).

# Bugs Galore: Treating Parasites

In the past two decades, pharmaceutical companies have made huge strides in parasite prevention and treatment. Gone are the days of having to use toxic flea and tick dips every week or exposing our families to bombs and sprays to rid the house of pests. The advent of monthly topical treatments for external parasites has made the lives of pet owners everywhere much simpler.

Unfortunately, many pets, particularly cats, have also died due to misuse or over-dosage of these chemicals. National poison control centers report thousands of cases of illness or death annually due to usage of topical pesticide products. Buried in veterinary research literature, it is also possible to find theories linking the increase in some cancers to the continual use of the monthly preventative chemicals.

Clients commonly voice concerns about their dogs succumbing to Lyme disease or other tick-borne diseases if a monthly parasite preventative chemical is not applied. It has been my experience that pets will still have ticks attached, even with the chemicals applied. I have diagnosed and treated Lyme disease many times in dogs that are "protected" monthly with a topical parasiticide. I do not use these chemicals on my pets.

Commonly used chemicals for flea and tick prevention include pyrethrins, fipronil, permethrins, imidacloprid, methoprene, etofenprox, dinotefuran, selamectin, moxidectin, pyriproxyfen, and others. These topical products spread throughout the pet's coat and are deposited in the oil glands of the skin where they are slowly released. Cats are extremely sensitive to many of these chemicals, and it is always important to read labels carefully to make sure you are using a product that is not toxic to cats. Side effects can include drooling, vomiting, diarrhea, hives, irritation at the site of application, lethargy, muscle tremors, seizures, and death. Long-lasting flea and tick preventive collars are also available (Seresto). Collars cannot be used on puppies less than seven weeks of age or kittens less than ten weeks old. I particularly do not like using pesticide-laden collars in multi-pet households where rough play may result in biting into the collar or in households with small children that may put the collar into their mouths or get the chemicals on their skin.

Oral products include spinosad (Comfortis and Trifexis), lufeneron (Program and Sentinel), and nitenpyram (Capstar) to kill fleas or prevent flea eggs from hatching. Most of these chemicals are neurotoxins for the fleas and/or ticks. Others are growth regulators that prevent hatching of eggs or development of larvae. Unfortunately, they can be extremely toxic to some pets as well. A new oral product containing afoxolaner (NexGard) is labeled for treatment and prevention of fleas and ticks. This product should not be used in dogs with seizure disorders, or dogs under eight weeks of age or under four pounds.        Side effects can include drooling, vomiting, diarrhea, hives, lethargy, muscle tremors, seizures, and death.

Alternative treatments do exist for prevention and treatment of ticks and fleas. Many herbal and essential oil products are now available on the market. Cedar oil can be very effective, but must be applied properly. For decades, farmers and owners of hunting dogs have known that using cedar chips in the dog house will keep fleas under control for dogs that live outside. Be careful with cedar oil products—and test them in small amounts before using them on your animals. I applied a cedar oil spray to repel ticks on my horses, and two of the horses had a severe reaction with blisters and peeling skin. I did find that product to be very useful, however, when sprayed on the walls of the stall to cut down on the fly population.

Diatamaceous Earth (DE) will dehydrate fleas, causing them to die. DE is nontoxic and can be used on bedding or on the pets. It is very drying to the skin and coat, unfortunately, and must be applied outside or in a well-ventilated area so your pet does not inhale the dust.

Lavender, peppermint, lemongrass, and geranium have flea- and tick-repelling effects. Herbal collars and scarves are available containing these herbs. Sometimes these can be problematic for animals that are prone to seizures and should not be used on those pets. Do not use citrus oils on cats since they can be sensitive to them. Washing pets in lemon juice and white vinegar makes it easier to comb out fleas by slowing their movement. This combination can bleach the hair, so test before saturating. Herbal and natural products usually require more frequent applications than the monthly spot-on or oral products, but they can be much safer.

Regular grooming and bathing, and keeping hair cut shorter during flea and tick seasons will make it easier to protect your pet. Keep your grass mowed short and limit pets' ability to get into shrubbery, wooded, or heavily mulched areas where parasites are more commonly found.

Heartworms are spread from infected dogs to healthy dogs through the bite of mosquitoes. It takes around six to nine months from the time of the bite to the development of mature adult heartworms in the dog's heart. Environmental temperatures must remain above fifty-seven degrees consistently for two to four weeks for mosquitoes to be active and the larvae to develop. For owners in northern climates, I cannot justify giving heartworm preventative year round. However, the American Heartworm Society now recommends year-round prevention for every state in the United States. The AHS is sponsored by at least eight major pharmaceutical companies, so we need to look critically at this recommendation.

There has been new evidence of heartworm resistance to some of the preventative medications. This has been seen mostly in the Mississippi River Valley. Ever since Hurricane Katrina hit New Orleans, more dogs have been transported from high-kill shelters in the South to low-kill shelters in the North. Many of those dogs were heartworm positive. The medication to treat adult heartworms, Immiticide (melarsomine), became unavailable for a time. This caused a dilemma for owners and practitioners and led to an alternative treatment to treat adult heartworms using a slow-kill method.

Research showed that adult heartworms have a commensal relationship with a parasite, Wohlbachia, which allows the heartworms to survive. The Wohlbachia is sensitive to the antibiotic Doxycycline. When dogs are given Doxycycline twice daily for one month and this is repeated every three months, the Wohlbachia die and the adult heartworms will also eventually die. The pet needs to be given a monthly heartworm preventative along with this to prevent any new infection from occurring. I have successfully used this protocol on quite a few dogs, and I actually like the slow-kill method. Now that melarsomine is available again, the American Heartworm Society recommends against using the slow-kill method with Doxycycline. There is debate over whether this has contributed to the recent resistance to heartworm drugs.

When I graduated from veterinary college, we used a product called Diethylcarbamazine, or DEC, as a daily heartworm preventative. Missing doses for even one or two days could result in the development of heartworm infection. Not long after graduation, ivermectin was discovered as a new preventative medication that could be used only once a month to prevent infection. Originally, this caused problems because owners were not used to remembering a monthly dosage, but this is now readily accepted.

The monthly heartworm preventatives work by killing off certain migrating stages of the heartworm larvae before they can reach the heart and develop into adult worms. Collies and other breeds of herding dogs have shown increased sensitivity to ivermectin

(Heartguard, Iverheart, etc.) products over other breeds. Research has found these dogs can carry a mutation in the gene known as the "white footed gene," the MDR1 gene. Because of this, many herding dog owners are very careful about medications given to their pets. There is a test available to discern which dogs carry the mutation.

Not long after the introduction of ivermectin came the introduction of milbemycin (Interceptor, Sentinel, Trifexis). Milbemycin has a somewhat broader scope of protection when used at the dosages currently used, providing protection from roundworms, whipworms, and hookworms. The makers of the ivermectin products fought back by adding pyrantel pamoate, an intestinal dewormer, to the ivermectin to cover roundworms and hookworms. More recently, the makers of Sentinel have added praziquantel, a dewormer effective against tapeworms, to their product, calling it Sentinel Spectrum.

I do not believe dogs need to be given a monthly dewormer for intestinal parasites, and I would prefer to test stool samples every six months and treat as needed. If a dog shows positive for whipworm infestation, I do recommend long-term use of a milbemycin heartworm preventative. Whipworm eggs are extremely hard to destroy, remaining viable in soil through drying and freezing cycles for years.

Selamectin (Revolution) is a newer topical product on the market that is labeled for protection against heartworms, fleas, one kind of tick, sarcoptic mange, and ear mites. The label states it should not be used on sick, weak, or underweight dogs. I rarely see dogs that need to be treated for all these parasites unless they are sick, weak, or underweight. It contains the preservative BHT, which can be toxic and has been banned nearly worldwide except in the United States. Collie dogs and other breeds with the MDR1 mutation will also be susceptible to side effects from Selamectin. I do not recommend the use of this product.

An injectable product using moxidectin (ProHeart) was introduced to the market, then pulled from the market, and is now back on the market. It is not recommended for use in sick, debilitated, or underweight dogs, or dogs that are losing weight. It should not be used in any dog with uncontrolled or pre-existing allergic disease. Dogs with the MDR1 mutation are extremely sensitive to this drug. If the dog has a bad reaction once the injection is given, the chemical will continue to be slowly released into the body—and there is no way to stop it. Reactions to the drug include drooling, loss of appetite, lethargy, ataxia, muscle tremors, and possibly death. I do not recommend use of this product.

Unfortunately, one of the topical products commonly used to treat flea infestation has added moxidectin to imidacloprid (Advantage Multi) to prevent heartworms, fleas, and intestinal parasites. Again, collie dogs and other dogs with the MDR1 gene mutation are extremely sensitive to moxidectin. I do not recommend use of this product.

Now that I have basically told you I do not recommend the use of most of these products, your head is probably spinning wondering what you should use. My preference is milbemycin. As of this writing, there has been no resistance seen to this product. In my practice, this product has shown fewer side effects and has been tolerated better by pets with seizure disorders and other illnesses. Unfortunately there are no products currently on the market that contain only milbemycin. One product combines milbemycin with spinosad (Trifexis), the other with lufeneron (Sentinel), for flea protection. I have seen more side effects from spinosad than lufeneron, so I choose the product with milbemycin and lufeneron (Sentinel). Spinosad should not be used in dogs known to have seizures. If I could get plain milbemycin compounded, I would.

I do not recommend giving heartworm preventative year round where I live (New Jersey). If I lived in the South where the temperatures are always warm and numbers of reported heartworm cases are high, I would consider year-round treatment. You can go to the website for the American Heartworm Society and look at maps of the United States to see the reported number of cases to decide if year-round prevention is warranted in your area. Unless you live in the Southeast or along the Mississippi River Valley, the incidence of heartworm infection is actually fairly low.

I also cheat and give preventative every six weeks instead of every four weeks, as the percentage of migrating heartworm larvae killed is still very high at six-week dosing intervals. The drug companies will never stand behind this dosing because it is off-label usage. I test my dogs each spring when the temperatures are warm enough for a long enough period of time that mosquitoes are active. In order for my dogs to become infected with heartworm, they need to be bitten by an infected mosquito that has bitten an infected dog. I live in an area where most people take good care of their pets—and there are few heartworm-positive dogs. If I lived in an area with a high population of untreated dogs, high mosquito population, and had dogs with poor immune systems, I would dose differently.

My dogs are not allowed to remain outside at dusk when mosquitoes become active. If we need to be outside in the evening I use a natural, herbal or essential oil spray to repel mosquitoes. By decreasing their exposure to the vector (mosquitoes) and the carrier (infected dogs), I worry less about them becoming infected. Currently, my dogs are given four milbemycin/lufeneron tablets (Sentinel) per year after having a negative heartworm test: June 1, July 15, September 1, and October 15. If it stays warm through November, they get another dose on December 1. The last dose of preventative needs to be given thirty days after the last mosquito activity. Please discuss this sort of program with your veterinarian (if they are not holistic, they'll say no way) before embarking on this dosing schedule. Look carefully at the climate and exposure level for your dog. The drug companies will not stand behind this dosing, and if your dog becomes infected, you will be responsible for treatment (which is expensive).

As long as I am going out on a limb by giving you my adjusted dosing schedule I will also let you in on the secret that I use a reduced dose. There is a link one of my clients found that shows the Safeheart study (NADA 140–915 http://www.fda.gov/AnimalVeterinary/ Products/ApprovedAnimalDrugProducts/FOIADrugSummaries/

ucm054862.htm) approved by the FDA on June 4, 1998. This approval was given for milbemycin to be marketed as Safeheart for prevention of heartworms. The milbemycin was present in the tablets at one-fifth the dosage currently in milbemycin products. Dogs up to fifty pounds would be given a tablet containing 2.3 milligrams of milbemycin, and dogs fifty-one to a hundred pounds would be given 5.75 milligrams of milbemycin. However, this product never came to market because the parent company (Novartis, makers of Interceptor and Sentinel) discovered that when milbemycin was given at five times the Safeheart dosage, it would also protect against intestinal parasites. This gave them an edge in the parasite-preventative market.

I currently use the lower doses for my clients who want to give the least amount of drug possible. Dogs under fifty pounds can take the tablets labeled for dogs two to ten pounds, and dogs fifty-one to a hundred pounds can take the tablets labeled for dogs eleven to twenty-five pounds. I do not recommend buying larger pills and cutting them. Again, remember that the drug company will not stand behind this dosing schedule—and neither will your veterinarian, most likely.

The advent of Internet pharmacies has resulted in many pet owners buying their medications and heartworm preventatives online at lower cost. While I admire the ability to save money, I caution owners about doing this. The companies that make the heartworm preventatives (at least the good ones) will guarantee their product if purchased through a veterinarian. If given as directed (usually monthly all year round), the company will pay for treatment if your dog should be diagnosed with heartworms or any of the intestinal parasites for which the product is labeled. Treatment for heartworm infection can easily run into hundreds or thousands of dollars. Even if you give heartworm prevention year round, your pet should be tested at least once a year for the presence of adult heartworms.

Clients commonly ask for alternatives to chemical prevention of heartworms. Black walnut has been touted as an effective preventative, but it is also very hard on the liver. When choosing black walnut for parasite prevention, I caution owners to also provide herbal (milk thistle) and food (leafy green vegetables) support to protect the liver. Wormwood and garlic have also been used anecdotally. Most reputable holistic veterinarians are not recommending use of these products. Homeopathic veterinarians use nosodes and other remedies for prevention, but there are many reports of animals succumbing to heartworm infection when taking these remedies. Doctors reporting high rates of success preventing heartworms using nontraditional remedies may live in areas where heartworm prevalence is low; therefore, the results may be skewed.

Healthy pets will generally not be bothered by parasites. I have seen households with many cats where one or two cats will have hundreds of fleas on them, but other cats in the household will have virtually none. Generally, parasites attack the old, the ill, and the weak. Keeping your pet in top form—with a healthy diet and healthy immune system—will minimize the effects of external and internal parasites. This means minimizing vaccines and medications, feeding a species-appropriate diet, and living a healthy lifestyle.

My current recommendations for parasite prevention:

- Sentinel for heartworm prevention. With responsible clients, I use the Safeheart dosing which is one-fifth the normal product dose, given during mosquito season. Dog must be tested for heartworms each year before starting preventative. For those who live in a warmer climate, a more protective dose would be achieved by dosing at one weight size lower than your pet's weight would normally receive. For those living in a high heartworm or tropical environment, give label dose all year round. (We once thought about moving to Belize. Due to the number of untreated dogs and high mosquito population, I would have treated with appropriate dosing all year.)

- Vetri-Repel by Vetri-Science (www.vetriscience.com) is an essential oil product for fleas and ticks.

- Best Yet Pest Repellant (www.cedarcide.com) for pets and yards contains cedar oil for fleas and ticks.

- Only Natural Pet Squeeze-On (www.onlynaturalpet.com) once a month spot-on herbal for fleas and ticks.

- Use Capstar (available through veterinarians or many online outlets) for quick-kill if you have a flea outbreak or Advantage for month-long kill (use once, only apply a second time if outbreak continues).

- Use Frontline if you have a big tick problem and herbal or essential oil products are not working in your area.

- Use Revolution for outdoor cats, which are hard to handle, as this product will kill roundworms, hookworms, fleas, and ear mites and will prevent heartworms.

Keep in mind that pharmaceutical companies develop and release new products frequently. These recommendations are based on products available at the time of writing.

# Water, Water, Everywhere:
# Treating Urinary Tract Disease

My fourth cat, LMNO, suffered from urinary tract disease. Okay, I know, what kind of name is LMNO for a cat? My first cat was Mr. P (short for Puff), then came P.S. (you know, an afterthought), and my son named his first cat Q, after the bad guy on Star Trek, which was his favorite television show when he was four years old. My husband told me we were not going to have twenty-six cats, so I needed to start combining letters of the alphabet. Right after we decided on the name LMNO for the new cat, there was a skit on Saturday Night Live about the "metric alphabet" and they actually combined LMNO into one letter: "Please LMNOpen the door." So I guess it was an okay name.

Anyway, back to his urinary problems. I adopted LMNO off the streets when he was about six months old. I fed all our cats dry cat food at that time (during my pet food salesman days). LMNO developed urinary problems by the time he was two years old. He had bloody urine and strained to urinate most of the time. He had urinary obstructions several times and had to be catheterized. Eventually, his problems became so bad, he had to have a surgical procedure called a perineal urethrostomy to remove his penis and make him into a her so he could urinate. It was pretty traumatic.

Chinese medicine says that the kidneys are responsible for life and death. They store the "essence" or "Jing" that we have at birth. When the kidneys deteriorate, the health does too. In Chinese medicine, the kidney system is responsible for reproduction, production of marrow to fill the brain, production of blood, and manifests as hair on the head. Pets and people who suffer from early graying of the hair may have a kidney deficiency. Those with reproductive problems need to have the kidney system supported with acupuncture, herbals, and food therapy. The kidneys are connected to the ears, just as the liver is connected to the eyes. Ability to detect sound diminishes with age as kidney function declines. The kidneys also rule the bones, and chronic inflammation of the kidneys goes hand in hand with arthritis. The kidneys are the organ of the water element, and they like moisture.

Chronic feeding of diets devoid of moisture causes chronic stress to the kidneys. Pets fed dry kibble will drink much more than their counterparts consuming high-moisture diets. (Imagine how you would feel if your diet consisted solely of dry cereal and crackers.) Urine of pets consuming dry food will be highly concentrated with an increase in crystal and stone formation. For years, we have treated cats for feline lower urinary tract disease (FLUTD) using antibiotics, urine acidifiers (dl-methionine in pet foods), anti-depressant and anti-inflammatory medications, and magnesium-restricted dry diets. In worst-case scenarios, male cats have their penis removed to allow the stones and crystals to pass through a larger, female type of opening. When did our society become so barbaric?

The first and most obvious change to make for these poor beasts is an increase in moisture in the diet! There is no reason to feed a dry prescription diet to a cat (or a dog). The addition of chemicals to the diet encourages the pet to drink more (adding salt), and acidifiers (dl-methionine) in the diet decrease the pH of the urine. This can have detrimental effects on other organ systems. There are two major types of crystals found in dog and cat urine. Struvite crystals are found when the pH of the urine is 7.5 or higher. This commonly occurs when an infection is present. Oxalate crystals, on the other hand, are typically found in urine with a pH of 6.5 or lower. By chemically altering the urine to avoid one type of crystal, the opposite crystal may show up instead if the pH swing is too dramatic. This is not a solution to the problem.

The pets at highest risk for disease are those that refuse to switch to a high-moisture diet. Cats are picky, and you cannot starve them into a diet change. Don't ever believe they'll eat if they get hungry enough. Cats will actually die while holding out for the food they want. My recommendation is to keep trying to get them to switch by gradually decreasing the amount of dry food offered while offering varied flavors and textures of canned or raw foods. Dehydrated or freeze-dried raw meat seems to be a favorite of many cats, and sprinkling this on top of the dry kibble may be a way to gradually get them to change. Once they like the meat, you can start adding small amounts of water and gradually increase until you are feeding a high-moisture diet.

For cats in crisis, medications will definitely be required. A cat with urinary crystals or urinary obstruction needs to be treated immediately. The long-term solution, however, resides in the addition of moisture to keep the kidneys happy.

Urinary tract infections are seen more commonly in female dogs since they have a wider opening and shorter urethra than males. Dogs with a vulva that is "tucked" into the folds of the groin are more prone to infection and are commonly plagued by yeast infections, which cause them to lick the area. Dogs with this condition may need surgical repair with a procedure called a vulvoplasty to avoid chronic infections. Dogs with loose stools or diarrhea may introduce bacteria into the vaginal opening when defecating or grooming. Male dogs rarely have primary infections. In males, they are usually related to prostate disease, kidney disease, inability to empty the bladder completely, or stones.

Signs of urinary tract infection include bloody urine, straining to urinate, lethargy, incontinence, dribbling urine, urinating in strange places, frequent urination, malodorous urine, and occasionally vomiting. Most dogs do not develop a fever with a UTI that is restricted to the bladder. Infection in the kidneys is more serious, and dogs will usually present with vomiting and fever.

Diagnosis of a urinary tract infection requires testing of the urine microscopically, looking for bacteria, red blood cells, white blood cells, crystals, or cancer cells. Treating with antibiotics without performing a microscopic analysis is bad medicine. If a UTI is diagnosed, a culture and sensitivity should be performed to determine the type of bacteria present and the appropriate antibiotic for treatment. Certainly, for dogs that have received multiple courses of antibiotics, the culture is essential.

Treatment with antibiotics usually requires ten to fourteen days to clear the infection. Probiotics should be given along with the antibiotics and for an additional two weeks to repopulate the bowel with healthy bacteria. An urinalysis should be repeated after giving antibiotics to be sure the infection has cleared.

Prevention of recurrent urinary tract infections lies in determining the underlying cause of infection. The underlying cause may include anatomical issues like the tucked vulva, a polyp on the bladder wall, an ectopic (misplaced) ureter, or an outcropping of the bladder wall called a diverticulum. Most pets less than one year of age will not have infections; when they do, it may signal an underlying deficiency in the immune system. Pets with repeat infections may have bladder stones that serve as a chronic source of infection. Radiographs should be taken to rule out stones. Tumors of the bladder are being seen with increased frequency and should be ruled out. Diagnosis usually requires an ultrasound study of the bladder. Pets with weakened immune systems from poor breeding, early spaying, poor diets, or over-vaccination will also be more prone to infection.

As discussed, treatment may include a course of antibiotics and probiotics. Increased moisture in the diet will promote urination and flushing of the bladder. In addition, there are many natural substances that can be used to help treat or prevent infection as well:

- ❧ Cranberry (contains proanthocyanidins which prevent bacterial attachment to the bladder wall) (Nutramax Labs Crananidin and Rx Vitamins Cranberry Rx are good products)

- ❧ Uva Ursi (decreases bleeding and inflammation, promotes urination to flush the bladder)

- ❧ Grapefruit seed extract (antiviral, antifungal, antibacterial, boosts immune system)

- ❧ Juniper berry (increases kidney filtration and helps flush the bacteria from the urinary tract)

- ❧ Marshmallow root (stimulates the immune system and soothes bladder inflammation)

- ❧ Parsley leaf (diuretic action helps flush the urinary tract)

- ❧ Glucosamine and Chondroitin (fifteen milligrams per pound of body weight strengthens the protective lining layer of the bladder to decrease invasion by bacteria) (Cosequin is a good product for this.)

- ❧ Chinese herbal combinations (can decrease infection, soothe the bladder, and decrease bleeding)

In recent years, I have noticed a big increase in the number of pets suffering from bladder stones. Bladder stones occur in two main types: struvite, which are secondary to highly concentrated urine and bacterial infection, and oxalate, which are related to high levels of calcium, genetic disorders, overuse of antibiotics causing a decrease in intestinal flora that feed on oxalate, and poor diet. Once stones are diagnosed, they are usually removed surgically. Small stones may pass, but particularly in males, the stones may lodge in the urethra, causing obstruction and death if not treated.

One way of avoiding stone formation is feeding a high-moisture diet, thereby decreasing the concentration of the urine. More moisture going into the pet results in more urine coming out of the pet, helping to flush the kidneys and bladder. Most pets diagnosed with bladder stones will be started on a prescription diet once the stones are removed. Commonly, these are dry formulations, which makes no sense because we need to flush the bladder. The diets are usually high in salt to encourage the pet to drink more. I do not use prescription diets.

I love to diagnose struvite stones because they are always caused by bacterial infection and are the easiest to treat. Once the stones are removed, a culture and sensitivity test needs to be performed to determine which bacterial infection caused the problem. Antibiotics should be given until the urine culture is negative. The pet should be fed a high-moisture diet (canned, home-cooked, or raw), and the urine should be monitored at least every three months for signs of infection. Dogs that return repeatedly with struvite stones requiring multiple surgeries have non-compliant or uninformed owners.

A good immune system is paramount to controlling infection; these pets need healthy diets and healthy guts, including the addition of good probiotics. Cranberry supplements may be helpful in preventing infection by not allowing bacteria to attach to the bladder wall. Do not feed cranberry juice with high-fructose corn syrup or sweeteners. Repeated use of antibiotics, medications, and over-vaccination will be detrimental; a healthy immune system is the key.

Oxalate stones are more difficult to treat. They are common in certain breeds like the bichon frise, miniature schnauzer, Lhasa apso, Yorkie, and shih tzu. These breeds may have a genetic predisposition. Oxalate stones occur commonly in pets with Cushing's disease, parathyroid tumors, and diseases associated with high calcium levels in the blood. Over-supplementation with calcium or vitamin C and certain foods like soy and wheat are common culprits.

Wait! Did I just say soy and wheat? It seems to me those are two major additions to the pet food industry in the past few decades. Other foods that are high in oxalates include spinach, sardines, sweet potatoes, white potatoes, beets, mustard greens, figs, almonds, and peanuts. Meats, on the other hand, are low in oxalates. It stands to reason these pets could be fed a low-oxalate, meat-based diet that could dramatically improve their lives.

Unfortunately, prescription diets for oxalate stones are based on providing a low-protein diet and do not include much meat. The ingredient list for one of the commonly used prescription products includes egg product, cornstarch, chicken fat, pork liver, sucrose (yes, sugar) rice, soybean oil, soy fiber, and a whole bunch of chemicals, vitamins, and minerals. I find this to be an oxymoronic diet since soy is high in oxalates—and there is no meat included.

Oxalate stones will not dissolve and must be removed. They are usually sharp and rough, causing pain in the bladder. Even if they are small enough to pass, I recommend having them removed to make the pet more comfortable. Male dogs may need to have a new opening made behind the penis to allow small stones to pass since the stones will reoccur in more than 50 percent of dogs. Potassium citrate is commonly prescribed to raise the urine pH and decrease chances of reoccurrence.

Drugs like steroids and furosemide can increase the risk of developing oxalate stones and should be avoided. Again, providing a species-appropriate diet with added probiotics, decreased vaccinations and medications, and a healthy immune system are the answer. I think I sound like a broken record.

Less common forms of stones include urate, seen mostly in Dalmatians, and cysteine stones, which are seen most commonly in bulldogs, Newfoundlands, Irish setters, bassett hounds, dachshunds, Chihuahuas, and Yorkies. These are less likely to be diet related and are seen more commonly due to genetic dysfunction.

Cancer can occur anywhere in the urinary system, but bladder cancer, most commonly transitional cell carcinoma (TCC), has been diagnosed more frequently in recent years. Scottish terriers, beagles, wirehaired terriers, West Highland white terriers, and Shetland sheepdogs seem to be predisposed. Perhaps this disease has always been a problem, and we didn't have the capability to diagnose it as well, but I think there is an increased incidence of occurrence.

The number one cause of this cancer in humans is smoking. Many pets are subjected to secondhand smoke and have no say in the matter. This is unfair. If you smoke, go outside or put your pet outside. Obesity, pesticides, lawn herbicides, and topical flea and tick products have been incriminated as well. Current treatments for TCC include surgical removal, if possible, radiation and chemotherapy, and use of the drug Piroxicam (an NSAID). The feeding of fresh vegetables seems to have some protective effect against this cancer. Avoid the chronic use of herbicides, pesticides, and topical insecticides. (See the chapter on cancer for further discussion on preventing and treating cancer.)

Any pet with kidney disease needs a high-moisture diet to keep the kidneys happy. Kidney failure can be caused by bacterial infections, tick-borne diseases, ingestion of toxins like antifreeze and melamine, and chronic inflammation from things like over-vaccination, over-medication, and toxins in the environment. Melamine, a chemical used to manufacture plastics, was added illegally to pet food ingredients like wheat gluten and rice protein sourced from China that killed over 13,000 American pets in the huge recall in 2007. A similar outbreak in Asia in 2004 resulted in the deaths of over 6,000 animals. Melamine causes kidney failure and formation of stones in the kidneys and bladder. When I visited China in 2008, all dairy products were recalled because melamine had been added to infant formula and milk, resulting in the death of infants. This happened again in 2011 and 2013. Melamine has also been added to feed products for chickens and swine; it is unknown what effect this will have on pets or people consuming the meat. Any products containing dairy may be contaminated, including cookies, candies, cocoa, and instant coffee mixes. Studies have shown the people who eat hot food off dishes made of melamine will excrete melamine in their urine. I grew up eating from melamine dishware, and now I will be cleaning my cabinets to dispose of them!

Kidney disease in its early stages usually goes unnoticed. By the time symptoms are noticed, kidney disease is usually fairly advanced. In the early stages, the only abnormality may be an increase in protein in the urine sample (good reason to take that urine sample for testing every year). As the disease progresses, creatinine and urea levels will increase in the blood. These are byproducts of protein metabolism.

Outward symptoms of kidney disease—loss of appetite, vomiting, diarrhea, foul odor to the breath, mouth ulcers, anemia, fatigue, and increased thirst and urination—may not be seen until late stages of disease. Luckily, the kidneys do a fairly good job even when they are not functioning at 100 percent. In humans, diabetes and high blood pressure are two of the main causes of kidney failure. There is no cure for kidney failure, and damaged kidney cells will not regenerate. The goal is to detect early signs of disease and protect the remaining cells.

Pets with kidney failure are commonly fed dry prescription diets with low moisture and low protein. I am not a huge fan of ultra-low-protein diets. When the kidneys are inflamed and failing, they lose protein into the urine. The animal's body will draw protein from the muscles, resulting in loss of muscle and energy. Rather than restricting protein to ultra-low levels, it is more important to address the quality of the proteins eaten.

Restricted intake of phosphorous may be required. Many grains are higher in phosphorous than meats; if you are going to prepare a home-cooked diet, you might want to check out phosphorous levels in the ingredients you plan to use. Processed foods commonly have phosphates added and should be avoided. If phosphorous levels in the blood begin to rise, the body will draw calcium from the bones to keep the calcium-phosphorous ratio in balance. Once a pet is in the late stages of kidney disease, it is imperative to work closely with the veterinarian to monitor the calcium, phosphorous, and potassium levels closely. Phosphate binders may need to be added to the treatment regimen to decrease absorption of phosphate from the intestines.

Diets for pets with kidney disease should include a lot of "baby" foods: eggs, sprouts, walnuts, almonds, black sesame seeds, berries, royal jelly, shiitake mushrooms, tofu, root vegetables, and beans. These foods help replace the kidney "Jing" that has been lost over time. If the pet is seeking warmth, warming foods like sweet potatoes, turnips, oats, and chicken can be added to the diet. If the pet is panting, hot, and dry, cooling foods like fish, rabbit, millet, tomatoes, string beans, and barley are good additions.

I am a huge fan of home-cooked stews for pets in kidney failure, but be sure to monitor calcium and phosphorus levels. A good multivitamin or mineral supplement may be indicated. For a natural, complete, prepared kidney diet, check out Darwin's frozen raw kidney diet at www.darwinspet.com. It is a meat- and organ-based diet, and most pets love it.

One of the biggest problems with pets with advanced stages of kidney disease is anorexia. They become nauseous and refuse to eat. Rotation in the diet can be important to keep them eating. Try new foods like a bowl of warm oatmeal or mashed sweet potatoes with cinnamon. Grated Parmesan cheese, garlic powder (not salt), or sugar-free tomato sauce can be used on top of the meal. Do not hide medications in the meal since this can make them turn away from the food. Offer small meals every few hours. Do not give a second helping if they like a meal. If they feel nauseous after eating, they will not eat that food again. Wait a day or two before offering the favored food again since this will keep them interested.

Nutritional supplements have helped immensely for pets with kidney disease.

- Renavast is a combination of naturally occurring peptides and amino acids that decreases symptoms and makes pets feel better, which helps improve the appetite. (Dose is one capsule twice daily for cats, and dog dosage is on the bottle.)

- Give omega-3 fatty acids (20 to 30 milligrams per pound of body weight daily).

- ❧ Give CoQ10 (30 to 200 milligrams daily based on size of dog), which can help decrease inflammation).

- ❧ Probiotics support the immune system and digestion. Azodyl is a specific probiotic that metabolizes urea waste products from the bowel to lower the urea in the bloodstream. Avoid probiotics with animal digest. I like Synacore or Rx Vitamins product Rx Biotic.

- ❧ Weekly injections of vitamin B12 help digestion and appetite as well as supporting formation of red blood cells. Give 250 micrograms (¼ ml) to cats and small dogs, 500 micrograms (½ ml) to medium and large dogs.

- ❧ Soluble fiber can be added to the diet from sources like oats, barley, fruits, and vegetables to help absorb toxins from the bowel.

There are many herbal and homeopathic support formulas available to treat kidney disease, but they should be prescribed after evaluation by an alternative therapy practitioner. Many owners will buy herbal combinations online that are not helpful and may be detrimental to the health of the pet. There is no "one-size-fits-all" herbal to support kidney failure. As in diet, the supplement may need to warm the body, cool the body, or support the kidney Jing.

Medications commonly prescribed for pets in kidney failure include ACE inhibitors to lower blood pressure, phosphate binders, calcitriol to increase vitamin D levels, subcutaneous fluids to rehydrate and flush toxins from the body, potassium supplements if potassium levels are dropping, and erythropoietin (a synthetic hormone to stimulate red blood cell production once the pet becomes severely anemic). These medications can be combined with natural therapies if needed.

# The Big C: Treating Cancer

When my grandmother was diagnosed with liver and colon cancer, my father and his brother sent me to talk to the doctor to get some answers on her condition. Having dealt in the past with medical doctors who looked down on veterinarians, I can say I was not too thrilled with my assignment.

As expected, the doctor was not very pleasant and resented having to speak with me. He marched into my grandmother's room and informed her that he was not pleased. The doctor was mad, but my grandparents were *furious*. In our family, we were not allowed to mention the word *cancer*. My grandparents did not speak to me for a week. Needless to say, I never asked her doctor for another update on her condition.

Fifteen years later, my grandfather was diagnosed with cancer. Once again, I was assigned the task of dealing with doctors. When my grandfather was placed on hospice care, I explicitly explained that we were never allowed to say the word *cancer*. Unfortunately, the first hospice care worker who arrived apparently did not get the memo. He chatted on and on to my grandfather about his impending care. When he finally said the word *cancer*, I was waving my arms and jumping up and down out of view of my grandfather.

My grandfather turned to me and said, "I do *not* have *cancer.* Get this guy out of here." Yikes.

Many people live in fear of cancer—whether for themselves or their pets. It brings up emotions associated with fear, pain, and loss. Cancer is the second leading cause of death in people in America and the leading cause of death in dogs over two years of age. We have every right to be afraid. But rather than living in fear, we could "take the bull by the horns" and be proactive in preventing cancer. Unfortunately, we live in a polluted, toxic world with questionable food and water supplies, but we can diminish our risks.

I know I repeat myself often, but I will keep repeating: eating fresh, organic, locally sourced, antibiotic- and pesticide-free foods is paramount to our survival. Yes, I know they can be hard to find. I know they are more expensive. I know it's hard to find nice restaurants that offer healthy options at an affordable price. I know packaged and processed foods are easier to store and prepare. But read the labels, people! How many chemicals that you can't even pronounce are listed on the side of the bag, box, or can? Do you have any idea what those chemicals do to the cells that make up your incredibly delicate, unique body? No? Well, neither do I—and neither do the folks at the manufacturing plants. But I can assure you there are bad things occurring because we read and hear reports of problems in the food chain every single day.

We need to stop overdosing on medication and antibiotics. Every drug has side effects, and we take more drugs to alleviate the side effects. Antibiotic resistance is a worldwide problem, requiring the use of bigger, better, stronger drugs. We are producing superbugs that will destroy us, such as unstoppable flesh-eating bacteria. We need to become a society in motion; sedentary lifestyles are leading to increased obesity. This includes our pets. Exercise is not a dirty word.

The immune systems in our bodies are incredibly sensitive. Constant stimulation with vaccines, chemicals, pollution, medications, and bad diets that include GMO grains, dyes, and chemical preservatives destroys the immune system. Destruction of the immune system causes poor digestion, endocrine disease, and cancer. It is *never* too late to improve diet and decrease toxin exposure. When someone comes to consult about a pet with cancer, the first order of business is cleaning up the diet and decreasing toxic chemical exposure.

Although there are many types of cancer, they tend to fall mainly into a couple of categories from a Chinese medicine perspective. Blood or qi stasis causes the congealing and decreased flow of blood and energy, forming a lump or mass. Qi, or energy, must be present to move blood. Traditional medicine studies have shown decreased and abnormal blood flow within tumors, so it would appear the ancient Chinese theory agrees with modern medicine.

Many of the herbal remedies used for cancerous lumps include herbs to move blood and soften hardness. With this condition, there will be a lack of energy, fatigue, and a feeling of heaviness. There may be pain or a history of pain. The tumor is only a symptom of a larger underlying imbalance resulting from emotional stress (dogs spending all day alone or kenneled in crowded conditions), poor diet, toxic chemicals, and pollution. Common cancers of this nature include mast cell tumors and hemangiosarcoma. These dogs may have tongues that are lavender or purple and may be coated in phlegm.

The second type of cancer from a Chinese medicine perspective is a yin deficiency with secondary phlegm formation. When blood becomes too dry (not enough moisture is present), phlegm results (think of mucousy secretions like snot). These animals are hot; they pant a lot. They can't get enough to drink. Many of them are overweight (or were) and have lipomas (benign fatty tumors) and poor digestion with gas, diarrhea, and vomiting. Their tongues are usually dark red (I call it toxic red). Most pets with lymphoma, lymphosarcoma, osteosarcoma, squamous cell carcinoma, and anal gland tumors will fall in this category. Herbs used to treat these cancers include yin tonics to cool and moisturize and herbs to clear heat.

In China, people with cancer are usually treated with Fu Zhen therapy, which is herbal therapy, in conjunction with chemotherapy. Ginseng, astragalus, ligusticum, codonopsis, atractylodes, and ganoderma herbs are combined to protect and stimulate the immune system to fight the cancer. Fu Zhen therapy is reported to increase survival times significantly when used in conjunction with modern treatments. In human medicine, patients are rarely treated with herbs alone, but herbal remedies can be used to stimulate the immune system, decrease side effects of radiation and chemotherapy, and aid in tumor reduction.

It is beyond the scope of this book to list herbal, vitamin, and glandular treatments for each cancer seen in pets. The list can be endless since each pet is different. There is no "one-size-fits-all" therapy. If your pet is undergoing chemotherapy or radiation, be sure to check with your oncologist before starting any sort of vitamin, herbal, or antioxidant therapies. Many supplements can interfere with traditional medicine therapies. It is imperative to work with a veterinary herbalist to achieve the best combination. I am including a list of some of the more common treatments:

- For any dog with a tumor that may rupture or bleed, like hemangiosarcoma, I dispense Yunnan Bai Yao.

- Si Maio San and Artemisinin (sweet wormwood) are commonly used for lymphoma and other phlegm-based cancers. Artemisinin should not be used in pets undergoing radiation. Artemisinin is usually given for eleven days, withheld for three days, and the cycle is repeated. Artemisinin dose is two to five milligrams per pound of body weight given twice daily on the prescribed cycle. Artemisinin should not be given with iron supplements or within three hours of a high-meat meal.

- Vitamin therapy can also help stimulate and protect the immune system. Vitamins A, B-complex, C, D, E, and selenium are commonly supplemented. Vitamin A, in particular, can kill cancer cells when given in high doses. It can also cause kidney failure, so work with your veterinarian or a veterinary nutritionist. Intravenous vitamin C infusion is becoming more popular for people and animals. Vitamin C in high doses will kill some types of cancer cells – pancreatic, liver, ovarian, prostatic, colon, and sarcoma cells – in particular. Increased effectiveness of some chemotherapy agents has been shown, however, other agents have decreased effectiveness when used with vitamin C (doxorubicin when used to treat lymphoma or multiple myeloma). Always check with your oncologist if your pet is receiving chemotherapy before using vitamin C supplements.

❖ Inositol hexaphosphate (IP-6) is a chemical found in beans, brown rice, corn, sesame seeds, wheat bran, and other high-fiber foods. It is a powerful antioxidant and stimulates production of natural killer cells to destroy cancer cells. I use this supplement in almost all dogs with cancer, at a dose of 800 to 1600 milligrams per day.

❖ CoQ10 is another wonderful antioxidant that can also protect the heart if chemotherapy is being used. Most dogs will tolerate a dose of 200 milligrams per day.

❖ Any pets undergoing chemotherapy should have liver support in the form of milk thistle, dosed at five to ten milligrams per pound daily, which may also help chemo drugs work better.

❖ Omega-3 fatty acids have antioxidant and anti-inflammatory effects when dosed at thirty to forty milligrams per pound; if your pet develops diarrhea with fish oil, try evening primrose, olive, flax, or borage oil.

❖ SAM-e is great for liver support, particularly for pets undergoing chemotherapy. Give 90 milligrams to small dogs, 225 milligrams to medium-sized dogs, and 400 milligrams to large dogs.

❖ Probiotics and digestive enzymes should be added to repopulate the bowel with good bacteria and ease the digestive process. Use probiotics in a vegetarian base, not probiotics in animal digest. I like Synacore and Rx Vitamins products like Rx Biotic, Nutrigest, and Rx Zyme.

- ❧ Mushrooms have been shown to have anti-cancer effects, and I include mushroom defense in most protocols. Clinical trials are underway studying the efficacy of medicinal mushrooms in treating canine cancers. Mushrooms can be added to the diet as well. Shiitake, reishi, cordyceps, and maitake are recommended. I'm Yunity is one of the best mushroom products currently available.

- ❧ Acupuncture can help pets feel better by improving appetite, decreasing pain, stimulating the immune system, moving blood, and improving energy.

- ❧ Electroacupuncture should not be used around cancerous areas.

- ❧ Cold-laser therapy should also not be used over cancerous tumors.

- ❧ Pets with cancer should never receive vaccines or be treated with topical pesticides and insecticides.

- ❧ Prednisone can be used judiciously in pets with cancer, and it can improve their appetites, making them feel better. Most complementary protocols can be used along with prednisone.

- ❧ Cats can be difficult to treat because they do not appreciate being made to take multiple supplements. Ask your veterinarian to choose the most important two or three for the cancer you are fighting.

Some tumors may respond to Neoplasene, an herbal product containing bloodroot extract. This product can be given orally, injected into the tumor or intravenously, or applied topically to tumors. Cancer cells will rupture and die when exposed to the extract. In theory, all cancer cells are susceptible. I have had varying results with this product, depending on tumor type. Ulcerated tumors of the skin seem to respond best. Cancerous tissue will become necrotic (die), and the tumor tissue will slough off in ten to fourteen days after application of Neoplasene paste. I have seen this with mammary tumors and tumors anywhere on the skin. If the tumor is not already ulcerated, the medication must be injected under the skin. I have seen severe allergic reactions when the product is used in this manner. I have never injected it intravenously for fear of reactions.

I have used Neoplasene orally, with moderate success, but it must be given with food or severe vomiting will ensue. The liquid is extremely bitter; some pets refuse to take it. It can be encapsulated, but it must be put into the capsules just before dosing because it dissolves the gelatin capsules fairly quickly. There are anecdotal reports of Neoplasene "curing" dogs with hemangiosarcoma after removal of the affected spleen. I have infused Neoplasene into the bladder of a cat with transitional cell carcinoma with moderate success, but no cure. I successfully treated a Labrador retriever with a malignant lipoma the size of a basketball, which was under his shoulder blade. The tumor was inoperable and finally got so large it cut off its own blood supply and developed a draining tract through the skin, leaking necrotic tissue. I injected the Neoplasene into the draining tract, and the entire tumor was gone within two weeks. It never returned, so I suppose we had a "cure." Further research regarding this product is warranted.

But what about the diet? First and foremost, take them off dry food. Dry food contributes to phlegm production. This is the time to pull out all the stops and go in search of organic, fresh, whole foods.

Cancer cells thrive on processed foods and diets high in simple carbohydrates. Avoid white potatoes, white rice, quick oats, or any food with a high glycemic (sugar) index. You can access plenty of glycemic index lists on the Internet. High-quality proteins and fresh foods that are rich with antioxidants can slow the cancer. Home-cooked or raw diets are best. If the pet is undergoing chemotherapy or radiation, a home-cooked diet may be preferable. Most oncologists will demand that the pet not be fed raw food.

Many pets undergoing treatment will become extremely picky with their food. It is more important to get calories in than to worry about balance and ingredients if you have a pet that is not eating. Offer different foods—and keep rotating them. Small amounts of tomato sauce (organic, no sugar added), grated Parmesan cheese, or dried garlic powder (not garlic salt) can sometimes entice picky eaters. Fish cooked in butter or sweet potatoes sprinkled with cinnamon are other options.

If you find one ingredient or food the pet likes, do not offer extra helpings. Overfeeding may result in nausea, and the pet will stop eating the one thing it liked. All foods should be fed slightly warmed and should never be fed cold, even if feeding raw meats. Do not warm foods in the microwave. You can put the meal in a plastic bag and put the bag in a bowl of hot water for warming.

Do not put medications in the meals. Pets need to eat, and many will walk away if the food is adulterated in any way. Pills can be hidden in bananas, organic no-sugar almond or peanut butter, liver, gizzards, or whatever you can manage. Try to avoid processed lunchmeats, ice cream or dairy products, and hot dogs for hiding medications.

Ingredients I like to include:

- grass-fed beef
- dark meat chicken or turkey (make sure the turkey is not injected with butters or oils)
- freshly caught ocean fish (not farm-raised fish)
- organ meats like heart or liver (up to 30 percent of the protein portion of the diet)
- broccoli (contains anticancer properties)
- spinach, purple cabbage, Brussels sprouts, and kale (to keep the liver happy)
- carrots—for vitamin A
- cooked eggs (as a blood tonic for kidney support)

❧ sardines (as a blood tonic)

❧ sweet potatoes, yams, and pumpkin (for soluble fiber and as qi tonics to move the blood and phlegm)

❧ barley (acceptable low-glycemic-value grain, which is cooling and draining for pets with blood stagnation)

❧ ground almonds (to help transform phlegm)

❧ pears, bananas, and apples (to help drain phlegm)

❧ mushrooms (to chase down cancer cells)

❧ fresh or dried ginger (to resolve stagnation and dissolve tumors)

❧ crushed fresh garlic (to resolve stagnation and dissolve tumors; garlic can entice anorexic pets to eat—up to one clove per thirty pounds of body weight per day)

❧ fresh organic blueberries or raspberries (antioxidants)

Processed treats should not be fed. All treats should be fruits or berries, pieces of hard-boiled egg, or pieces of meat. Because this diet is low in carbohydrates, pets may have a difficult time maintaining weight. You may have to feed three to four times daily if weight loss is an issue. High-quality probiotics must be added to the diet, and I also recommend adding digestive enzymes. Since 70 percent of the immune system resides in the gut, the gut function needs to improve. For a more in-depth look at feeding to treat cancer, check out my YouTube food webinar at http://www.youtube.com/watch?v=-vHe3E4RN7s.

In addition to high-quality food and elimination of toxins, exercise and interaction play key roles in healing. All the therapies in the world are not as important as attitude and ability to *live* while treating cancer. I have seen clients spend every day hauling their pet from one veterinary specialist to the next, having the pet poked and prodded every day, hoping someone, somewhere, will give them a cure or the answer they desperately want to hear. Sometimes they seem to forget the feelings of the pet that would definitely enjoy a trip to the park or a walk in the neighborhood instead.

One of my clients had a wonderful older dog that was her dancing partner. (Yes, I said dancing. It's a great sport.) Misty developed cancer in her upper jaw, even though she was not vaccinated and was fed an organic raw diet. Even with the best care, cancer can still appear.

Misty's owner struggled with the decision about how to proceed with treatment. The oncologist gave her decent odds the cancer could be stopped with radiation, so the owner decided to go forward. Six treatments under anesthesia would be the protocol.

Misty hated the treatments. Misty loved to go for long walks. By the fifth treatment, which didn't seem to be working because the tumor was still getting bigger and destroying more jaw tissue, Misty refused to get out of the car at the radiation center. Once pulled and lifted out, she refused to go into the building. I realize the traditionalists would argue that we shouldn't let the dog dictate the treatment—and the treatment wasn't working because she hadn't finished the full dose of radiation—but this owner realized how much Misty was suffering from the treatments. She decided to honor Misty's wishes. Instead of going to radiation therapy, they went for walks. They walked miles and miles for hours and hours. They went everywhere. When Misty would come for acupuncture treatments, I would only use a few needles. If I used too many, she would hide and cower under the chair. After each treatment, she and her mother would walk to the river near our practice and walk for an hour or two.

Weeks later, when it was finally time for Misty to cross the Rainbow Bridge, she walked for four hours before her owner walked her into the veterinary office. Misty's owner realized it was more important to spend time enjoying each day than to prolong a life of suffering.

Since cancer can be a heart-wrenching subject, I will leave you with a couple of success stories that will make you smile. Deedee, a standard poodle, spent the first few years of her life as a breeding female. She was owned by a quality breeder who fed raw diets and didn't over-vaccinate. Deedee was adopted by very special people who also fed a raw diet and avoided vaccinations. Unfortunately, because Deedee was spayed later in life, she developed mammary cancer. The mass seemed to appear overnight and grew rapidly. The biopsy came back with the dreaded news that the tumor was an aggressive form of mammary cancer, and the prognosis was guarded.

We had a long discussion about traditional versus alternative therapies, and the owners opted to avoid chemotherapy. I had never treated a case of mammary cancer using herbs, so this presented a new challenge. I combed books, journals, and the Internet, and I asked veterinary herbalists how to proceed. I came up with a protocol that included IP6, Artemisinin, Sanshedan Chuanbeiye, mushrooms, omega-3 fatty acids, and CoQ10. The owners continued the raw diet. Deedee became our new, shining star, role model for alternative therapies. She is happy, has had no regrowth or spread of the cancer, and is two years out from the original diagnosis.

Another favorite is Lally, a cocker spaniel. Lally had been treated for mast cell skin cancer with multiple surgeries and two rounds of chemotherapy at the veterinary college. When the masses continued to grow after the second round of therapy and became too invasive to be surgically removed, the doctors said no more could be done for her. The owner sought out alternative care as a last resort. Of course, Lally needed a diet change so her owner opted for home cooking. She started taking probiotics, IP6, Artemisinin, mushrooms, omega-3 fatty acids, CoQ10, and an herbal called stasis in the mansion of the blood.

Within a month, the tumors began to shrink. A year later, the owner laughingly said if it wouldn't cost so much money, she'd love to make an appointment with the doctors at the university just to point out that something *could* be done to save Lally. Lally decided at some point that she did not like taking a lot of medications. We had to choose the most important supplements and decrease the medication load. She has not had any increase in tumor size or number, even with less supplementation.

Do not be fooled into thinking all cancer diagnoses are death sentences. Do not be fooled into believing all cancers can be cured with chemotherapy, radiation, or alternative treatments. There will always be outstanding stories on the Internet with testimonials spouting miraculous cancer cures. Each case is different and must be treated individually. Do the best you can with the resources you have available—and remember to live each day to the fullest.

# Old Age: Not for Sissies

Old age is not a disease. Old age can be challenging. Old age should be celebrated because you survived your youth.

As pets age, the effects of poor nutrition, over-vaccination, and environmental pollution become magnified. Many pet owners decline to deal with the problems of old age and choose euthanasia or place the pet in a shelter. I hear the common complaints like:

- *He seems to be in pain.* This argument might work with me if diagnostics and treatments have been used to try to alleviate pain. How about giving him some supplements or medication to decrease the pain? How about a workup to discover the source of the pain?

- *She urinates on my rugs.* This argument might work with me if diagnostics and treatments have been used to try to stop the house soiling. How about treating the infection, bladder stones, incontinence, or kidney failure? Maybe her arthritis hurts and she can't get up to get outside.

- *She can't see or hear well.* Neither can your great-grandmother; it's not a reason to kill her.

🐾 *The kids want a new puppy they can play with that can run around.* Alternatively, your kids could learn a lesson in compassion and caring for an elderly being. You could have them walk the older dog gently around the yard. They could read stories to the older pet.

🐾 *I'm moving three hundred miles away and the trip will be hard on him.* It will be hard on him—or on you? Riding in a car is not traumatic for most pets, especially if they have been trained to ride in the car over a lifetime.

🐾 *I can't afford the veterinary bills associated with aging.* You signed on to care for this pet for life. You did not sign on to care for him only during his youth. I understand circumstances can change over time, including loss of employment or housing. But please remember the love this pet has given to you—and don't bail on him when times get tough. Find a new home or rescue group where the pet can receive appropriate care. Most rescue groups will take senior pets, and there are new senior sanctuaries becoming available.

Aging pets will start to fall apart. My oldest spaniel, Lora Lu, developed urinary incontinence a year ago. I have tried chiropractic treatment, acupuncture, and herbs, which have helped a little, but she still leaks. Sometimes she leaks a lake in our bed or on our sofa. She now wears adorable little doggy diapers at all times. Hue said he would never change diapers again after his children were grown. He was wrong.

Lora has minimal hearing and usually doesn't hear us calling her. She developed glaucoma and needed to have both eyes removed. Now she bumps her way around the house and yard. We have to be vigilant that gates remain closed so she can't wander from home and get lost. She suffers from dementia at sundown (like sundowner's syndrome in people) and needs to have medication to keep her from pacing and barking for hours each evening. She has heart disease and high blood pressure, requiring a handful of medications and supplements twice each day.

Many people would say we should put her down and end her suffering. I say, "What suffering?" She loves life. She loves to go for walks in the stroller. She loves sitting outside with us under the shade tree. She *loves* to eat and is the first one to dive into the bowl at mealtime. She loves snuggling in the big chair with Hue. It requires extra time and patience, and yes, money to care for Lora Lu. She has a team of veterinary specialists that helps with her care, which does not come cheap, but I made a commitment to Lora Lu when she was rescued from the puppy mill that she would be with me for life—and I stand by that commitment.

My sister has a fifteen-year-old corgi, Comet, who has not been able to walk for more than a year. He has a cart to use, but he seems fairly content to drag himself around. Six months ago, he started leaking urine and developed a bad odor. My sister had him checked, and the veterinarian assured her it was due to his spinal disease and inability to walk, nothing more.

By the time she brought Comet home for the holidays, my parents were dreading the thought of a leaky, stinky dog in their house for a week. When I saw Comet, it was obvious he had a raging infection with an odor that permeated the house. I cultured the urine and grew some nasty bacteria, which had caused a secondary skin infection. Treatment required shaving all the hair off his belly and hindquarters, washing daily with antibacterial soap, application of tea tree oil creams, and a long course of antibiotics and probiotics. I also added Adequan for his joints and Duralactin for inflammation. Miraculously (or not) the odor disappeared, and the urine leakage stopped. My parents seemed to be the most thankful! Caring for Comet requires a huge commitment of time and money for my sister, but she is committed to giving him a long, pain-free life.

Dumping old pets at the local shelter is only one step better than dumping old pets along the road. Older pets with medical issues stand very little chance of being adopted, and most of them will be euthanized. Imagine living your life with your family and suddenly being dropped off in a strange environment with people you don't know. Your vision and hearing are not good, and you feel confused. Not a pretty scenario, is it? (Actually, this may be a fairly normal scenario and a good comparison to what is done with many older people in our society.) Private rescue groups and breed-specific rescues are usually willing to take in older pets with medical issues. If you truly cannot afford to care for your senior pet, I implore you to contact one of those groups.

At some point, you will know it is the right time to let your senior pet cross the Rainbow Bridge. Things that may help you make the decision include:

- pain that is no longer responding to treatment
- anorexia and weight loss to the point of malnourishment
- no interest in surroundings or people
- depression
- loss of bowel and bladder control to the point where you cannot keep the pet clean and sanitary
- open wounds or tumors that cannot be closed or removed and have dead or chronically infected tissue

The decision to euthanize can be extremely difficult. I have seen people struggle with this decision many times. If you have done everything humanely possible for your pet, but they are failing and struggling, you will know when the time is right. The decision of when, where, and how the procedure should be carried out is a personal one.

I recommend always having an intravenous catheter in place with sedation and pain medication on board before proceeding with the final injection. If you want to have the procedure performed in your home or garden, ask your veterinarian if that service is offered. If the procedure will be done in the office, ask which time of day is the quietest with the least number of clients in the building.

Try to remain calm and talk soothingly to your pets at the end. Let them know you love them, and they will always hold a special place in your heart. This is the final act of compassion you can offer to your dearest friends.

# Future Generations

When I first became interested in alternative therapies, many of my colleagues considered me to be "out there." Ridicule, snickering, and jokes were the norm. The American Holistic Veterinary Medical Association was not formed until 1982, only a few short years prior to my foray into chiropractic therapy. It was easy to ignore the ridicule because I was seeing such great results with my patients.

Over time, those same doctors started referring patients for alternative care, hoping for help when there was nothing left to offer. Some were just trying to shuttle their hopeless cases to someone else. Now, I am happy to say, some alternative therapies are becoming mainstream. Acupuncture has become extremely popular, and most veterinary clinics in my area now have at least one veterinarian practicing acupuncture. I found in my early days with alternative medicine that having one doctor performing acupuncture—while not truly believing in holistic healing—leaves the patient with minimal healing effect. Prescribing foods and medications that will continue to cause degradation of the immune system will continue to contribute to disease.

Food therapy is less popular with traditional veterinarians, and the American Veterinary Medical Association has actually issued a statement against feeding raw foods to animals. The Delta Society, one of the largest pet-therapy groups in the nation, has excluded any pets that are fed raw diets, warning those pets may harbor bacteria that could be spread to children and adults with weakened immune systems. I have never seen this happen, but there are many reports of people dying after handling dry pet food contaminated with salmonella. Of course, safe-handling practices must be followed when handling any raw meats—whether they are being fed to pets or cooked for human consumption.

The American Veterinary Medical Association has recently started an investigation into the use of homeopathy to treat animals, saying there is no validity that it helps, and pets may be succumbing to diseases that could be treated using more traditional methods. I do not practice homeopathy, but I know many veterinarians who are extremely successful using that therapy. If a governing body becomes successful in outlawing one alternative therapy, what is to stop them from attacking another? Luckily, when the vote came before the AVMA House of Delegates, there was no statement made against homeopathy. For now.

Holistic veterinarians strongly support limited vaccinations in pets. Vaccinations have almost eradicated many diseases that used to kill pets, but repeatedly vaccinating year after year has proven to be unnecessary for many diseases. Each animal has a different level of exposure to disease, so each vaccination schedule must be tailored to the individual animal. For years, good pet owners have followed annual vaccination protocols, which are presented by their trusted veterinarians but are outdated.

Chiropractic therapy is less popular than acupuncture, but it has become easier to find practitioners. There has been ongoing debate regarding who should perform chiropractic manipulations on animals. Human chiropractors state they are the only doctors that should treat the spine, and veterinarians state they are the only doctors who should treat animals. The stress forces on the spine are very different for two-legged humans versus four-legged animals. I feel human chiropractors should treat humans, and veterinarians should treat animals. Ideally, those who would like to treat spines of animals should complete human chiropractic school as well as veterinary school, but that would require more years of college than most people would like to attend.

Herbal supplement usage in pets has become very popular. Many clients come to the clinic with a bag full of products they have purchased online or at stores to give their pets. Unfortunately, most of those products are not regulated by the Food and Drug Administration, and there is no quality control. Many of the supplements are just placebos, containing no active ingredients. Many are toxic to pets or can cause symptoms to worsen because they are not being used correctly. I can't emphasize enough how important it is to work with a knowledgeable veterinarian before purchasing supplements for your pets.

The future is bright for the use of alternative therapies in healing animals. I have had the pleasure of training other veterinarians who are interested in using holistic treatments for their patients, and I love their excitement about alternative medicine. For pet owners who are seeking a different form of veterinary medicine, it is becoming easier to find holistic practitioners. You can find a holistic practitioner in your area by going to www.AHVMA.org, the website for the American Holistic Veterinary Medical Association. Once you find someone in your area, set up an appointment to meet the doctor and tour the clinic. Ask for references from current clients.

My journey into traditional veterinary medicine—followed by the unusual path that led me into alternative veterinary medicine—has been long and rewarding. I am thankful to all my family, clients, patients, and staff who have been along for the ride of a lifetime. It's been a joy.

# Index

# B

bacteria | 27, 58, 60, 182, 204, 208, 211, 221, 224, 225, 227, 230, 232, 233, 234, 237, 252, 253, 254, 255, 262, 265, 275, 279

bacterial overgrowth | 223, 224, 227

B-complex vitamins | 105

BHA | 167, 169, 236

BHT | 167, 169, 236, 244

black walnut | 247

Bladder stones | 254

blindness | 38, 84, 85, 86, 210

Blood | 51, 80, 81, 94, 101, 146, 190, 192, 231, 234, 236, 263, 268, 269, 271

blood pressure | 26, 59, 60, 83, 84, 85, 135, 138, 139, 140, 146, 150, 151, 152, 230, 258, 260, 275

bone meal | 166

Bordetella | 201, 205

BPA | 135

Bromelain | 105

Bugleweed | 138

by-products | 57, 137, 166, 169, 174, 177, 178, 258

# C

calcitriol | 260

calcium | 139, 151, 152, 153, 163, 179, 180, 183, 185, 235, 254, 255, 258, 259

Calicivirus | 201, 210

cancer | 3, 27, 58, 59, 86, 93, 167, 168, 178, 189, 196, 202, 211, 220, 221, 223, 253, 256, 261, 262, 263, 264, 265, 266, 267, 269, 270, 271, 272

canned foods | 160, 167, 175, 232

Capstar | 241, 249

carbohydrates | 96, 104, 107, 115, 121, 123, 124, 129, 137, 140, 158, 159, 160, 172, 173, 225, 226, 231, 235, 267, 269

carrageenan | 175, 176, 177

Carts | 103, 104, 116

cataracts | 83, 86, 124

cedar oil | 241, 249

Cervical Formula | 66

Cervical Vertebral Instability | 66

chemotherapy | 156, 220, 257, 263, 264, 265, 267, 271, 272

Chiari malformation | 90

chiropractic | 39, 40, 41, 45, 47, 50, 51, 57, 65, 93, 100, 102, 112, 114, 274, 278, 279

Chlamydia | 201, 211

chocolate | 58

chondroitin | 66, 108, 111, 115

Chromium | 151

citrus oils | 242

cobalamin | 224

Cold Laser Therapy. *See* laser therapy

Comfortis | 241

congee | 222

CoQ10 | 66, 84, 87, 105, 140, 146, 151, 260, 265, 271

corneal ulceration | 85

Coronavirus | 201, 206, 212

Cranberry | 254, 255

Craniosacral | 44

cruciate | 102
Curcumin | 105
Cushing's disease | 49, 86, 124,
    132, 133, 138, 139, 141, 201,
    230, 235, 239
Cyclosporine | 79, 81

# D

Damp | 51
dandelion leaf | 146, 152
Degenerative Myelopathy | 93,
    100, 103
dental disease | 60, 61, 158, 173,
    175, 194
Deramaxx | 66, 117, 119
desoxycorticosterone pivolate | 142
diabetic | 86, 108, 120, 121, 122,
    123, 124, 159
diarrhea | 19, 110, 118, 134, 135,
    139, 140, 141, 152, 172, 187,
    189, 199, 204, 206, 219, 220,
    221, 222, 223, 224, 226,
    230, 232, 233, 241, 252, 258,
    263, 265
Diatamaceous Earth | 242
digestive enzymes | 172, 182, 221,
    226, 230, 235, 236, 265, 269
Distemper | 37, 39, 58, 95, 199,
    201, 202, 203, 204, 211
diuresis | 153
dl-methionine | 173, 251
DNA Testing | 104
Dog Gone Pain | 66, 92, 103, 110,
    116
Dorzolamide | 84, 85, 87
Doxycycline | 208, 243

Dry Eye. *See* KCS
DRY EYE. *See* KCS
Duralactin | 91, 92, 111, 115, 275

# E

ear infections | 133, 172, 175, 181,
    230, 237, 238
Eosinophilic Myositis | 215
essential oil | 44, 52, 241, 246,
    248, 249
Ethoxyquin | 167, 168, 169
Etogesic | 117
euthanasia | 121, 163, 166, 273
exercise | 48, 56, 61, 72, 101, 104,
    106, 107, 115, 128, 129, 130,
    131, 134, 145, 147, 149, 159,
    269
exocrine pancreatic insufficiency |
    221, 223, 224, 227

# F

FDA | 108, 113, 166, 168, 183, 247
feline immunodeficiency virus. *See*
    FIV
Feline Immunodeficiency Virus.
    *See* FIV
Feline Infectious Peritonitis | 201,
    212
Feline Leukemia | 200, 201, 211,
    213
FIV | 156, 212
Flax seed lignans | 140
fleas | 24, 52, 53, 59, 157, 232, 236,
    241, 242, 244, 245, 248, 249
Florinef | 142
flower essences | 44, 51, 52

Influenza | 201, 207, 216, 217
Inositol hexaphosphate | 265
insulin | 49, 120, 121, 122, 123, 124, 158
Intervertebral Disc Disease | 100
ivermectin | 95, 96, 105, 243, 244

**J**

jerky treats | 183
Jing | 66, 94, 189, 251, 259, 260
Juniper berry | 254

**K**

KCS | 79, 80, 81
Kelp | 134, 193
Kennel Cough | 201, 205
keratoconjunctivitis sicca. *See* KCS
ketoconazole | 139
kibble | 38, 39, 56, 72, 73, 80, 120, 121, 127, 129, 172, 220, 251, 252
kidney disease | 27, 56, 59, 60, 136, 173, 175, 189, 190, 194, 230, 252, 257, 258, 259, 260
kidney failure | 119, 139, 141, 150, 158, 179, 208, 230, 257, 258, 259, 260, 264, 273

**L**

L-arginine | 151
laser therapy | 39, 66, 90, 100, 101, 103, 104, 113, 116, 266
Latanoprost | 84, 85, 87
L-carnitine | 151
L-Carnitine | 138, 146

L-Deprenyl | 139
Leptospirosis | 58, 201, 204
L-glutamine | 226
lick granulomas | 113
Licorice | 134, 232, 236
lipomas | 193, 263
liver disease | 38, 39, 230
lufeneron | 241, 245, 246
luxating patellae | 69
Lyme | 58, 201, 208, 209, 217, 240
Lymphangiectasia | 220
lymphoma | 156, 263, 264
lymphosarcoma | 263
Lysodren | 139

**M**

macadamia nuts | 58
Magnesium | 146, 152
mannitol | 84
Marshmallow root | 254
massage | 51, 112
mast cell tumors | 263
MaxiGuard Gel | 60, 174
MDR1 gene | 244, 245
melamine | 163, 183, 257
Melatonin | 140
Metacam | 117
methimazole | 135
methocarbamol | 66, 103
Metronidazole | 206, 233
microchip | 198
milbemycin | 95, 96, 244, 245, 246, 247
milk thistle | 87, 96, 141, 265
Milk thistle | 87, 94, 137, 152
mites | 171, 232, 236, 244

Traditional Chinese Veterinary
    Medicine | 51, 96
tramadol | 103
Trifexis | 96, 244, 245
trilostane | 139
T-Touch | 44
tumors | 59, 85, 86, 135, 136, 139,
    189, 192, 193, 197, 200, 201,
    213, 255, 263, 266, 269, 271,
    276

# U

urinary crystals | 173, 252
urinary tract disease | 28, 159, 175,
    250
urinary tract infection | 252, 253
Uva Ursi | 254

# V

vaccination protocol | 214, 215
vegan | 150, 166
vegetarian | 150, 166, 266
vertebral heart score | 149
Veterinary Orthopedic
    Manipulation | 40, 66, 103,
    116
Vitamin A | 134, 264
Vitamin B12 | 227, 260
Vitamin C | 105, 110, 116, 255,
    265
Vitamin E | 105, 110, 134, 146,
    151, 232, 236
Vitamins | 151, 152, 183, 223, 226,
    227, 235, 236, 254, 260, 264,
    266

vomiting | 75, 118, 135, 139, 141,
    150, 172, 199, 204, 206, 219,
    220, 221, 222, 223, 224,
    230, 241, 253, 258, 263, 267
vulvoplasty | 252

# W

West Nile Virus | 216, 217
Wobbler's Syndrome | 64, 66, 67,
    100
Wohlbachia | 243

# Y

Yang | 51, 116, 186, 187, 188, 189,
    191
Y/D | 136, 137
yeast | 167, 232, 237, 238, 252
Yin | 51, 94, 116, 137, 186, 187,
    188, 189, 192, 263
youtube | 169, 190, 269
Yunnan Bai Yao | 264

# Z

Zubrin | 117
Zymox | 238